D1572031

Traveler's Tales

Traveler's Tales

The Wanderings of a Bird Hunter and Sometime Fly Fisherman

Michael McIntosh

Down East Books

Copyright © 1997 by Michael McIntosh
ISBN 0-89272-420-X
Book design by Faith Hague
Color Separation by Roxmont Graphics
Printed and bound at BookCrafters, Inc.
5 4 3 2 1

Down East Books / Camden, Maine

LIBRARY OF CONGRESS CATALOGING-IN-PUBLICATION DATA

McIntosh, Michael.
    Traveler's tales : the wanderings of a bird hunter and sometime
fly fisherman / by Michael McIntosh.
        p.   cm.
    ISBN 0-89272-420-X (hardcover)
    1. Bird hunting—America—Anecdotes. 2. Fly fishing—America—
Anecdotes. I. Title.
SK316.A45M35 1997
799.2'4—dc21   97-24322
                                                         CIP

To Vicky,
for the rest of the journey

I am a part of all that I have met;
Yet all experience is an arch wherethro'
Gleams that untravell'd world whose margin fades
For ever and for ever when I move.

Ulysses
Alfred, Lord Tennyson

Contents

Foreword

GREAT OUTDOOR LITERATURE endures for the same reason that any great art endures—it speaks to the timeless, to those aspects of human experience that transcend the trivial restrictions of time and place. Outdoor art has endured the longest through human history because it was first. Cave paintings depicting the hunt, hieroglyphs of the sun and the earth, crudely but lovingly drawn pictures of animals and birds—all signs of man's wonder at the mystery of his place in the world that is his home.

It was his first enemy and his first friend. He fought against nature for his very survival and then, in turn, worshipped its spirit, a spirit which man perceived as not unlike his own. And we've never lost that ancient paradox. We no longer hunt out of desperate necessity, yet we hunt nonetheless; we no longer develop religious dogma out of natural phenomena, yet we still can find in nature the surest window on ourselves.

Had you told me only two years ago that those words were written by Michael McIntosh, and moreover that he'd written them almost twenty years earlier, I'd have raised a dubious eyebrow.

Like most of us who are addicted to the outdoor press, I

knew McIntosh primarily as a technical writer, perhaps the best in the business: a specialist in fine English and American shotguns, the author of books like *Best Guns* (1989), *A.H. Fox: The Finest Gun in the World* (1992), and *Shotguns and Shooting* (1995). For years I'd admired his columns in magazines like *Sporting Classics*, *Gun Dog*, *Shooting Sportsman*, and *Double Gun Journal*, without for a moment suspecting he had a literary side. Oh, sure, now and then those magazines ran one of his accounts of an actual hunt, usually in some exotic locale the rest of us could only dream of one day reaching. For all the elegance and clarity of his prose, however, these were essentially "how-to" stories—in most cases discussing how to get there, what kind of gun to bring, what to wear for the weather and terrain, how much it'll cost you to duplicate McIntosh's experience (usually an arm and a leg).

Then in 1995 I met the man for the first time. A year earlier I'd been asked to write a column of my own for *Shooting Sportsman*, and that September I was invited to the magazine's first annual reader/writer wing shoot at the Paul Nelson Farm in Gettysburg, South Dakota, to hunt pheasants. It was there that I first laid eyes on Michael McIntosh. He looked like a male model posing as an outdoor writer: six feet tall and commensurately slim, with a thick thatch of silver-white hair and beard on his ruddy Caledonian pan, from which winked wise but humorously bright blue eyes. A fragrant, well-rubbed briar pipe seemed permanently clenched in his jaws. His voice was rich and mellifluous, an actor's voice of the old school (which figured when I later learned he'd aspired to the Shakespearean theater in his misguided youth). Now, however, he employed that voice to utter some of the funniest and vilest jokes I've heard this side of the late Gene Hill.

I knew Mac could shoot well, of course, but even so he astonished me, both at sporting clays and in the pheasant fields. He was shooting a splendid old John Wilkes London sidelock, and on one drive I saw him snatch down six high, fast-moving cocks in a row from the hard blue skies of Dakota, recharging his barrels between birds with the speed and surety of an English loader. All of the birds hit the ground stone dead. Okay, I thought, he can practice whereof he preacheth. But what does he know about *real writing?*

Plenty, as it turns out. After all, in one of his earlier incarnations he was an English instructor at Missouri Western College. That night over dinner and post-prandial libations, and later throughout that memorable week, we discussed the state of literature in every spare moment, both classical and contemporary, indoor and out. Not just gunning legends like Frank Forester, Nash Buckingham, Burt Spiller, Gordon MacQuarrie, Caroline Gordon, or William Harnden Foster, but the *real* writers as well, from Henry Fielding to Cormac McCarthy to Annie Proulx, with stops at Tolstoy, Turgenev, Maupassant, Faulkner, Hemingway, McGuana, Harrison & Co., all of whom share to one degree or another our awe and love for the natural world, and our rage at what's being done to it.

But the most outrageous thing of all, we agreed, is that in the literature of the millennium, hunting books have become an endangered species. Since the late 1960s, hard-core outdoor writing has been shunted out of the literary world's mainstream. Any book with so much as a BB gun in it, fiction or memoir, is immediately suspect. And, if it should happen—God forbid—to feature a protagonist, male or female, who actually enjoys hunting or even target shooting, the book is usually cast beyond the pale. What used to be called sporting literature is now ghettoized— sport, in contemporary urban usage, being a term reserved for the spectator variety, involving balls, teams, fans, and uniforms.

With *Traveler's Tales*, Michael McIntosh breaks out of his "how-to" mode and reveals himself as the literary man he actually is. The stories in this exceptional collection all deal with wing shooting and/or fishing. The locales range from Michael's native

Midwest—Iowa, Minnesota, South Dakota, Arkansas, Ontario, Manitoba—to the proper West—Montana, Colorado, Alaska—and as far abroad as England, Spain, and Hungary. Some of the best stories are set south of the border, from Mexico to Brazil and clear down to Argentina, where Mac is widely known as "Barba Blanca"—White Beard.

The writing is generous, colorful, assured, evocative, and in some of its words and phrases, capable of evoking epiphanies worthy of Wordsworth. Consider this passage from "Ducks Over Delta," the story set in Manitoba: "When the far shore finally looms up, black on black, you clamber out, following the thin beam of the flashlight into a tiny clearing hacked from a stand of bulrush and marsh grass and phragmites, cover that looks dense as a wall. You sort your gear and uncase your gun, investigate the direction of the breeze, braille some coffee out of the thermos . . . then you listen to the *thunks* and splashes as the guide sets the decoys somewhere in the dark . . . You wait to hear the sweet, slithery whisper of wings cut the graying darkness . . . There is a certain moment in a marsh when I invariably think of a Words-worth poem . . . a single line from 'Tintern Abbey,' the one that reads 'connect the landscape with the quiet of the sky.' "

That's beautiful enough by itself, but best of all I love the verb "*braille*." Think about it. Remember . . .

Or this description of typical bobwhite quail cover in the north-central reaches of Mexico, south of Brownsville, Texas: "These birds are entirely wild, and habitat therefore is the key both to how many there are and how best to hunt them. In Tamaulipas, the countryside is a patchwork of grassland and grainfield, laced with thickly grown fencerows and interspersed among tracts of classic Mexican bush that range from tiny to vast. Where there's bush, the birds use it as daytime cover, roosting in short grass or stubble nearby and stirring at sunrise to feed their way into the thick stuff. Once there, their safety is absolute, because 'thick' hardly describes it. It is a villainous mélange of scrub so densely packed with catclaw, Spanish dagger, jumping cactus, and other blood-letting vegetation that just the sight of it is enough to make a rattlesnake whimper."

So rattlesnakes aren't capable of whimpering; so what?

The quote that introduces this foreword came from an introduction that Michael wrote in 1979 as a prelude to a collection of essays by our late, great, mutual friend, John Madson. Now out of print, this book, which Michael both assembled and edited, is called *Out Home* and deserves a second life. It ranks right up there with Madson's other superb collections, *Up on the River* and *Where the Sky Began*, near the top of America's canon of great outdoor literature.

So, too, does *Traveler's Tales*.

—Robert F. Jones

Introduction

I WAS A DAYDREAMER as a kid, able to lose myself in some self-spun fantasy at a moment's notice. I was also a reader and just as quick to be transported through pages of print to some faraway place where adventure loomed.

I remember spending an entire summer evening when I was eight or nine, lying on the back porch watching broken clouds scud across the face of a full moon, blowing just fast enough to make it seem that they were standing still and the moon was moving. And I remember imagining that the moon was a ship under sail, a brave schooner coursing white-ribbed seas toward some distant shore, and wishing that I was on the fore-deck, feeling the wind in my face and anticipation in my heart.

Not long after that, my mother asked me what I wanted to be, and I said, "A wanderer."

I am now no longer a kid except in spirit, but otherwise not much has changed.

I never became a sailor, but I did become a hunter. I have not been a wanderer in quite the same way I imagined back then, never quite reached the status of footloose vagabond always on the move, like a leaf that remains in one place only until the wind blows once more. Looking back, however, I am sometimes astonished to think of where I've been.

Being a hunter—and, of late, a fisherman once again—is part of it. Being a writer is the rest. Had I known on that long-ago night that owning a small talent for tinkering with the language could be the key to adventuring in far-flung places I might have taken up the craft as a full-time occupation sooner. Or maybe not, and it really doesn't matter; what's important is that my good fortune of being able to make a reasonable living as a writer has brought the additional good fortune of magazine assignments that have sent me across three continents and into places ranging from the subarctic tundra to the equatorial rain forest, from exotic cities to country villages where the local tongue is as incomprehensible to my ear as a differential equation.

They've seen me lodged in every sort of dwelling, from tents to the Duke of Bedford's country estate; led me to dine on everything from *haute cuisine* to biltong, linty from my pocket; and had me washing it down with such diverse libations as water from a wild Alaskan spring to home-distilled *pálinka* from a reused plastic jug.

They've also seen me blistered by the tropical sun; drenched in prairie rainstorms; pelted by snow and sleet; eyed by bears and *federales*, crocodiles and Russian soldiers; and treated with warmth and kindness by strangers whose languages I can neither speak nor understand.

It's been wonderful.

Through it all has run the common thread of birds to hunt and, sometimes, fish to catch, and this in turn has led me to understand that no matter how different the landscapes and the customs might be, the bonds among sportsmen are truly universal. What differences might exist between a Brazilian fishing guide's approving "*Grande peixe!*" as he nets a good peacock bass and a Hungarian loader's quiet "*Bravo!*" when you've taken down a high, fast pheasant are only a matter of form; the content is the same.

This holds for companions as well. Companions are crucial elements in both sport and travel; bad ones can sour the pleasantest trip while good ones can turn adversity sweet. In my experience, the latter have far outnumbered the others, and in a way this is a wonder, because in many cases your full complement of companions is a matter of potluck. You might book a shooting trip with one or two friends, but you'll most likely share a lodge—and the shooting as well—with other hunters, especially if you're after doves or driven game. Running across the occasional jerk is inevitable, but you'll find them surprisingly few. I've met hundreds of people in hunting and fishing lodges and camps, but I can literally count the obnoxious specimens on one hand. I can honestly say that the best people I know are those I've met because of shotguns and fly rods.

Actually, that's not surprising. We all love the same things, and love knows no barriers of space nor time nor differences in background and lifestyle.

So, these are some stories from where I've been and what I've found there. They cover about ten years' time, from the mid-1980s to as recently as last season. Writing them was as much fun as being where they took me, because writing allows me to relive the experience and attempt to capture in words a sense of place and a sense of what I saw and heard and smelled and felt.

Nearly all of them were originally magazine stories, created from the working habits I've developed over the years. It's long been my custom, for instance, to take notes only to the extent of recording how names are properly spelled. It also is my custom whenever possible to wait at least three months—or better, six— between making a trip and writing about it, which is about the only way I've found of turning a failing memory to advantage. For me, time has a nice way of filtering things so that what I remember months after the fact are the sort of salient details that best serve a story.

Curiously, though, rereading these pieces as I've put this book together has brought much of the memory flooding back and prompted me to expand some of them to include things the original versions simply could not accommodate because of length. Being free of the limitations of space is one of the sweetest differences between writing magazine stories and writing books, especially to someone whose mind tends to meander like a cow elk browsing a vegetable market and most especially when the subject matter is as full of incidental experiences as travel often is.

In part, this is a chronicle of history, albeit a very personal one, and that has presented some choices. A project such as this makes a revisionist approach rather tempting. In the end, though, revisionism strikes me as valid only when it clarifies the facts, not when it obscures them. I was, for example, married to a woman named Susan during the time some of these stories took place, and she sometimes traveled with me. We aren't married now, haven't been for several years, and I could easily have edited her out. But that would in some cases obscure the truth of what happened, which makes for poor history.

It's ironic perhaps that the lovely lady who now shares my life doesn't appear in any of these pieces, but that's just one of the quirks in how time and events unfold. If I someday put together a second volume of such stories, you'll get to meet her. Meanwhile, if we should happen to run into each other somewhere in the world and you notice I'm with a tiny, beautiful, blonde-haired woman with a dazzling smile and one blue eye and one green, I promise you'll be as taken with her as I continue to be.

In some ways travel is its own reward, but in the end we really weren't meant to travel alone.

Copper Creek Farm
Camdenton, Missouri
January 1997

Acknowledgments

THIS BOOK OWES MUCH—almost everything, actually—to the magazine editors who've sent me off hither and yon in search of stories, and to the outfitters and hosts who've done their best to see that I found them.

Thanks go to editors Chuck Wechsler of *Sporting Classics*, Silvio Calabi and Ralph Stuart of *Shooting Sportsman*, Jim Butler of *Fly Rod & Reel*, Steve Smith of *Game & Gun*, Daniel Coté of *The Double Gun Journal*, and Dave Meisner and Diane Vasey of *The Pointing Dog Journal*. That all the various parts came together in their present form owes thanks to Tom Fernald, Karin Womer, and Chris Cornell of Down East Books.

I'm grateful to outfitters and hosts David Gregory and J. W. Smith of Rod & Gun Resources, Jack Jansma of Wingshooting Adventures, Jon Hollinger of Aspen Outfitting Company, Larry Grisham, Chris Goll of Rainbow River Lodge, Bill Moore and Bob Hunter, Tom Kennedy of Lansdowne Lodge, Dick Wallin of Sports Afield Duck Club, Robin Hurt of Sporting International, Alain Drache, Roger Mitchell and Jan Roosenburg of Holland & Holland, Frank Ruiz, Mike Okray of Hunts West, David Dees, Rick Hodges of The 74 Ranch, David Schuster of Herradura Ranch, Philip Marsteller of Amazon Tours, Robert Brand of Hacienda Paloma Blanca, Barry Batsell and Eduardo Maraboto of Sunbelt Hunting, Bob Ellsworth of La Rucia Ranch, and Bob Tinker.

And thanks to The Usual Suspects, the dear old friends whose good companionship lent sparkle and charm to these and other days—Ted Lundrigan, Bill Habein, David and Theresa Gregory, J. W. and Dawn Smith, Jon Hollinger, Jack Jansma, Bill Teesdale, Special Ed Smyth, Bob Schneidmiller, Ed Hayes, Wayne Latta, Joe Pryor and all the Hungarian Crew, Downwind Bob, Tim Leary, Dave Maass, Herb Booth, Chuck Wechsler, Bob Winn, and Dan Foster.

I'm especially grateful to my "twin brother," David Trevallion, both for being a great traveler and for not getting me tossed into a Russian pokey.

To all of you, here's to the days we've had and the days to come.

Prologue

Not Yesterday I Learned to Know the Love

WHEN HE RAN HIS DOGS in field trials, my father wore a pair of knee-high laced boots with his pant legs tucked inside. From my point of view, which at the time wasn't much higher than their tops, they were the most fabulous boots in the world. They meant bare, brown fields and lean, hard-running dogs and a gun and the promise of quail.

At first, those boots were at the center of it all, the prime criterion, lending shape and dimension. Then Dad showed me the real heart.

Try as I might, I cannot remember exactly when nor exactly where. I was no more than six or seven, very young, not yet a bird hunter. Dad took me along to a field trial—in eastern Iowa or western Illinois, I can't say which. It was the first time I ever saw dogs at work in earnest.

The fads of language unfortunately have gutted the word of all meaning nowadays, but it was awesome, and I was awestruck. It was a new world, beyond imagination—a world of men and dogs, judges on horseback, and everywhere I looked, boots just like Dad's. It was shrill silver whistles, the crackle of cornstalks underfoot, nose-twitching whiffs of horseapples faintly steaming in bright, cold air.

When the time came, Dad fetched his dog. A few men drove tall, boxy, wood-sided station wagons with dog boxes in the back, but in those days, most dogs rode in car trunks. Cookie was waiting, eager and happy, in the cavernous space of Dad's 1948 Olds, and she seemed to tremble in an anticipation I didn't understand. Dad clipped a short leather leash to her collar, told her to heel, and we walked to the line, she on his one side, I on the other.

The other dog was taller, a big male, every muscle aquiver. Keeping a finger hooked in her collar, Dad unsnapped the leash, rubbed her ears, and in response to some signal I didn't recognize, said simply, "Birds."

In the next instant she was gone, launched by an uncoiling of energy I could almost feel in the aftershock. Down the field she went full-stretch, sweeping a great arc. The big male was out there, too, cutting curves of his own, and we set out to follow.

I don't know how long it took. In my mind that day, there was no room for time. All I know is that Dad suddenly went off at a trot, and I remember churning through the corn stubble, thumping along as if pursuing the fading pale of grace. Then he was there again, in front of me, and he reached down and lifted me to his own height.

She was a few yards off, immobile as a monument, half bent, her forelegs crouched, her tail straight out and so rigid I imagined it would twang if you brushed against it.

And Dad said, "Look at that. Did you ever see anything so beautiful?"

I had not. Not even the boots.

Nor has that same perfect beauty dimmed in the thousands of times I've seen it since.

All the principal players in that little drama are gone now— first the dogs and then Dad—leaving me, like Ishmael, to tell the tale. It's never slipped far from memory in all these years, but it came back especially clearly not long ago. I was talking with a young friend who's just discovered what bird hunting can do to your soul, and he confessed feeling confused over choosing a dog, pointer or flusher, lacking any great experience with either one. He asked what I prefer, personally, and I told him that I can imagine hunting upland birds with something other than a pointing dog—because I've done it—but I can't imagine it feeling quite complete. He wondered why, and I told him the story I've just told you.

He mulled it over for a few minutes and then asked, "Would I feel the same way?"

From the mouths of babes and beginners . . .

The most honest answer I could think of was "maybe." If you have a dog that's interested in hunting, one that's intelligently trained, one that builds upon its own experience—maybe. Maybe, too, if your expectations are realistic, if you're tolerant enough to grant the dog its imperfections, patient enough to do a lot of teaching before you expect a lot of learning, secure enough not to burden the dog with the responsibility of your own self-image. Secure enough, in other words, not to see the dog as the sole arbiter of whether your hunting buddies think you're a hero or a dork.

Most of all, I told him, how you feel about hunting will shape how you feel about your dog. If action is the main appeal, a flusher might be just the ticket. But if the connection between yourself and the bird is what reaches right down into your gut and takes hold with both hands, then nothing forges that link like a dog on point. In that moment, the dog is a bridge between two worlds.

I don't know whether any of it made sense to him. It's the sort of thing everybody has to learn for himself, out of his own emotions and experience. But it set me thinking about the inward territory I've covered in the company of dogs.

To my father, "bird dog" meant English pointer, and except for a brief fling with a setter named Pudge—which happened before I was born—he was a pointer man all his hunting life. That meant I was a pointer man, too, or a pointer boy, at least in the beginning. It also meant that what I learned of dogs early on, I learned from Cookie.

If you were to go back in the Field Dog Stud Book, you'd find her as Accolade's Wig-Wag, whelped in 1945, daughter of Accolade, descendant of The Texas Ranger, who carried a fair measure of clout in the field-trial world of the early 1940s. I don't know how she got her kennel name, but as a tyke I heard often enough how she came to be Dad's dog.

Her litter belonged to one of his best friends, who owned a neighborhood tavern as a means of funding his real passion, which was to breed pointing dogs and hunt quail. By one of those not-uncommon quirks, the puppies outnumbered the bitch's teats by one, and Doyle was about to dispose of the least-promising specimen when my parents showed up. Dad was dogless at the time, having given his big setter to a friend when he left for the war. My mother, probably somehow influenced by my own imminent arrival, laid claim to the pup and fed her with an eyedropper until she reached weaning age.

Cookie was the best Dad ever owned. I still have the First-in-Derby trophy she won at an Illinois field trial in April 1947. Her ribbons have long since disappeared, but some brittle, yellowed clippings in Dad's scrapbook speak of her—and of an age when local newspapers in the Midwest reported such events.

She was the first friend I remember. Almost from the moment I could walk, or so my mother's stories went, the kennel was my main destination at any given time, and I do remember climbing inside the doghouse and curling up close to that warm, hard-muscled body with the soft, floppy ears that never seemed to tire of being rubbed.

I didn't shoot my first quail over Cookie; that came as a chance encounter during a rabbit hunt. But the first pointed bird I ever shot was one of hers and so was the next and the next, until I lost count. When she grew old and eventually died, my heart broke. I believe Dad's did, too, because he didn't own another dog for a long time after.

Between them, Cookie and Nancy, my rat terrier who lived to be eighteen, shaped my feeling for dogs. With Cookie I first felt the breathtaking swoop my spirit makes in the moments between the point and the flush. From Nancy I learned the ideal of uncomplicated love. Naturally, I sought to combine the two.

Armed with all the certainty of youth, I decided early on that those who insisted gun dogs should not or could not be "pets" were full of crap clear to their eyebrows. There would, in short, be no kennel dogs at my house. For a long time I cherished an image that alternated between fields and fireside. In the fields, we were tireless hunters, my dog and I, ever intense, ever on the verge of high deeds; afterwards, by the fire, the faithful dog would sleep peacefully on the hearth rug while I sipped cognac and relived sweet memories. True to the nature of youthful certainties, I perceived all this from the outside looking in, as if it were some graceful old diptych painted in a mellow palette, firmly convinced it would be so because I wished it so.

Not surprisingly, there were a few false starts—first a pointer, chosen for obvious reasons; followed by a lovely, rambunctious setter named Dolly; followed by another pointer who ate a dictionary, a pair and a half of my wife's shoes, and the neighbor's cat all in one afternoon; followed by a period of no dog at all, during which I began to question whether having a gun dog as housemate and constant companion was really such a bright idea after all.

About that time I accepted a teaching job in northwest Missouri, where the bird hunting was even richer and more varied than in the Iowa corn country where I'd been living. By the following summer, doglessness was becoming burdensome. My office-mate, a linguistics professor who hadn't the slightest interest in hunting, phoned one Saturday afternoon from Illinois, where he'd gone to visit his family, and said he'd found a litter of eight-week-old Brittany pups at a flea market for $25 apiece. At first I thought he was putting me on, finding pups at a flea market and all, but he assured me it was no joke. The owner was being transferred in his job and rather than fool with pups during the move, he chose the clearance-sale, loss-leader approach. Rob said he was going to buy one for a pet, just because they were especially pretty, and would get one for me if I wanted it.

I'd never bought a dog sight-unseen in my life, and haven't since, but the next thing I knew, I heard myself telling him to pick the largest female in the bunch.

The red gods must have been on my side for a change, because two days later, Rob delivered a little orange-and-white package that stole my heart forever.

Almost every pointer and a great many setters have eyes like hawks—a flinty, piercing gaze that makes you feel as if they're surveying the condition of your underwear or your moral rectitude. Something to do with their intensity as hunters, I suppose. In that summer of 1971, I was not much familiar with Brittanies and had in fact hunted behind a sum total of one, but their easygoing nature appealed to me. One look into my new puppy's eyes and I was a goner, for her and for the breed. If you searched an illustrated dictionary for the definition of love and sweet devotion, those eyes are what you'd find.

Ginny's training amounted mainly to come, sit, and some playful retrieving. As it turned out, that's all she needed. At four months, she pointed and held four successive single quail from my house covey. They were the first live birds she ever saw. A month later, we opened the bird season together with a nine-covey day, each one handled with great finesse, and never looked back. I haven't given a moment's thought to owning another pointer or setter since.

Thus I came to understand that the miscues and false starts were nature's way of telling me my thinking was altogether screwed up. I suspect every young Nimrod fantasizes about owning the ultimate bird dog, the one that streaks across the fields leaving a trail of charred, smoking stubble and foxtail behind, never out of touch or control, slamming into classic points from light-speed, guided always by an infallible, full-choke nose. After the hunting, said noble beast turns into the canine equivalent of David Niven, urbane and impeccably mannered, at ease in the drawing room, laconically graceful by the fireside.

It finally dawned that my treasured images were as compatible as fire and fuel. I can't say it's impossible to find a slashing, hard-driving hunter who turns into a lounge lizard indoors—but I can say I've never seen one, at least not a young one. More to the point, I also realized that my approach to hunting had undergone some change. The half-bloodthirsty kid whose idea of a good day's hunt meant scouring two counties at a canter had, by his mid-twenties, come to enjoy a slower pace. He slowed even more by his mid-thirties, and now, mid-fifties approaching, he is a rambling putterer—still looking for birds, but given to detours and intermissions, as apt to search for arrowheads as for likely cover, fond of sitting by streams listening to water over stones or perching on a fallen log to hear the woods go about their business of living.

For that kind of hunting, a big-going dog just doesn't cut it. Which isn't to say I don't appreciate the hard-runner's sheer athletic drive; a few of my friends have such dogs, and I love to hunt with them—but I don't want one of my own. The typical Brittany pace, slower and closer in, is my pace as well. Their points may not be quite so dramatic, but they're no less intense and they touch the same places in the heart.

This I learned from Ginny in the too-few years we had together. She died three months short of her fifth birthday, brought down by strychnine-laced peanuts that some neighborhood clod dropped into a mole run and left uncovered.

Then came Katie, a snipe-nosed genetic aberration who

wore the most gorgeous coat ever grown by a dog—thick waves and curls of deep, rich cordovan red interrupted only by a narrow white blaze on her chest and two white feet. Sweet, tragic Katie, who accumulated catastrophe as other dogs pick up cockleburs; who lost the sight in one eye from some mishap I never understood; who lost her bearings and strayed off for five brutally cold December days before turning up at a farmhouse five miles from home; who lost blood from being shot by some rifle-wielding scum alive today only because I never learned his whereabouts or name; who lost more blood and much of her sense of balance after being blindsided by a passing car; who finally lost it all dashing out of the bushes along the driveway at dusk one evening, going under the wheels of my own car.

And that was Katie, who died in my arms as I sat sobbing in a pile of sere November leaves. She was like some exotic flower struggling to bloom in a climate suited only for thorns. She haunts me still.

There was no gun dog in my house for almost two years after Katie, which is a long time to be without a key component of one's soul. But the horror of that awful night slowly faded, and I found the missing piece once more, in a suburb of St. Paul.

It was the single most beautiful litter of puppies I've ever seen, begotten by Spick's Brimstone Buster upon Sunshine Taffy II, dogs of similar bloodline whose pedigrees show a list of Field Champions and Dual Champions as long as your arm and in which eight members of the Brittany Hall of Fame appear a total of thirty-two times—the stuff of raptures, I suppose, to one more impressed by pedigrees than I.

I am, though, impressed by beauty, brains, and demeanor—qualities Taffy and Buster owned in abundance. And Lord, what pups they made. There were eight, as I remember, four of each sex, and even at six weeks and five days, they formed one of those rare litters from which you could close your eyes, grab one, and come out with a beauty. Thanks to the help of a friend, I had first pick among the females and spent the afternoon playing with them, looking for one to give me the sign, whatever it might be, that she and I would connect in some special way.

Watching them rollick and tumble, I noticed that one in particular, a lovely little creature with an almost perfectly drawn facial mask, preferred exploring the yard to chewing on her sisters. Each in turn puppy-pointed a grouse wing, showing about equal enthusiasm. And then mine revealed herself.

The wing was tied to a fishing rod by a length of thick white string. After a couple of play-points, the adventuresome lass who'd caught my eye earlier ignored the wing as I twitched it away from her and went for the string instead. I've always believed dogs have more capacity for reason than we think they do, and from the way she behaved, I could almost see the wheels turning inside her head: The wing always followed the string, and she couldn't catch the wing, therefore . . .

Now, I have no idea if that's why it happened the way it happened, but said pup left with me the next morning, and she's been with me ever since. To the AKC, she is October First, which is when the woodcock season used to open here in Missouri. To me, she is variously Tober, Tobe, Toby, and frequently Dingleberry. Her passions include woodcock, anything remotely edible, quail, any bed or form of upholstered furniture, and cowflops— not necessarily in that order. Her desire to hunt is a precise match for my own, and as a retriever I'd put her against any of any breed, simply for the ability to find and fetch whatever falls. In the twelve seasons we hunted together before she retired, she failed to find exactly one downed bird, and that one was my fault, not hers. Otherwise—dead, wounded, or merely dinged; runner or hider; in the open or the brush; in thick grass, water, snow, leaf litter, or dust; it was all the same to her. If it was down, she'd have it sooner or later.

Like many another Brittany I've known, she had a penchant for wanting to get eyeball to eyeball with the birds she pointed and thus didn't always earn high marks for deftness in handling game. She was a slow, close worker, so she didn't find as many birds as her hot-footed colleagues. Having an alpha personality and having hunted mostly alone, she was dead certain to muscle in on another dog's point unless I was close by, and she was steady to flush as a six-pack of nitro.

In short, my aging friend is an imperfect gun dog. As I am an imperfect man, we get along just fine. Hard times or good times, her devotion is absolute, her love unearthly in its simple perfection. And when she shines, she shines like a bouquet of suns.

It was the last hour of the last day of the week we spend each year among the grouse and woodcock of northern Minnesota. It's always a long week in terms of knee joints and leg muscles, incomprehensibly short in the terms of my heart. As Tober and I came down the steep old farm path toward the creek, the Blazer in sight at the top of the next rise, I was thinking more about the knees and beat-up muscles than about my heart.

Tobe was tired, too. This Minnesota gig was usually her first intensive work of the year, and she was eight then. For a half-hour or so, she'd stayed mostly at heel, by choice, but as we drew near the creek, she caught some tendril of smell she liked and slid under the fence to check it out.

From the way she vacuumed around in tight circles, it was clear that a grouse had puttered this same hillside in the recent past. Slowly, she wound a tortuous upward path. I looked at the slope, thought of my aching knees, and gave her a tentative "come," more question than command. I already had three birds in my vest and really didn't care if there should be a fourth. She paid no attention to me, working higher still in the scribbly gestures a dog makes when following the foot-scent of a grouse. One more "come" and a soft whistle got the same response, so I sighed, clambered over the fence, and followed slowly behind.

Thirty yards and about ten minutes on, she picked up the pace, and I came on edge. A moving grouse in open woods surely wasn't going to sit still for the kind of nose-to-nose point Tobe is wont to make.

Then she simply stopped.

At first I thought it was the scant remains of a cabin, twenty feet off her nose. On second look, it was just one fallen tree that happened to land on top of another. But together they formed a breastworks logical for a grouse to use as shelter—and an equally effective screen to block any shot I might have at a low flush.

How many grouse would stay put, knowing full well the fix it was in, while I struck off, gained the elevation and came in from the side? One in fifty, maybe.

I told Tobe that staying cool was the name of the game and moved off sideways. Still fearing a wild flush, I figured ten steps were all I could risk. Suddenly, I wanted that bird more than gold or salvation. A few slow yards uphill brought me to where any flush would at least be in sight, and then I moved back to inter-sect the invisible line from her nose to the bird, so plain you could draw it without a ruler.

It ended without drama. Five paces on, a grouse whirred up, straight away; I caught its path in almost a throwaway gesture with the gun; it fell dead, and my dear, dear girl trotted over, picked it up, and brought it in, eyes shining.

My eyes shone, too, as I hopped stone to stone across the creek while Tobe splashed through, stopping for a quick drink be-fore we tackled the last hill up the pasture. Her shining, I suspect, was in the satisfaction of a job well done. Mine came from forty years of love lodged firmly in my throat.

Part I

Heading North

- ▶ *Minnesota*

- ▶ *Canada*

- ▶ *Alaska*

Spirits in the Woods

I been up and down that river
From one end to the other end,
And I ain't found no heaven
Anywhere I been.

—old Delta blues

FOR THOSE OF US in whom kinship with the Earth flows strong and deeply, heaven is where spirits coincide, where the landscape matches the contours of our hearts. It's the place where we cease to be an errant puzzle-piece, where the fit is perfect beyond thought. You won't know where it is until you're there, and where you find it depends on which end of the river you're looking from. And even old bluesmen can be wrong.

My corner of heaven begins north of the Crow Wing River, reaches east to the St. Croix and the big lake, north at least to the Rainy River. It's country where deciduous woods mingle the southern fringes of the boreal pines, country freckled with blue lakes and veined with slender streams that run tea-colored from tannin leached out of the soil. On moonless nights, the aurora shimmers the northern sky like distant jeweled curtains rippling at the open windows of the gods.

I have a notion that we don't find our particular patches of heaven until we've reached an age to appreciate them. I was born and grew up less than two hundred miles from Minnesota's southern border, but for some reason I didn't set foot in the state until exactly the midpoint of what I assume to be my allotted threescore years and ten. I went there to spend some time with grouse, and grouse are part of what has taken me back, year after year, ever since.

I believe there are more grouse in Minnesota than anywhere else on Earth. But there's more to it. What meaning there is in the week I spend in northern Minnesota every fall is an accumulation in time, by now as many-layered yet tightly unified as a pearl. It is the essence of what hunting ought to be—which is to say that it is a microcosm of life itself.

Part of it is country—wonderful, wild, shaggy country. I can find something to love about any landscape that's still the way nature made it, but the Minnesota woods steal my soul. For one thing, there's plenty of it; Minnesota has about 26,000 square miles of forest—an area slightly larger than West Virginia, roughly the size of Vermont, New Hampshire, and Massachusetts combined. Most of it lies on the eastern side of the state in a vast carpet that in some places goes on for miles unbroken even by a road.

It's also beautifully diverse woodland: oak and hickory mixed with a dozen or more species of evergreen, with aspen, alder, tamarack, and elegant white birch. The understory is lush with gray dogwood, highbush cranberry, hazelbush, willow, ferns—enough plant life, all told, to send a botanist into raptures.

Its size, diversity, and the ways it's managed all combine to make the Minnesota woods rich living space for grouse. Ironically, man himself has contributed much to this wealth of habitat, even at times when he was hell-bent on raping the countryside for every penny it could yield. A hundred years ago, the lumber barons plundered northern Minnesota, just as they did the rest of the great forests in the upper Midwest, leveling thousands of square miles of virgin timber in less than a generation. Some areas, too fragile to regenerate themselves, were destroyed forever, but through most of the northern woods, second-growth timber flourished, and so did the grouse.

Bonasa umbellus thrives in young, thick woods, finding his livelihood in buds, shoots, berries, catkins, leaves, and seeds from the scores of different plants that colonize a sunny opening in the woods. He'll continue to thrive there until the trees grow tall and old enough that the canopy blocks the sun and vegetation dies out on the forest floor.

Now, timber management helps keep much of Minnesota's forest land in prime condition for grouse. Cutting, mercifully, is no longer done on the scale it was at the turn of the century, but enough trees are felled every year for pulp and firewood and the sawmills that you can find good habitat in almost all of the eastern counties. The country I hunt is in some places a patchwork of tiny hayfields laced with trails sown in sweet clover. Some days, the field edges and the trails fairly teem with grouse.

Access to good hunting is abundant, too. An enormous amount of Minnesota land is in federal, state, and even county ownership, and the hunting on much of it is as good as you'll find anywhere. Obviously, the farther you go into the country, away from the cities, the less gunning pressure there is. I've hunted some pieces of public land for years and have yet to meet another hunter there.

What I have found there are birds and dogs and friends, happiness and pain, love and sorrow—life rendered to the essence.

The experience centers on two birds, grouse and woodcock, each in its own way a distillation of spirits.

The one is a spark of cosmic energy dressed in feathers, so firmly integrated with its environment that grouse and Minnesota woods are a mutual definition. The northern Indians heard voices of the gods in the beat of a drumming grouse. For many years, even ornithologists believed that the bird made the sound by striking its wings against its breast. We now know that drumming, primarily a means by which cock birds attract hens during the mating season, is actually a sonic boom produced by air momentarily trapped and compressed between the bird's cupped wings and its body. But even if the image of a cock grouse pounding its chest in a primal display of sovereignty isn't good biology, it's close enough to the spirit of truth. Some grouse drum year-round, and hearing that ghostly, resonant cadence in the October woods is enough to make you believe that the Indians probably were right, after all.

For all the sophistication that science has brought to bear, the grouse still holds some mysteries unrevealed. Biologists have yet to find the cause—or even a consistent set of causes—for the cyclical ebb and swell of grouse populations. Every ten years or so, after a steady annual increase in numbers, the population crashes almost overnight. It apparently has nothing to do with weather or predation or any observable phenomenon—the birds simply disappear in a quantum stroke and almost immediately begin increasing until the cycle turns again.

There is some evidence that the aspen tree, which offers grouse so much in terms of food and shelter, also plays a role in the population cycle. In response to high numbers of birds feeding heavily on its buds during the winter, the aspen generates a chemical, coniferyl benzoate, that suffuses the buds and makes them unpalatable to grouse. Moreover, it happens as a chain reaction, so that when one aspen starts producing coniferyl benzoate, those nearby do, too, until the phenomenon sweeps across vast areas. The cycle happens everywhere grouse live, but it's considerably more pronounced in the Upper Midwest, with its virtually unbroken aspen belt, than elsewhere.

Even so, despite a profuse outpouring of effort and carefully documented monographs, even the most knowledgeable grouse biologists, particularly if they also are grouse hunters, won't argue very strenuously against the notion that the population cycle is the work of the gods.

You can find a satisfying number of birds in Minnesota even in the down years. Most of the coverts I hunt are private land, places that see no hunters other than our little group. Finding birds takes a bit more effort when the cycle is at its nadir, but always there are enough. Public land isn't much different: if you get far enough from the cities and far enough from the roads to outdistance the weekenders and ribbon clerks, you'll find grouse in Minnesota. The big woods really are that big.

The up years are almost beyond belief—utterly so for hunters accustomed to populations in which four- or five-flush days are the stuff of fireside stories. In those years, fifty flushes before lunch is not unheard-of; it's a marvel that so relatively few acres of woods can harbor so many birds.

And every year, reliable as leaves, there are woodcock. The resident birds are usually gone by mid-October, the coverts filling and refilling with migrants. If the wind holds in the south for two or three days at a time, which it often does, the alder runs and certain stands of doghair popple will be stiff with birds. There's a certain forty-acre patch of alder swamp south of Leech Lake where I've more than once moved three dozen woodcock in two hours' time, and there's a little upland corner about five miles away that's almost as good. And those are only two of many.

You find such places largely by accident and remember them for the rest of your life, even when the timber grows old and out of favor with the strange, gentle, long-nosed little birds that seem to come from somewhere out of space and time, linger a while, and then move on.

I do all of my Minnesota hunting within a ten-mile mile radius of one small town, and in nearly twenty years of going there I've come to know the countryside and the people about equally well. It isn't Lake Wobegon, but it could be. The prevailing accent is a musical lilt from the back of the throat, so nearly everyone sounds like Butch Thompson. The younger faces have the healthy glow that comes from living in a cool climate; the older ones crinkle in fine creases when they smile. Ole and Lena are the main characters in most of the jokes you hear over coffee at the local restaurant. As in every town everywhere, there's a share of rounders and layabouts, scofflaws and dolts, but the best of these large-hearted, generous-spirited Minnesota people are proof that Garrison Keillor's stories are fiction only in the strictest sense.

It starts, officially, when I roll into Ted's driveway—Tober growing restive in her traveling crate, I stiff and creaky from fourteen hours on the road. The yard light is on. For a lot of those years, Dixie, the sweet old Labrador who flushed and fetched more grouse than most dogs would see in three lifetimes, usually barked once before she recognized my voice and then put her graying muzzle into my hand. Salty, a little white setter held together by sheer centripetal force, always deferred to Dixie's claim on first pets and hung back until I called her, at which Tobe would set up an aggrieved clamor in the back of the Blazer. Then Ted has me wrapped in a bear hug and a smile that feels like home.

Inside, there's a warm fire and hugs from Cheryl and Mister Max, my buddy who arrived in this world one cold February night in 1982 and who has helped make it a better place ever since. If Bill isn't there already, he soon will be—grizzly-bearded Bill who calls himself a blacksmith but who actually is a jackpine genius. He could start with a pile of iron and an idea and make anything from a stove to a door lock or a six-ton machine that'll turn a tree trunk into a finished building log in less than a minute.

None of us is thinking much about work, though. For the next week, Ted's law partner will care for the clients, and the CLOSED sign will stay up on Bill's workshop door. Tonight, before I haul my gear down to the log cabin by the brook, there will be good whiskey by the fire, a long briefing on where the birds are hanging out, some loose plans about which coverts to visit first—all of it laced with stories told in verbal shorthand, in the way of men who've covered many miles together.

At this latitude, October in its second week is a moment on the cusp. Grass is still summer-green, the trees molting autumn plumage. The woods change almost overnight from a postcard picture to a starker, leaner beauty. Some leaves still cling in the popple thickets, trembling in the slightest breeze as if anxious at being left behind. The patient tamaracks—odd, bog-loving trees that masquerade as evergreens—take the final curtain-call of autumn color, showing brilliant yellow against a backdrop flattening into subtle shades of brown and gray. These are hunter's woods.

I imagine that even hell itself looks pretty good in October, but northern Minnesota weaves its magic around every sense. There's a smell about these woods that I've never smelled anywhere else, a ripe sweetness that seems to transpire from the earth itself. It may come from the knee-high stands of wood fern turned coppery-brown from frost, or from something else entirely. What matters is that it's there, mixed with the poignant scent of spruce. Sometimes, moving through the woods, we'll cross the musky thread of stink left by a whitetail buck in early rut. For all that these hunting days can feel like moments forever locked in time, the wild smell of deer is a reminder that the country is in a headlong rush toward winter.

So, too, is the early snow that sometimes comes to the north country in October. It rarely lasts half a day, but hunting those woods on a brilliant blue morning carpeted in white is a wonder. No year passes without someone remembering out loud a certain Sunday afternoon when we hunted in the first thick flurries of a new snow, great cottony flakes sifting silently down through the windless woods and a fresh fall of woodcock in the alders along the swamp.

We hunt, always, in a pastiche of sound: boot soles scuffing the forest floor; the woody clack of stems and branches as we push through the undergrowth; dry whispers of twigs on canvas vests and nylon-faced pant legs. For years, you could close your eyes and know by bells and footfalls which dog was where. Dixie ambled next to Ted, moving almost in a doze until she picked up the foot-scent of a grouse. Then, nose down and tail waving, she'd trot off along its invisible, twisty course, and presently there would be a bird in the air. Old Dixie trained us well.

The middle distance, gunshot range, would be busy with dogs, Tobe crossing back and forth, bell jingling, Bill's springers, Tootsie and Rosie, turning merry circles in the leaves and brush. Farther out, wrapped in the clear notes of a Swiss bell, Salty glided in larger sweeps, probing the woods with her full-choke nose.

With both flushers and pointers working in the same platoon, there is little room for complacency, because the sound of wings can come with little warning. According to where we are, we can predict to some extent what the sound will be—a woodcock's eerie twitter or the fine, rolling roar of a grouse—and then in a few magic seconds, one of us will reach out to close the circle.

Grouse hunting, more than any hunting I know, is a constant communion with spirits. What predictability there is belongs mostly to woodcock. Hunt for grouse, and you find yourself in a chess game with the red gods, playing on a board that only they can see. Approach a grouse from an angle that gives it clear flight to the best escape cover you can see—the angle, naturally, that gives you a straightaway shot—and the bird is likely to fly straight for your head. Spend enough time with them, and you'll forever wonder why some grouse flush a hundred yards out if you think too loudly and why others sit in trees and simply watch while you pelt them with sticks, yell, or call in a marching band underneath.

Other game birds are creatures you hunt. Grouse happen to you.

Exactly how they happen to you can change from day to day, bird to bird, moment to moment, almost. There was that Thursday, for instance.

It was the first sunny day in almost a week. We'd hunted in rain, sleet, and drizzling mist, and the birds had for the most part gone wherever it is that grouse go when the weather is weird. But Thursday came up cool and fine, with high, fluffy clouds in a sky the color of cornflowers. The morning offered some reasonable shots, and I shot them reasonably well. Two birds in the bag by lunchtime always suits me well.

In the afternoon, we hunted Uncle Willie's farm, a textbook landscape of grouse cover. The dogs found birds almost immediately, in a big patch of gray dogwood at the edge of the south pasture. Ted eased in behind a stylish point and met with one of the rarest, loveliest moments in grouse hunting—a double flush. The two birds came up not three feet apart, actually bumped into one another breast to breast, and parted as if in slow motion, just as Ted's shot charge passed cleanly between them. One flew west, the other north, and no one fired again.

There were more grouse in the balsams at the north end of the pasture. Ted shot one over another point, and I killed a young-of-the-year bird, wise beyond its time. That grouse flushed wild, tried sliding along the forest edge behind the screen of trees and almost made it work.

Fifty yards beyond, Ted took another and so did I. By then we were fairly herding grouse ahead of us, pushing north toward the alder bottom at Goblin Creek. There were birds there, too, the smell of them lying heavy as fog, and the dogs started to come unglued. Everywhere they moved, more grouse roared out.

Trying some off-the-cuff strategy to get things under control again, Ted angled west toward an old, dried-up beaver pond that we knew the birds wouldn't cross, and I turned east, thinking to cross the creek among the alders, gain the higher ground, and, if not pin the birds for a moment by an unexpected approach, at least see their flight path into the jackpines beyond.

It wasn't the best-laid plan, but it went awry quickly enough. The alders grew there in such a horrid tangle that a snake couldn't have made that crossing, much less a none-too-agile hunter burdened with a shotgun. I stopped at one point to catch my breath, nearly horizontal and spread out among springy alder whips like a palsied spider, and realized that even if I died there, I wouldn't touch the ground until my weathered bones finally separated and fell one by one.

The birds were long gone by the time I caught up with Ted, who was sitting in the grass drawing plumes of smoke from his pipe and trying not to laugh. I flopped down next to him and spoke coarse words about the ancestry of *Bonasa* and all his tribe.

"Those birds made fools of us."

"Unh-huh," Ted said. "That's their job."

And Ted, whose job it is to commemorate such things—and who sometimes calls me Lord Byron, for reasons I take to be flattering—named that little alder hell Byron's Demise. Grouse, and the places where you find them, have a way of bringing you to the very bone of what hunting is about.

Every year, Ted and Bill take me to some new place they've found, but the sweetest moments are those in the old, familiar coverts, the ones with names, the ones where the ghosts of memory gather. Places like Covey Top, the Disco, Wagonwheel, Luke's Luck, Bee Sting, Leonard Woodcock, Sam's Rest, Mike's Revenge, the Cursing Cover, Ray Charles, Hail Valley. Places that have touched our lives, places where the cycle of life is a constant affirmation.

And so, every year, we visit Laura's Woods.

We never knew Laura Pedersen, but we know something of her spirit. She sleeps in a grove at the shoulder of a gentle hill where a meadow slopes south to a tiny stream. From there, the land tilts up again, through woods that were prime for grouse when I first saw them. Now, only pockets of cover remain. Laura's grave is a tiny circle of grass in the slowly opening woods. The original stone, carried from the meadow, stands at one side, weathered smooth and white. A newer stone, this one polished granite from somewhere else, tells us that Laura was born November 2, 1881, and that she died May 17, 1898. Some of her brothers and sisters—old, old people in whom the fire of life still burns fiercely bright—have told us of a girl, gentle as spring, who died of pneumonia in the blossoming of her sixteenth year.

To anyone who might be watching, it might seem odd that men in hunting clothes would abruptly turn from the old, grass-grown road, follow a now all-but-invisible path to this little clearing and stand hatless and silent, looking down. A few autumns ago, Ted and I faced each other across Laura's grave and wondered at the mysteries of death. When we'd last stood here, his daughter had been alive and so had my father. Now both, like our days already spent in these woods, were part of time and space beyond every reach but that of memory. And we were forever changed.

When we turned to go, I looked back, as I always do, with the hope of seeing this place again. A few minutes later, at the other end of Laura's Woods, Tobe sprung a big gray grouse that sailed off among the trees, looping down toward the creek. Ted and I looked at one another, both knowing exactly the piece of cover where, if we chose, we could flush him again. Instead, we turned north up the old road arched over with trees, heading for the car. We'll meet that grouse soon enough, next year, during the week that always breaks my heart and always makes it whole again.

Father's Day

FATHER'S DAY CAME LATE in 1991. It was Ted's idea.

He broached it over the phone one late-summer day while we were making hunting plans for October: "What do you think about reserving an afternoon to hunt with our fathers' guns?"

I thought it was just right. Ted's father and mine never met one another, but they were both bird hunters and they made bird hunters of us. They both lived long lives that ended, not so long apart, in more struggle and pain than either deserved, and they left behind sons who loved them fiercely and who still carried all the pangs of loss. How better to celebrate remembrance?

I'd thought before of taking Dad's gun along on one of my trips to the north woods, as a way of completing some unfinished business.

Dad bought his gun in 1935, used it for just under fifty years, and then gave it to me. By then, it had brought to bag an impressive variety of game—quail and pheasant, prairie chickens, woodcock, snipe, ducks, geese, and rabbits—and I determined to finish out its record, at least on the species common to the Midwest. Since Dad lived his whole life in Iowa, where the mourning dove is cast in the same regard as house wrens and goldfinches, the gun had no claim on the little gray chaps. I live in Missouri, though, so getting it blooded in the dove fields was easy enough.

And then there were grouse. In all his days, Dad never hunted ruffs, which is a pity, because he would have loved them.

And I'd love to take him through some coverts I know, but that time is past. Perhaps taking his gun instead would be the next-best thing.

Perhaps. Have you ever longed to do something you know will soothe your spirit but didn't because the time never seemed right? That's how it was with Dad's gun and grouse. Two years passed after he died, then three, and each October I left his gun behind. But then Ted, his own father just a few months gone, suggested we set Father's Day on a new schedule—or, as he put it, "carry the old clunkers around for a while and see if we can hit anything."

Ted's father and mine were of the generation that fell truly in love with repeating guns, Ted and I of the one that rediscovered the double's exquisite delights. For my Dad, the Remington Model 31 pump was the *ne plus ultra*, for Ted's, the Remington Model 11 autoloader, and those were the guns they left us. Compared with our own favorites, they're heavy and graceless, and we'd both prefer they were Purdeys—but neither of us would trade them even-up for any of London's best, because . . . well, you know why.

Grouse were not easy to come by in that year, even in the lovely coverts Ted shares with me. Not that we were in any danger of being skunked, because the last grouse on earth will flush out of those thickets, but when the population cycle starts to fall, the hunting hones down to a fine, demanding edge. For three days we thrashed and strove, flogging brush and doghair popple, taking the shots as they came, admiring the fugitives, and paying high honors to the ones that didn't get away.

Father's Day came on a gorgeous afternoon, the sky impossibly blue above a landscape flowing with sunlight. The poetic part of me saw it that way; the hunter in me surveyed the atmosphere and decided it was going to be too bloody warm for comfort. I could feel a trickle of sweat down my neck even as I drew

Remington gun No. 10784 out of its fleece-lined slip and shoved two of my pet handloads into the magazine.

Ted did the same with a massive old humpback. I'm so used to seeing him with either a Parker or L.C. Smith in his hands that I looked twice, to make sure I was hunting with the right guy.

We started across a pasture laced with tendrils of scruffy brush, cover about as ungrouselike as cover can be. Even the dogs couldn't take it very seriously. When they hit the ground and started nosing the air like three radar screens, I figured they were casting for the nearest water.

Given their respective natures, I suspect the black dog and the Brittany were doing exactly that, but we hadn't gone a hundred yards when Salty the setter veered off north as if she knew something. When she does that, Salty always knows something, and Ted veered off with her. I was about another hundred yards toward the woods when I heard the shot and saw the black dog heading in for the fetch.

I waited at the edge of the timber until Ted caught up, still smoothing feathers on a handsome second-year cockbird.

"What's a grouse doing in this crap?"

"Oh, there's always one out in these necks," Ted said. "You know, this gun really feels weird."

Ten minutes later, I stood in the woods and stared up at a grouse in a tree.

"Your turn," Ted said, grinning.

"Throw or shake?"

"Your choice," Ted said.

"Shake."

Ted walked over and took hold of the tree, which was no bigger around than your arm. I stepped in beside him, having learned a long time ago where to stand if I'm going to have a crack at a grouse bailing off a limb.

"Ready?"

"Ready," I said, gun butt tucked neatly under my arm, muzzle pointed right where the bird was looking.

He shook the tree, the grouse flew, about where I thought it would, and I killed it. My Brittany girl was waiting like Nellie Fox under an infield fly, and Ted and I were exchanging Father's Day congratulations, so I forgot about the bird and looked down to see why I couldn't get my thumb on the top-lever. Because there was no top-lever, and only then did I think to jack the slide.

Now I grew up shooting a pump gun—in fact, the very pump gun I had in my hands. But that was a long time ago, and I have lost the touch. Once, I could get off two shots that sounded like one. Last time I shot a pump was at skeet, and the gun was a little .410 that looked like fun, so I asked to try it. Singles were fine, but I went through four sets of doubles on Station 1 before I could remember to shuck the damn thing for the second shot. Then when I did, I somehow managed to slam my little finger between the forend and the frame. It was not a pretty sight.

I looked at Ted. "This gun feels really weird." Ted smiled.

After half an hour, I realized I'd forgotten how to carry a pump gun. Hunting in the woods, I usually hold a gun by the grip with my right hand and let the barrels rest on my shoulder. It's an easy position from which to get started after an unexpected flush and leaves my left hand free to fend off the brush. Moreover, the width of a side-by-side's twin tubes keeps the gun stable and in line with my hand.

But it only works with a side-by-side. Any other gun keeps falling over one way or the other, so the grip and trigger are at right angles—which is to say, wrong angles—to your hand. Unless, of course, you keep a tight hold on it, which makes your arm tired . . .

I was thinking about all this and fumbling around trying to decide which was the least awkward way to let Dad's gun fall against my shoulder when the next grouse came sizzling past from somewhere in Ted's direction. I turned toward it, wrestled the gun into something like a shooting posture, lost the safety, found it, poked a shot well behind, pulled the trigger again, remembered the slide, short-shucked, jammed the action, and ended up sending nothing more after the now-vanished bird than several brief words of Anglo-Saxon origin, delivered with a volume and vehemence that might have been deadly at closer range.

"Having trouble?" Ted called over, his voice juicy with the effort of not laughing out loud.

"You might say," I answered, feeling my own tongue thicken but not sure whether I was going to laugh, cry, or just howl like a ruptured coyote.

I was right about one thing: Father's Day was too bloody warm for comfort. By the time we got up to the edge of the big clearcut, we had our shirts unbuttoned, sleeves rolled to the elbows, and hats in our game bags. Both our vests were soaked through. We'd had a total of fourteen flushes, eight of them shootable, and carried precisely one grouse apiece.

Ted suggested we split up, work the clearcut edge in opposite directions, and meet on the far side. Okay by me. He started off down the hill, and I crossed a pasture corner toward the trees.

The clearcut reached right to the fence, where a clump of popple had been recently felled. Tobe slid under the wire, took a whiff at a little pile of leafy slash, and struck a point. Whether the bird had wandered out after some easy picking on the aspen leaves or had been cutting clover in the pasture edge was impossible to tell, but it was in a serious pickle either way—pasture on two sides, clearcut on another, Tobe holding it tightly in sparse cover, and the nearest standing trees a good twenty yards off. So I eased through the fence, thinking, here's where Nimrod is going to do himself and Dad's gun right proud.

Actually, there was one tree left, a wrist-sized popple next to the slash pile where the bird was, and I figured to pick up the flush at the tree and take the shot between there and the woods. The bird was understandably nervous and took off right on cue, heading exactly where it was supposed to go.

Once upon a time, disengaging a cross-bolt safety while mounting the gun was for me as unconscious an act as flicking a tang safety is now, just a little pressure from the middle joint of my finger as it curled toward the trigger. In retrospect, that amounts to two distinct motions with a fine and delicate line between—in retrospect. At the time, I simplified things by pushing the safety and pulling the trigger all at once, so the muzzle was swinging toward the bird and the gun was about halfway up when I cut a silver-dollar-sized chunk out of the popple tree.

The bird never looked back, and I was afraid to look at Tobe, because I knew exactly what expression I'd see on her face. Instead, I took a deep breath, blew it out, opened the gun, shook out the live round, dropped it in my pocket, and strolled around the top side of the clearcut, keeping well out from the trees for fear there might be another grouse nearby. Ted's side was thicker, so I reached the meeting point before he did, found a stump, and sat down with Dad's gun across my knees.

"Well, old-timer," I said to it, "one of us was not meant to be a grouse hunter today. But you got your bird."

Ted came toiling up the hill, his face streaming sweat, and sat down, too.

"I thought I heard you shoot down there," I said. "Hit anything?"

He nodded. "Somehow." He looked at his father's gun. "I can't shoot this damn thing," he said. "I'm not even sure I can carry it all the way back to the truck."

"I think we accomplished what we set out to do."

"Yes," my dear old friend said, "and I'm glad."

We looked at each other and said, in perfect unison, "Because now we don't ever have to do it again."

I like to think that two fathers were together somewhere when Father's Day came late, watching their sons trudge back through the rich, slanting sun, seeing us not as we were but as the boys we used to be. Watching and smiling.

Golden Hours

I'VE HEARD IT SAID that the Almighty does not subtract from a man's allotted time the hours he spends fishing. I don't know whether this is true or if it's just wishful thinking on the part of anglers or tackle manufacturers or both. Nor do I know whether the same deal extends to hunting grouse and woodcock. It certainly seems no less worthy than flogging some innocent body of water, but I haven't questioned the Almighty on that account—and as I'm not operating from what you might call a strong bargaining position where the Almighty is concerned, I probably won't.

I will, however, continue to hope that all my poking around the woods looking to make some connection with *Bonasa umbellus* and *Scolopax minor* has been an exercise in credit rather than debit. If it truly is time earned and not time spent, then I figure I'm due to live about 180 years. Which would be fine with me, because I wouldn't at all mind the chance to make up a bit of lost time.

When I was a kid, ruffed grouse were conspicuously absent from the woods of southeastern Iowa, so it was a while before I made their acquaintance. Woodcock, though, were a different story. I don't remember them being abundant—which may have had more to do with my not really knowing where to look than with actual population levels—but I do remember that the little chaps got their hooks into my heart well before I graduated to double-digit birthdays.

We were quail hunters, Dad and I, and the woodcock we bagged together were always adjuncts to the pursuit of bobwhites, encounters more of chance than design. Even so, every one of them stands sharp in my memory, from the first time I saw a woodcock on the wing—flushed from a little willow-thatched spring seep in one of Granddad's fields—to the last time Dad and I hunted together, twenty-five years later. From the moment I held the first one in my hand, woodcock were mystery and beauty and a sense of wildness so vast that it overspilled the boundaries of thought. Those early birds were my trophies, to my mind the most intriguing game a hunter could aspire to find. Since then, I've given them a full measure of time on their own account, and nothing has happened to change my mind or diminish the feeling.

Which I suppose explains a few things that some people seem to think require explanation: Such as why a grown man is willing to make long trips by automobile and flying machine for the sole purpose of wading through alder swamps, river-bottom jungles, and other unseemly places looking for specimens of a six-ounce bird that has a three-inch bill, eyes on top of its head, a brain that's upside-down, and a taste for earthworms. Such as why that same man would willingly associate with bird dogs and with other men known to perform similar acts of lunacy. Or why his fondest dream is to one day posses the wherewithal to spend several thousand dollars on having made to order a 28-bore self-cocking hammer gun specifically for hunting woodcock.

Such questions used to trouble me, because I thought I should be able to come up with clear, well-reasoned answers. No more. Pose them to me now, and I'll simply tell you that woodcock are like jazz—if you have to ask, you'll never understand.

I've asked the same questions of myself, mind you, and more than once. Especially when I've come out on the wrong side in the game of woodcock roulette—which involves a long, expensive trip whose success rests solely upon the question of whether you and the birds will be in the same place at the same time. Duck hunters have a keen appreciation of the time-honored statement, "you shoulda been here last week"—but only because they heard it first from woodcock hunters.

Everyone who knows woodcock knows they're migratory birds, but those who know them best understand that woodcock often approach the idea of migrating as if it's a notion that just occurred to them. They'll hang around their coverts for days on end, loafing and doodling as if they have no intention of seeing the next county. Then the wind shifts or stars collide or something happens that only a woodcock can see, and an hour later they're all gone.

Out of a hilltop loafing covert in Minnesota, I once sprang a bird that twittered up, flew through my shot swarm, and settled back down about twenty yards off—all typical of the way woodcock behave. I walked over, flushed him again, missed him again, and then I guess he decided, what with being in the air and all, that he might as well migrate. I had a long view over the surrounding woods from that spot, and the last I saw of him was a tiny speck in the sky, heading south, clearly without any intention of landing anywhere that side of Iowa.

How could anyone keep from falling in love with a bird whose impulses lie so close to the surface?

Which is not to say it's always easy to appreciate. I once flew from home (Missouri) to Nova Scotia (a hell of a long way) for the express purpose of hunting woodcock in one of the classic Eastern woodcock-hunting grounds. I spent three days crawling through coverts on the order of dreams and flushed exactly one bird, which of course flew straight from me toward the fellow I was hunting with, so neither of us had a safe shot.

Just last fall, I drove to northern Minnesota (not quite so far but still a hell of a long way) for the same reason. Every mile, in the song of tires against the road, I could hear my pal Ted's voice from the phone three days before. It was a lovely refrain: "We're covered up with woodcock, covered up with woodcock, covered up, covered up . . ." In five days of hunting hard I saw three, all of which flushed within thirty yards and two minutes of each other and all in front of Ted, who put them neatly to bag with three barks from his little Westley Richards 20.

I could go on, but you've got enough stories of your own to know exactly what I mean.

Fortunately for us, though, woodcock and grouse like much the same sort of digs, and since grouse don't migrate, sudden disappearances by the one don't affect availability of the other.

I was past thirty before I shot my first ruff, so they never have occupied quite the same emotional territory as some other birds—which is not to say the feeling's any less, only that it's different. The older I get, the more I believe that some things come along at just the time when we're best prepared to appreciate them. That first one was a big, red, northeastern-Iowa cockbird, hard found and hard won, and my life hasn't been quite the same since.

As a clan, grouse have become something of a pet preoccupation with me. I've hunted all the prairie birds and a couple of the alpine species and intend to keep at it until I've met every one. If there's anything unexciting about grouse I haven't found it. I love them all, in their ways, but ruffs seem to me to have more sheer wild energy, more complex ways of interacting with their environment, more of that combination of qualities that make game birds game, than all the rest put together. In the presence of ruffs, I've been hornswoggled, bamboozled, duped, and made to play the fool; I've sweated and sworn, shivered in rain and snow, crashed around the woods like a drunken moose, gone as leg-weary as I hope I'll ever be—and offered many a silent prayer of thanks for the privilege. I'd hunt every day of the season if I could.

It's fulfilling enough to spend time solely with one or the other, but the sweetest hours of all are those where you move from grouse to woodcock, woodcock to grouse, where habitats shift and blend, where sometimes the posture of your dog is the only clue you have for guessing which bird is about to flush.

In those hours, hunting is a symphony. Woodcock fill legato passages, gentle and softly voiced, sweet violoncello sprites on woodwind wings. Grouse are percussion crescendos, brass-bold, hammering thunder, martial, stirring.

Years ago, Ted and I discovered a magic place in the midst of yet another magic place. It was a Sunday afternoon, one of those days that only come in October, the woods washed in buttery sunlight under a sky as blue as my lady's eyes. We were just crossing the first fence when one of the Norwegian bachelor farmers who own the place came rattling by in his pickup, and we turned back to talk with our old friend. He and his brother have been kind hosts to our hunting for more years than any of us like to think about.

"Yah, der's a buncha grouse in 'er dis year," he said, pointing to the piece of woods we call the Green Field covert. "Prolly soma'dem woodcocks you fellers like, too. You guys hava good time, now." And off he went, down the old road toward the house.

Has it ever occurred to you that the decentest people you ever met were farmers or bird hunters? Ted and I waved the dust cloud away from our faces and grinned at one another.

The dogs were in splendid form, Ted's as a matter of course, mine for a change, performing at that level of grace and deftness that can take your breath away. Salty nailed the first grouse dead solid on the up-slope trail, and Tober got the next where the hilltop trail intersects. Not many things are capable of spoiling a day that puts a bird in each of your vests twenty minutes from the truck.

By the time we reached the west edge of the woods a couple of hours later, it would have taken a dreadful accident or a nuclear attack to put a blemish on things. Ted had four grouse. I had three and the bittersweet memory of blowing both barrels at what may have been the easiest shot any grouse ever presented any man. I could only smile and shake my head, it was that bad.

Now we had a choice. We could turn north and catch another piece of woods that stretches on unbroken for another mile, or turn south for a short walk to the road and then head east back toward the car.

"How's your back?" Ted asked. This was in the old painful days before I had a triple fusion and some stainless-steel buttresses installed in my lumbar regions.

"Hurts. I think I've pushed it enough. You go on if you want. I'll wait for you at the car."

"Nah," Ted said. "One more's a limit, and there's gotta be a few birds between here and there. I've never been in this corner down by the road anyway. Let's have a look."

That corner down by the road now has a name of its own. Ted dubbed it Leonard Woodcock. Have you ever run across one little patch of woods, to all appearances no different from about ten zillion acres around it, that for some unfathomable reason was a woodcock resort? That's Leonard Woodcock. In the years since we've tried to recognize just what it is about this place the woodcock like. Whatever it is, it covers no more than an acre at most and it's invisible to me. But so far as the woodcock are concerned, it's Club Med, the Riviera, pick your own metaphor. I know a few other places in that country where they pack in to the same extent, but they're all places where even I can see why. This one, I just can't figure out.

I couldn't begin to tell you how many birds were there that Sunday afternoon. Every point could have covered half a dozen. It was like walking into the biggest nest of ground wasps ever. The dogs were as bemused by it all as we were: Point, shoot, still on point, two steps and shoot again, two steps and point again, over and over until we both had limits and the dogs were on the brink of hysteria.

When we reached the car and laid out our birds, there was little to say that wasn't obvious when left unsaid. Ten woodcock and seven grouse is no bad afternoon. Not that the feeling is exponentially greater than having one each apiece, but finding a new woodcock covert in an old familiar place isn't something that happens every day.

With these birds, time plays a certain role that it doesn't play with others. Leave quail habitat alone and it will always harbor quail, other things being equal. Do the same with the places grouse and woodcock like, and they'll eventually forsake it. I know some coverts where finding one or the other was a certainty twenty years ago, or even ten; now there's only the scenery of aging woods, where birds live only in the memory of an aging hunter. So we seek younger places and think about the old ones, and in doing so renew something within ourselves. It's as if somehow those hours past aren't gone at all, nor even tarnished with passing years.

So, if in the end the Almighty chooses to log them against my account, the reckoning will hold a certain justice. Those were the hours that really counted anyway.

Grouse Without October

I KEPT HEARING HER BELL when no bell was ringing, and I caught with the corner of my eye flashes of white where nothing white was moving.

Even the crackle and chop of her footfalls were there, a counter-rhythm under the sound of my own, but they ceased every time I stopped to listen.

It was an odd thing, like an old familiar song played slightly out of tune or a once-comfortable glove with two fingers missing—faintly perverse, a level world gone the merest fraction on the slant.

After two days, I looked at Bill and said, "This just doesn't feel right."

He drew back from the long thoughts in his curling pipe smoke, knowing exactly what I meant. "Nope," he said, "sure doesn't."

We had reasons for choosing the covert we were in, and they didn't all turn on the fact that it's a reliable place to find grouse in a year when grouse are hard to find. As Bill put it when we turned down that particular gravel road, "Gibby's woods oughtta be okay for two old dogless hunters . . ."

He was right, of course, but there's okay and then there's okay.

I don't mind being an old hunter. In fact, I enjoy my hunting days more now than I ever did when I was a young hunter—and when I was a young hunter, the world began and ended with birds and guns.

But I do mind being an old dogless hunter. I mind that very much, because the older I get, the more clearly I see that the duality I once recognized is actually a triad, bird and gun and dog, complete, indisseverable.

As I measure time, it was an extraordinary October, because for the first time in ten years the other October, the one the AKC knows as October First, didn't go with me to ramble through the Minnesota grouse coverts we love so well.

It started ten days before, with my sweet old Brittany girl sprawled unladylike, flat on her back in my lap, snoring through a movie. Far as she's concerned, books and the VCR are of value only because they're tickets to uninterrupted belly-rubbing. That's when I noticed the mass, too large and indistinct to be called a lump, hovering under the skin down low inside her left hind leg. Alien topography on a familiar landscape.

Next day, Doctor Jim Wilsman tried his hand on the same place.

"Could be a hernia," he said, "or just some fatty tissue surrounding a lymph node. Feels like a hernia, though. Best have a look inside."

Monday morning, we both looked, Jim behind the scalpel and I stroking her throat while she inhaled anesthetic through a trach tube. Her tongue lolled impossibly long. The same tongue that's been slurping my face all these years. She looked so vulnerable, lying there in the surgical trough. I kept my hands on her, transferring what I hoped was life and energy.

"Hernia," Jim said finally, nudging aside a wad of fat half the size of a tennis ball. I peered over his shoulder. There in the jumble of tissue, surprisingly bloodless, I could see the rent in her abdominal wall.

Three layers of sutures and a few recovery hours later she was home, dopey and sore and out of sorts, sleeping heavily on the love seat and rousing herself only for creaky trips outdoors and to her water bowl. Dinnertime came and went, scarcely remarked upon—and it's a significant sign when Tober is indifferent to food. It was a long night for me, while she slept.

She was in fine fettle the morning I left for Minnesota, ready as always and clearly worried that something was amiss. Physically, nothing was. There was some swelling, predictably, but the incision was knitting tighter by the day. I would have postponed the trip for another week, but I was committed to a magazine story on duck shooting in Canada, with grouse week to follow, and no way would I risk that tender, still-sutured belly in the brush. I left her sulky, almost outright angry, as I drove off regretfully in the early morning dark.

For two weeks, she was there and not there. I could hear the faint tinkle of her little brass bell every time the wind shifted, had to remind myself to look closely at every hit and falling bird. Without realizing it, I'd grown careless of marking falls, gone complacent in the knowledge that she was on the job.

At night, no immovable object occupied the exact center of the bed. No imperious morning barks summoned me to the cabin door. No need to look for an out-of-the-way turnoff for the periodic airings-out. No one to talk to for hours on the road. It was an experience left incomplete.

Next year, I kept telling myself. Next year will be just like always . . .

But this year my old friend Bill sat with me dogless in the woods and smoked his pipe while a thin sheen glistened on his eyes. I was dogless because of an unexpected surgery, temporarily dogless, but Bill's Rosie was gone, really gone—sweet, silly Rosie, whose fire burned white-hot from the moment of leaving home to the moment of getting back, who rejoiced in the smell of grouse and the thunder of wings. A shattered shoulder and a needle laden with mercy took Rosie down almost at the same moment I watched Doctor Jim tie the last knot that put October well.

Hunting is an exercise in futures. Somewhere a bird is waiting, and the moment is waiting for the triad to gather. It's always ahead, always waiting.

Time is waiting, too, cruel as well as kind. And in the end, time is all we really have.

Grouse, Ducks, and Strange Little Sprites

NOVA SCOTIA REACHES OFF the eastern continental rim like a short, brawny arm flexing a stony fist at the North Atlantic. From jetliner altitude above the Bay of Fundy on a clear autumn afternoon, the Isthmus of Chignecto, which joins the province to New Brunswick and the rest of North America, seems improbably narrow, scarcely more than a thread. You wonder if even a mild northwest wind out of the Gulf of St. Lawrence wouldn't change the landscape below from a peninsula to an island. Compared with 4,700 miles of coastline, seventeen miles of dry land seems at best a tenuous grasp.

A friend of mine, speaking from experience greater than my own, once remarked that people who live on islands are different from people who don't. She never said whether the same differences, whatever they are, apply among those who live on quasi-islands, but the comment came back to me about the time the plane touched down at Halifax. Since I was to be here for the better part of a week, I had a momentary urge to find a telephone and demand an explanation.

I still don't know what she meant, but if she's right, then perhaps I should be an islander. Or a Nova Scotian, at least, since I always feel at home among people who truly love the land. Coming to Nova Scotia felt like meeting an old friend for the first time.

I imagine that many of us harbor a special feeling about certain parts of the world that we've never seen, places that for one reason or another have caught our fancy and never quite let go. I don't remember exactly how Nova Scotia came to be one of those places for me, but it happened long ago. The north country rings deep chimes in my soul anyway, and given my ancestry, I suppose a place called New Scotland would predictably hold a certain charm. At any rate, explainable or not, it's a place I've always wanted to see.

The view from ground level seemed promising enough. From the airport at Halifax, Paul Rogers and I drove north along the four-lane highway, bound ultimately for the village of Upper Stewiacke and Lansdowne Lodge. Paul, a young man with a boyish face half-submerged in a luxuriant growth of beard, works as a hunting guide in the fall and farms during the rest of the year, and we talked of his land and the prospects for the coming season while I watched miles of woods brighten and fade in the lowering sunlight.

I had come to hunt grouse, woodcock, and other such birds as might be fair and legal game. Paul said he'd flushed several grouse on his own farm while choosing where to build tree-stands for deer. Where the highway bridged a small stream, I looked down at the tag-alders and asked if the woodcock were in.

Paul grinned. "Woodcock," he said. "There's a strange little sprite. They're here when you find them."

Which was exactly what I wanted to hear. Any guide who guarantees woodcock is pulling your leg.

I asked, too, about Lansdowne Lodge and Tom Kennedy, who owns the place and who was then still no more than a voice over the phone.

"Tom's the best in Nova Scotia," Paul said. "He doesn't

guide so much himself any more, but he has seven of us working for him, including two sons, all master guides. Took me a long time to get where I felt I was good enough to apply to be a guide for Tom."

It was dark when we turned off the main highway and headed east through Brookfield and Middle Stewiacke, darker still when we arrived at the lodge. A hundred yards across the clipped lawn, the Stewiacke River glittered in the moonlight. Lansdowne is a fishing as well as a hunting lodge, and along with the St. Mary's, the Stewiacke is the most famous salmon river in the province. In the main room at the lodge are Atlantic salmon and brown trout, mounted and photographed, to make even me, who fishes with all the intensity of a window shopper, wish for a fly rod and waders.

Tom Kennedy is a big man with a grizzly beard and a soft Canadian accent, and he knows exactly what another man needs after flying half a continent. I sipped the whiskey while he filled out my hunting license and his wife Marion dipped a bowl of chili from a pot simmering on the stove. The Olympian gods feasted on nectar and ambrosia only because they didn't have Scotch and Marion's chili.

By law, no one may hunt in the province of Nova Scotia on a Sunday, so I spent the next morning talking with the other Lansdowne guests and taking photographs along the river. From a bank lush with ferns and wildflowers overlooking a pool, I could see the shadowy forms of fish, some of them as long as my leg, lying just at the current's edge. A few feet out, the river flowed slick and powerful, leading out of sight around the next bend.

After lunch, I talked over the next day's hunting with Todd Kennedy, my guide, and Tom's youngest son, Russell. Woodcock? Todd had seen a few but hadn't been out in a day or so, and you know how it is with woodcock . . . Right again. If the birds weren't in, there was some wet pasture in the river bottom that usually held snipe. Later, we drove west to the Lansdowne goose leases on Cobequid Bay, the inlandmost reach of the Bay of Fundy, where the guides were digging hunting pits under a sky laced with skein after skein of Canadas trading from the bay to their cornfield feeding grounds and back again.

Nova Scotia isn't as far north as you might imagine. Virtually the entire province lies between 44 and 47 degrees north latitude, which puts Lansdowne Lodge at almost the same parallel as Minneapolis and St. Paul. The surrounding ocean tempers the climate to a surprisingly moderate range, and with rain in the offing, the weather can be almost tropically close, even in the early days of October.

Monday came up with a thin overcast and shirtsleeve temperatures. One other guest, an amiable gentleman from Long Island, was there for bird shooting, too, and we'd agreed to hunt together. We strove mightily for what seemed miles through tag alders and grass, thrashing cover that looked like a woodcock's dream, and flushed a single bird that flew from me directly toward Russell, the only path out of 360 degrees that could keep me from shooting. Strange little sprites, indeed.

The afternoon outing produced additional sweat and snipe that scaled off on a tailing wind, moving fast enough to leave shot charges languishing in their wake.

Todd and I stood at the windows next morning and watched rain dripping from the eaves. When hunting in duck weather, hunt ducks, so, rubber-booted, we struck off for the drainage ditches that lace the river-bottom fields.

I don't know about you, but I like to walk in the rain, truly do. I like the sound of it pattering on my hat, like the soggy thump of boots on wet turf, and like the way the fields look with distances foreshortened in the haze. The black ducks seemed to be enjoying the day, too, loafing in the narrow, shallow ditches, offering jump-shooting that I suspect is as demanding as jump-shooting gets. But for Todd, who probably wasn't sharing my enthusiasm for a tramp through the rain, I might be there still, because after a couple of hours I hadn't the faintest idea where to find the truck and didn't really care.

The rain slackened at midday and finally stopped altogether as Tom and Todd and I drove the back roads south of the river, deciding on which pieces of woods to probe for grouse. According to the map, no spot in all of Nova Scotia is more than thirty-five miles from the ocean, but even from the old clearcut at the top of Berry Hill, the illusion of vast woodland is strong. There, you can look out, in every direction, toward gently rounded hills under a dense cover of mixed timber—balsam and spruce, hemlock, birch, pine, beech, maples going red and gold, and old apple trees sporting russet fruit. When John Cabot made landfall not too many miles north of here on June 24, 1497, he thought he was in northern Asia. I understand the man's confusion; I thought I was in the hinterlands of Elysium.

Farther on, where the narrow, sandy road runs between an old stone-walled pasture and the woods, a grouse strolled out of the fence corner, gave us a half-indifferent look, and walked off into the woods.

The Lansdowne goose hunters, two from Connecticut and two more from Massachusetts, came in that evening with nineteen Canadas, one bird shy of a daily limit among all four. I made a note in my journal to bring a goose gun and proper cartridges next time. In any case, the next two days, the last of the trip, were for grouse.

I figured out a long time past where grouse go when it rains, or at least where some of them go. The Berry Hill woods are unutterably beautiful in a soft rain, and we moved quietly among the trees, searching out the evergreen patches while Tie, Todd's sweet-natured little English springer, cut close, busy circles around us. As I expected, the birds were in the pine thickets, and as I further expected, we heard more of them than we saw. It's tough habitat to shoot in, hard enough for two or three men, who might get shots at birds the others flush, almost impossible for a single hunter unless the red gods smile and lavish him with luck.

True to form, Lady Luck found me napping. I stepped into a room-sized clearing in a stand of spruce and dug out my bandanna to wipe the rain off my gun. In the next instant, a grouse blew out of a tree in front of me and bored straight in overhead. Had I been ready, I might have made the incoming shot; as it was, the first one went behind and the second, going away, printed a brief circle on the spruce boughs where the bird had disappeared a heartbeat before. I've killed grouse that way, but not this time.

After the rain, we tried some river-bottom woods. The birds there were edgy, rocketing off through the still-clinging leaves, offering only sound or the merest flicker of wings. Grouse will be grouse, wherever they are.

And so, as it turned out, will ducks. Heading back to the lodge, Todd suddenly slowed the truck and pointed to a tiny pasture pothole just a few dozen yards off the road, the water dotted with ducks.

"We have permission to hunt this farm, and I have a few decoys in the back," he said. "Are you game?"

Is a pig's butt made of pork? We drove closer to the pothole, and as the ducks lifted off, I grabbed some stick-up silhouette decoys and my gun. I invited Todd to bring his own gun and join me when he'd parked the truck a safe distance away. By the time I got a half-dozen flatties stuck in the margin, the birds were already circling back overhead.

They were teal, greenwings all, and as is the case when you're lucky enough to find the one place where ducks want to be, the decoys were unnecessary. There were a couple of trees next to the water, and just standing next to them proved concealment enough. The fleet little chaps gave us some good shooting for the last hour before dusk, and we repaid the favor by taking only two or three apiece before giving them back their pothole for the night.

It's said that the farther into the wilderness you go, the tamer ruffed grouse become. Maybe, but I have a hard time swallowing that one. For all I could see, these Nova Scotia birds get only a little more gunning pressure than the grouse on Mars, but they're nobody's patsies. We never had a problem finding grouse, only finding a way to get the shots. We tried the woods on Berry Hill again and then moved into the river valley once more. Fortune flirted coyly, giving me birds at arm's length and taking them out of sight before I could move the gun, coquettishly offering double—and, in one instance, triple—sound flushes, showing me all the faces that early-season hunting wears, reminding me at every turn why it's always called hunting.

The wind shifted that evening, quartering out of the northwest. I was booked on an early flight to Boston and from there west toward home. The sunrise promised a magnificent day as I said good-bye to Tom, and we agreed that the wind should bring along a fall of woodcock. A couple of hours later, looping over the Bay of Fundy for a short stop at Saint John, New Brunswick, I noticed again that slender land bridge at Chignecto and hoped that the newly risen woodcock wind would stay mild enough to leave Nova Scotia where it is, where I can find it next time.

Grouse on the Mississippi

GROUSE HUNTING is as much a seeking after tradition as it is the pursuit of a bird, and the tradition has as much to do with *where* as it does with *how*.

Since the ruffed grouse is native nowhere but North America, it probably was the first bird the New World colonists hunted purely for sport. So if you ask a grouse hunter to describe the classic landscape, he'll likely paint you a picture out of William Harndon Foster and Burton Spiller and a lineage of artists from A. B. Frost and Lynn Bogue Hunt and Aden Ripley, through generations of obscure illustrators, to such modern masters as Ogden Pleissner and Bob Abbett. He'll talk of old hills and broad valleys patchworked in hardwoods and evergreens; of a countryside laced with stone fences and dotted with gnarled orchards, where grouse peck at apples shriveling with early frost, where the woodcock come and go along their ancient flyways.

It makes a fine, romantic picture and one that hasn't entirely disappeared. The New England landscape still offers the woods and the stone fences and the tiny, clapboard villages, and if you squint a bit, you can see yourself with dog and gun, strolling beyond the last house at the edge of town and into the woods, into the past, into tradition.

Sharpen the focus, however, and you're likely to see yourself bumping against village constables quoting gun laws and leash laws, against NO TRESPASSING signs, against backyards where grouse woods used to be, and against largely empty woods where grouse and woodcock used to be. New England grouse hunting ain't what it was in Foster's day, nor Spiller's, nor even in the days when you and I were young.

Which is not to say that you can't find good grouse and woodcock hunting in a classic landscape, only that it's sometimes hard to come by in the northeastern United States. But eastern Ontario—well, that's another story.

Like Huckleberry Finn, my old friend Jon Hollinger was born and raised on the banks of the Mississippi River—in Jon's case, the one that runs through Lanark County, Ontario, past the village of Ferguson's Falls. You won't find the town on most maps; it's too small, and it's a mile or more off the concrete ribbon of Highway 7, which slants across the province from Peterborough to Ottawa. But if Ferguson's Falls has suffered any ill effects from the indifference of cartographers or the lack of traffic thundering through, they don't show. The houses are snug and tidily kept, and one of them is a comfortable old two-story structure of hewn logs with a backyard that slopes down to a wide bend in the river. Here you can spend a chilly October evening with your feet stretched out toward the woodstove and play back in memory a day spent in country so like the images of traditional grouse hunting that it's almost a trip back into time.

And in a way, it is. No one knows exactly what happened to Huck Finn after he lit out for the territory to escape Aunt Sally's plans to adopt and "sivilize" him. What happened to Jon Hollinger after he left the banks of the other Mississippi is considerably clearer; he became, among other things, an outfitter, and among the shooting trips he offered until recently are a few days back home with Lanark County grouse, and accommodations in the old family home.

He first described the hunting and the countryside to me over the phone on an August day when October and grouse seemed far-off prospects. But as we talked, I was looking at an old, New Englandy grouse-hunting print that hangs on my study wall, and the more he said about the Lanark County landscape, the more he described what I was seeing at the moment.

"I only book three trips there per year," he said, "and only four guns at a time. Any more and I'd feel as if I was overworking the coverts. For me, these are trips back home. They're something special."

Indeed, they are. Even without 150 years of family history in one place ("There are seven generations of us buried there," Jon said later, pointing to the churchyard cemetery as we drove past), anyone with a love for the north woods and the traditions of grouse and woodcock can feel at home in Lanark County. It's all there—the undulating hills covered in oak and maple, hickory and beech, hemlock, birch, cedar, larch, pine, old apple trees, and a hundred kinds of understory shrub; fences of stone and split rail; rocky pastures and broad vistas; deep woods and shaggy edge.

The birds are there, too. Jon, like Master Finn, spent his early years roaming the woods and swamps, and he can take you to coverts where you'll find the umpteenth-great grandchildren of grouse he knew years ago. Peter Little, Jon's nephew, keeps a day-to-day eye on things through the season, and together they make sure you spend your time hunting, not prospecting.

Weather, though, is a less dependable commodity. We got in a good morning the first day—Jon and Peter and Marty Lichterman and John Esposti and I—but at noon the lowering sky finally gathered and cracked. I have hunted grouse in the rain, and I've loved it. I have also turned sharply toward the car at the first sprinkles and loved that, too, and that day I was not dismayed at the prospect of a pub lunch and an afternoon frittered away on whatever pastimes the local culture provides.

I don't know what most people do on a rainy afternoon in Perth, Ontario, but we visited the local billiard parlor, housed on the second floor of a side-street building. With tables for snooker and pool and a bank of video games along one wall, it's a hangout for the Perth high-school population, several representatives of which were in residence at the time.

Perhaps they are unaccustomed to being invaded by five men in hunting clothes. It's hard to know what goes on in a teenager's mind. At any rate, one group clearly were puzzled by something about us, and after some earnest whispering and side-long looks, one of them sidled over.

"Um . . . well . . . my friends were wondering why you guys are dressed so funny." This from a spike-haired adolescent draped head to foot in black, outlandishly baggy—but presumably cool—attire.

"We've been hunting grouse," Jon said, and I searched her face for signs of some impending remarks on the benefits of peace and love, delivered from the lofty wisdom and utter certainty of fifteen years' tenure on earth.

She hesitated a moment, said "Oh . . . yeah," giggled, smiled the sweet, open smile of the child she was. Amazing, the things you can find on a hunting trip.

We found better weather after that, and good hunting—for grouse, woodcock, and even a few black ducks in a reedy backwater upriver. That the grouse population cycle had broken over its peak was clear all across the north country that year, but among the three states and one foreign country where I hunted grouse in October 1990, only Minnesota surpassed the Lanark County woods.

When the cycle starts the downward arc, hunting changes. The birds are cagier, because the population doesn't contain as many young-of-the-year, Mortimer Snerd types that know no better than to hang out on logging roads, trails, and in open woods. We found a few such simpletons, of course, because you always do, but for the most part, the Lanark County grouse were veterans not to be trifled with nor taken lightly, lurking in the densest thickets and employing all the fiendishly clever tricks that make *Bonasa umbellus* the prince of upland game.

Time and again, they gave us straightforward, simple choices—thrash through the hairy stuff for birds or take the easy going and enjoy the scenery; shoot at a blur streaking beyond a thick screen of twigs and branches or don't shoot at all; hunt, really hunt, or stand a high chance of going in empty-handed. At times like that, every bird is a trophy.

Sometimes, though, the trophies of memory are more poignant than those that end up on the wall or the dining table—because sometimes the sheer whims of chance open some strange and lovely windows. It always seems to happen with a particular bird in a particular circumstance, and those are the birds that remain in mind more clearly than the rest.

Jon and I met this one first as a sound-flush deep in a patch of woods. Since neither of us saw even a flicker, we reckoned his line of flight as straight away. Jon said we were heading for an old trail with a narrow strip of cover on the other side and a pasture beyond, so, figuring on a reflush at the trail, we toiled up the hill while Lefty, Jon's Labrador, cut back and forth a few feet ahead. We stopped on the trail, scant yards apart, and there next to a fallen log, not fifteen feet in front of me, stood the grouse, a big gray cockbird alert as a spring. I froze, the grouse bobbed his head a couple of times as grouse do, ducked under the log, and turned back to watch me watch him.

By this time, Jon was walking my way, and I told him, as low-voiced as I could, what was going on. He eased up beside me, and we both stood there, watching the grouse watching us. Lefty, unaware, nosed around Jon's feet.

I've seen this sort of thing before—adult grouse in the East and Midwest that behave like the fabled fool-hens of the western wilderness, where you'll find blue, spruce, and ruffed grouse alike so tame and nonchalant you can bop them with a stick. They're not dumb, just uneducated, because they have never been hunted and in fact probably have never seen a human being. You can expect such naiveté out West—and from very young birds anywhere—but it's always a surprise to me when I come across a full-grown eastern bird that acts like a callow freshman. It's also a pleasant surprise, because it means the local hunting pressure is light indeed.

Anyway, nothing continued to happen for about ten seconds, while everyone waited for somebody to do something. "Let's send Lefty in," Jon murmured. "Okay," I said. "He has to flush straight away or to the left." The cover soon petered out into pasture on the right, and of course, we were blocking the way to the woods behind us. Of course. Jon nodded and sent Lefty in.

Lefty went around the end of the log, and the grouse hopped on top of it, now keeping one eye on us and the other on the dog. Lefty struck the foot scent right away, glued his nose to the ground, and nearly batted the bird off the log with his tail. The bird simply moved aside. Not only had this lad never seen a human, but he clearly had never seen a four-legged predator, either.

I started to say something pertinent and got as far as "For cryin' out . . ." when Lefty suddenly put the puzzle together and raised his head. And then the grouse figured out a few things of his own. One instant, they were nose to beak; in the next, the bird roared over our heads the way Mantle used to smoke line drives and was halfway back down the hill before either of us could make a full turn.

I got off one fumbling shot that I knew was too high when I pulled the trigger, and Jon added two more in exactly the same place. Then we looked at one another and stood laughing like lunatics until *we* had to go sit on the damn log. I don't believe we've had a conversation about ruffed grouse since then without one of us bringing up The One That Blew Our Hats Off.

I don't know where he is right now, but I hope he's still in those woods, siring a dynasty. One thing is certain: Whoever meets him next will get a far different reception. That bird changed from a neophyte to an old pro in about three seconds.

But I do hope to meet him again, or one of his offspring— or any other Lanark County grouse, for that matter. It's one of those places that make up the where of a lovely tradition, one of those places that are like walking into a fine old painting of a world you thought was gone forever.

Ducks Over Delta

From the middle of Waterhen Bay, you can count the lights of St. Ambroise, lined up like candles against a velvety black eastern sky. There are thirteen, each one representing a neatly kept frame house and, in total, about 90 percent of the local population.

The lights of Winnipeg define a faint horizon in the southeast. Portage la Prairie, smaller but nearer, glows more brightly to the southwest. North is depthless black, a hundred miles of Lake Manitoba, and beyond that, hundreds more miles of lakes and ponds and potholes scattered through a wilderness that eventually fetches up against the high Arctic. You might be adrift in the cosmos for all else you can see at this hour of the morning, save those few homey lights of town. Once they're counted, there's nothing to do but watch them recede in the distance, listen to the oarlocks creak and the wavelets plant wet kisses on the bow as Raymond Lamirande pulls the boat slowly across the bay.

When the far shore finally looms up, black on black, you clamber out, following the thin beam of Raymond's flashlight into a tiny clearing hacked from a stand of bulrush and marsh grass and phragmites, cover that looks dense as a wall. You sort your gear and uncase your gun, investigate the direction of the breeze, braille some coffee out of the thermos, and arrange your left glove on your hip-booted knee so the liquid that missed the cup might one day evaporate. Then you listen to the *thunks* and splashes as Ray-

75

mond sets the decoys somewhere in the dark. When that's complete and he, too, is tucked into the cane, as you wait to hear the sweet, slithery whisper of wings cut the graying darkness—then you go back to counting the lights of St. Ambroise. If it all goes according to plan, you'll be too preoccupied later to notice them fade and finally wink out as dawn rises over the Delta wetlands.

There is a certain moment in a marsh when I invariably think of a Wordsworth poem. In actuality, there are two such moments, at sunrise and sunset, and it's only a single line from "Tintern Abbey," the one that reads ". . . connect the landscape with the quiet of the sky." At those moments there is no clear distinction between water and air; the marsh seems to float suspended between identical elements; up and down are so completely irrelevant that you only know which is which if your feet are wet and your head isn't.

Delta is one of those places where the phenomenon is especially strong. If you're a hunter with an eye for ducky-looking real estate, you won't need to look twice to recognize it as prime country: flat, endless acres of water and rushes under the enormous Manitoba sky. You'd certainly guess you aren't the first to thread its meandering channels or cross the bays in search of the fine miseries that attend the hunting of ducks, but Delta wears its history lightly, gives no signs that it's been one of the most famous wildfowling sites in North America for almost ten generations—or a hundred generations, if you count the native peoples who enjoyed its bounty.

The history (part of it, anyway) is more apparent in St. Ambroise. Among those baker's-dozen lights along the eastern side of Waterhen Bay, at least ten belong to families who have plied these marshes since time out of mind—as watermen and guides, builders of duck boats and carvers of decoys. Their names are etched deeply in local tradition—Ducharme, Lamirande, Lavallee, Lipine, St. Goddard. And under yet another of those lights stands the bobbin upon which all the threads are wound.

Jimmy Robinson created the Sports Afield Duck Club— and apart from life itself, the only thing that could have created Jimmy Robinson is a novelist with a sense for characters who can be caricature and reality all in one. Raconteur, entrepreneur, trap and skeet shot, duck hunter, fisherman, hail-fellow of the great and near-great, and contributing editor to *Sports Afield* for forty-odd years, Jimmy Robinson was a sort we aren't likely to see again. He opened his first lodge at Delta Marsh in 1935, in a farmhouse on Portage Creek, and in 1958 built the rambling shingle-sided structure in St. Ambroise, on a road that dead-ends at the shore of Lake Manitoba.

Dick Wallin, for twenty years Jimmy's hunting and fishing partner, as white-bearded as I, owns it now. The main room is a shrine not only to the memory of Jimmy Robinson but also to those who've known the ducks on the Delta Marsh. They stand in photographs, rank upon rank: Ernest Hemingway, Clark Gable, Gary Cooper, Ted Williams, and Robert Stack have all hunted here. So have Walter Hagen, Roy Rogers, Robert Mitchum, Dean Martin, Robert Taylor, Nash Buckingham, and Grits Gresham. I don't know whether Mary Hemingway, Alice Faye, and Dolly Parton really came to hunt ducks or just make the place look better, but their photos hang there, too, along with about two thousand other faces that ring only faint bells, or none at all, in my memory. Whatever else there is to say, Jimmy's camp has been a popular place.

Some David Maass prints dominate the little dining room, just as David Maass has dominated all other artists in capturing the feel of gunning at Delta. Dave was my roomie and hunting partner there in the fall of 1993.

The more I chase around the world after birds that offer keen levels of sport, the fonder I am of hunting certain ones with certain people. I've spent sweet days at ducks with some fine friends, but hunting ducks with Dave Maass is something special. It's like seeing the greatest waterfowl art ever painted and living it at the same time. Be it Delta, the Arkansas green timber, a Minnesota slough, here, there, or anywhere the ducks might come, I find it all the better if I know it's Dave making the rustles, bumps, and crunches in the nearby dark. I can't think of anyone who knows ducks better or loves them more.

It's a Maass painting when they come, sleek and hard-edged with dawn, swinging down the wind with a graceful sweep and a straight-ahead speed that takes my breath away. Canvasbacks, bluebills, mallards, pintails—name it and it flies over Delta, and David's painted it, caught in that heart-stopping moment just before you rise up in a clatter of weeds, just before you and an incredibly beautiful bird come in touch as predator and prey. Sometimes the predator gets the edge, sometimes the prey. The prey has wings, a wary nature, and a superb sense of life in three dimensions; the predator has an analytic mind and opposable thumbs—sometimes all thumbs. But whichever way it works out is the right way.

No matter what part of the marsh we hunt—Lake Francis, Waterhen Bay, or some pool known only by a local name—and no matter who takes us out—chief guide Lawrence St. Goddard and his son Mel; the brothers Ducharme, Paul and John; George Lavallee; Raymond Lamirande—morning on the Delta is a world out of time, vast and silent except for the stirring of a chill October breeze.

Finally, the night begins to crack, flame-colored and fulgent. When the light is enough to just make out the decoys bobbing on the tiny swells, wooden working blocks carved by Duncan Ducharme, Delta becomes a world of wings. Near and far, they stitch the sky in skeins and lines and loose, busily shifting knots, pinions beating quick tempos to music felt rather than heard.

Someone, usually the guide, speaks a soft "Mark!" and you

watch them come—dabblers riding high, swinging around for another look, spilling air from cupped wings in their descent, or divers barreling in low to the deck like formations of fighter planes on a strafing run, exulting in sheer velocity.

You consult oracles, labor over ancient mysteries. How many passes are enough? Which one represents the key moment when they'll either succumb to the seduction or flare? Wait or not? Now or next time?

In the end it's a throw of the dice, a leap of faith, a surrender to instinct. You stand up and take your chances, pick a bird, get the gun moving, look ahead and hope it's enough. As I don't shoot ducks very often and therefore don't keep the rhythms finely honed, far enough is usually about twice what I think it should be, and I sometimes get thoroughly peeved with myself for shooting sloppily despite knowing better.

Not that it's so important. The birds still in the air are the real prize, the ones that go beating away, chasing the fading echoes of gunfire. Those birds are tomorrow, next week, next year, something to hold in mind like the image of a fine painting. Those birds are—as Al Hochbaum, former head of the nearby Delta Waterfowl Research Station, put it—fulfilling their destiny to ride the wind. Mine is to spend some time with them now and again, with a treasured friend, out here where it's sometimes hard to tell the difference between the landscape and the sky, out here where the difference hardly matters.

Grouse at the End of the Rainbow

SEEN FROM THE AIR, the river curls like a shaken-out line that half-remembers the confinement of coils. You can't hear it for the distance and the roar of the DeHavilland engine, but its glossy sheen promises a voice that mutters and sings.

And then it drops from sight as the pilot banks into a landing approach, drawing a bead on a lake that seems impossibly tiny after the trip across the huge expanse of Lake Iliamna to the north. The tall island at the center heightens the illusion, so it's not till the floats actually plow the surface that you realize this "tiny" lake is a half-mile across.

Big country, Alaska is, especially seen for the first time. You need a while to readjust your sense of scale.

In the meantime, as you round the island and head for the north shore, your sense of having found the right place settles in right away. By the time the floats crunch lightly against the gravel beach and you clamber out, hop ashore, shake hands with Chris Goll, knock down a welcoming snort of something warm offered on a silver tray, and take a first good look with your feet on the ground, there's no question at all that Rainbow River is going to do just fine as a home in the wilderness.

You stash your gear in one of the little cabins, hike up the hill to the main lodge, find the other half of your welcoming snort, and stand for a few minutes at the big windows looking out across the lake. There you see hills dressed in the colors of September, and beyond them, the faint, distant ridges of the Aleutian Range. Now the feeling expands into that pleasant moment on the cusp between a long trip finally ended and the promise of adventures soon to come. Just the chance to finally have a look at Alaska was enough to whet a good edge of anticipation; to do so while hunting birds and fishing for trout had honed it keener still.

The plan was to make a couple of flights up to the tundra for ptarmigan and to fish the home river for rainbows. As it was late September, the salmon runs were well past; this meant the sanitation crew of bears and ravens and eagles had all the dead fish cleaned up, and we could work the splendid rainbow fishery without the nuisance of snagging spawn-sluggish salmon.

If this last sounds impressively knowledgeable coming from a diehard gun and bird-shooting writer, I have to confess it's something I've learned since, not something I knew at the time. Up to the moment I waded out from the bank the first morning at Rainbow River, my fishing career had been in almost total eclipse for better than ten years. In fact, but for a single day on the Bighorn and a fruitless morning on the Pere Marquette I hadn't cast a fly at the promise of a trout in almost twenty years. Being for all good purposes a rank beginner at the art of salmonid fishing was one reason why I'd pleaded and whined until Jon Hollinger agreed to go with me to Alaska—that and the fact that Jonny and I have hunted birds and shot clays and generally knocked around the world together long enough to be of a mind on what's really important about it all. He's a better fisherman than I by an order of magnitude, and besides enjoying his company I figured he could keep me from doing anything really embarrassing, short of turning a fly into an earring.

As it turned out, Chris assigned us a guide who's good at handling the piscatorially challenged. If you read the fly-fishing magazines you'll see Larry Tullis's name as a by-line. When you do, pay attention; he knows what he's talking about.

It turned out, too, that his approach to fishing is similar to mine, which is to say that the point of the whole exercise is to get a fish onto the end of your tippet. As one who believes that shooting a beautiful bird with an ugly gun is marginally sinful, I understand a certain measure of purism—but I don't understand those who feel compelled to apologize for catching a trout on a woolly bugger and pretend they'd rather be fishing a quill Gordon.

Larry handed me a hank of combed-out orange yarn lashed to a hook. "Flesh fly," he said. The rainbows, carnivorous and cannibalistic, had been feeding on dead salmon for more than a month, and anything that looked like a scrap of salmon flesh could trigger a strike. "Cast it up and across and let it drift," Larry said. I did. "Mend your line." I did that. "Bigger mend; you're still getting some drag."

I followed his direction on the next cast, and on the one after that a fish took halfway through the drift.

I love the rainbow's penchant for going airborne. This one leaped immediately and then tore off upstream, making the reel spin and the line sing in the rod guides. Life lived in swift water builds strong bodies. The fish's power surged and throbbed through the rod. He wasn't especially big by Alaskan standards—four or five pounds, I reckoned later—but he felt big, and that was good enough. By the time I got him into the shallows I was as firmly hooked as he was. I didn't say anything about it, but as I watched him ease back out toward the current under Larry's coaxing the thought crossed my mind that things were going to be different for me in the foreseeable future.

Discovery is one thing, rediscovery quite another. In those few minutes, one of the fondest passions of my youth came flooding back, filling some blanks and niches that I wasn't even aware still existed. The silky flow of water around my knees, the flex of the rod, and the sheer wild strength of the fish combined to make me feel more complete. It suddenly felt exquisitely good to be a fisherman once again.

It didn't hurt that I landed another, slightly larger rainbow a few minutes later and yet another just before we headed in to lunch. A better angler might have caught more fish—and in fact Jonny did—but I wouldn't have felt any more excitement if I had. I was pleased, too, that I landed every one that struck (actually I landed every fish I hooked on the whole trip, a fact you may file solely under Beginner's Luck). The last one of the morning was a real acrobat, tail-walking nearly the full width of the stream back and forth until I felt like doing the same thing out of sheer exhilaration.

It would be difficult to overrate the quality of the fishery. The rainbows are both plentiful and sizeable. The lodge record currently goes to a thirty-nine-inch twenty-three-pounder landed and released in early September 1994. I'm told the dry-fly fishing is superb at certain times of the year.

In the afternoon Chris took us on a turn through the woods behind the lodge to see if we might flush a spruce grouse or two. That the only ones we found were simply sound flushes screened by the dense conifers was no real disappointment compared with the pleasure of roaming the woods. Hunting puts you in touch with the landscape in ways that fishing cannot—although walking on the deep layer of mosses and tiny trailing plants that form the forest floor is not greatly different from wading. It's like strolling across a great feather-tick mattress, and it's tough on your legs—but it's great stuff for sprawling on when you take a breather.

Later, as the medicinal properties of bourbon whiskey worked the ache out of my knees, I remarked that hunting spruce grouse was more demanding that I'd imagined. Chris Goll has a certain grin that reminds me of a bobcat who knows how to pick the latch on a henhouse door. "Weelll," he allowed, "there is a way that's kinda fun . . ."

The sun had not topped the eastern mountains as we piled our guns into the jet-boat down at the landing and Chris invited Dana to come aboard. Dana is a big, calendar-handsome German shorthair with a field-trial-class background and a deportment that's as businesslike as a cash register. Cuddly she ain't, but we soon found that she's a gas in the woods. We pushed off, crossed the lake, threaded the twisty channel leading to the river, and turned upstream.

Chris told us to keep an eye on the gravel bars; on the third one I saw why—two spruce grouse puttering and picking. Landing the boat at the far end of the bar, we uncased our guns. You can walk these birds up, Chris told us, but be ready because there'll be more than what we saw. He was right. The two in the open flushed at about twenty yards, and when Jon and I dumped them with a shot apiece, about fifteen more blew out of the willows, heading for the streamside woods. Thus the fun began.

Dendrapagus canadensis is not generally well-regarded as a game bird; in fact, spruce grouse are often dismissed as the proverbial fool hen, willing to sit still while you kill them with a stick. That's mainly, I suspect, because through most of their range there isn't nearly enough hunting pressure to build much wariness into the gene pool. I've seen wilderness ruffed grouse behave just as naively.

But get some spruces scattered through a grove of trees, and the whole complexion changes. A few'll still sit and stare at you halfwittedly, but the rest will suddenly turn from bozos to brigands, bailing out when you least expect it in the initial power dive characteristic of all grouse that sometimes perch in trees. They're strong, nimble flyers when they want to be, and that combined with surprise makes them highly sporty birds.

I've seen dogs point grouse in trees but none as consistently or with as much skill as Dana. Catching the scent, she'd stop, roll her eyes upward in a parody of long-suffering resignation. We couldn't always be sure exactly which tree was the source, but if nothing happened when we walked past her, Chris gave each trunk a lusty whack with a club he'd picked up and that usually was enough to get some action.

As the gravel bars are virtually their only source of grit, the birds gather there every morning, and we played the game several times over. It's as much fun as any grouse hunting I've ever done, demanding enough that collecting a daily limit of fifteen would take some real effort.

Brown bears and moose are elements of Alaskan fauna I especially wanted to see. We got a good look at a moose on our way fishing one morning when we rounded a bend in the boat and almost ran into a magnificent bull standing hock-deep in the stream. I'd seen moose before but not that close. I almost believe we could have ducked down and run right under his belly without touching him. Mercifully, Larry throttled back instead, and the moose crossed the river in a brisk trot, cleared the six- or seven-foot bank in one leap, and disappeared like a shadow into the undergrowth.

We found bear sign aplenty—huge tracks on the sandy bars and big piles of bear flop full of wild berries (pie filling, Chris calls it)—but no animals. The local bruins, Chris explained, are mainly nocturnal, and as if to prove the point, one decided to rearrange the stainless-steel racks in the lodge meathouse that very night. It sounded like an earthquake in a junkyard.

The day-shift bears live to the northwest, up on the tundra, and they were out in full force the afternoon we flew up to the Battle River to check out the ptarmigan. The Battle is a fairly short river that runs between two lakes; at the downstream end, the valley is two or three miles wide, all treeless tundra. In one pass over it I counted eleven bears of every shade from chestnut-brown to dishwater blonde—big bears, medium-sized bears, and one enormous chap who looked up at us like an old dog whose midday siesta was being interrupted.

Maneuvering the Super Cub down onto the lake near the mouth, Chris said there'd be no ptarmigan shooting today. Too windy.

So what?

When the wind blows, the birds head for the willow brakes.

Again, so what?

They get into the willows and snuggle up with the bears. Jonny, who'd mentioned an aversion to bears no more than fifty or sixty times in the previous three months, said he'd really rather fish than hunt ptarmigan anyway.

This we did, though we still shared the river with the bears. Every so often, one would appear on the bank or a gravel spit a couple of hundred yards away, swing its head a bit to get a fix on our scent, and presently amble off. One sow with three almost-grown cubs smelled us as she came moseying downstream and hustled her charges out of the water to lead them around us. Being goofy about animals—or possibly just goofy—I loved having them around. Looking up from a good tussle with one of the Battle's tough, hard-running rainbows to find a bear watching me curiously from the far bank made it all just that much wilder and more wonderful.

I could say as much of Alaska itself. I've gone back twice since Jonny and I spent our good days at Rainbow River. If the red gods are willing, I'll go there yet again.

But as with some other things, the tug of Alaska will always be tinged by that first visit. No matter what memories might ultimately accrue, there'll always be a spruce grouse in there somewhere and a rainbow trout leaping on the tether of a fly line out of a lovely, curling river that mutters and sings.

An Alaskan Adventure

THE RIVER THAT FLOWS into Nakalilok Bay has no name, but the salmon don't seem to mind. They come streaming in from the cold North Pacific, running along the Shelikof Strait, riding over the sandbars at high tide, threading at low tide the narrow inlet to Nakalilok. There they pause, crowding the main channel, their sleek, sea-bright bodies packed in growing ranks facing upstream, the entire throng focused like a single organism.

Their remaining future is brief. They'll force their way upriver against the current, struggling through stony shallows to find the right spot, deposit eggs and diaphanous clouds of milt, and presently die. Their bodies, decomposing even while they still live, will litter the banks and make a feast for the bears and the eagles and the ravens.

It is not a prospect to inspire optimism, but the fish of course are unaware of what lies ahead. As they wait, their systems adjust from salt water to fresh and they leap repeatedly, ridding themselves of clinging, parasitic sea lice. It would take a pretty far-gone anthropomorphist to assign any aesthetic sensibility to a fish, but at least there's some poetic symmetry in the notion that perhaps they leap to have one last look at this incredibly beautiful place where they, like generations of their ancestors, first came to life.

I know this: Rounding the seaward headland in the little

bush plane and dropping down toward the tidal flat on a landing approach was my first view of Nakalilok Bay, and for days after I savored every look as if it might be *my* last—the gray-green, late-summer slopes cut with stark, bare faces of rock, volcanic Mt. Chiginagak rising cloud-shrouded in the northwest, and the beetling scarp of the Aleutian Range looming beyond.

At the moment of my first look, I was on sensory overload. A couple of hours earlier, I and the young pilot at the controls had set out from King Salmon, flying south, low over the tundra. At the mountain pass he'd planned to use as a gateway to the southern coast of the peninsula, we ran into a vicious rainstorm blocking the way and so swung west. Our route through the next good pass took us right alongside a mountain burdened with a glacier on its flattened summit, with great fingers of ice reaching down like the tendrils of some parasitic plant.

It was one thing to fly along seemingly within arm's reach of the slope—and quite another to see a neon mountain. The glacial ice has become so compressed over the past million-odd years that it absorbs almost the entire spectrum, reflecting only brilliant blue. With color saturation enhanced by the overcast sky, the ice fields simply glowed as if lit from within, breathtaking in their eerie beauty. Flying into Nakalilok, I was still spellbound by the memory of it.

I've known my old friend J. W. Smith long enough to recognize Nakalilok Bay as the sort of place that would appeal to him. I imagine he came across it long ago, sometime during the nearly thirty years he's spent in Alaska as a game warden, general bush rat, and outfitter. His camp was on the western ridge, set high up from the river to minimize nighttime bear traffic in the village of snug, hard-floored tents that he and his wife, Dawn, and the guides set up every summer. You have to take a second look to see them even from the air, because they're drab-colored and tucked neatly into the alders—the cook and dining tent that's the social center of the whole thing, the shower tent with its bounty of propane-fired hot water, the latrine tent, and all the guest tents connected by a little maze of trails.

As we skimmed down onto the tidal shingle, I could see fish leaping all over the bay. Pete and Stan, the week's other two fishers, were standing thigh-deep among them, and I was ready to haul on my waders, string up a rod, and get out there, too, as soon as we taxied to a halt. But then J. W., whose job sometimes is to impose adult supervision on my enthusiasms, had an arm around my neck and was hauling me up the hill to a warm glass of whiskey and dinner and a couple of chairs perched where we could watch the river turn silver and then gunmetal gray in the long, late-August twilight.

Although driven by a common genetic imperative, each species of salmon has its own timetable for the spawning run. Legions of chums and pinks had already made their way upstream, and the late arrivals jammed the bay. The first few silvers were in as well, prowling alongside the crush of pinks and chums like indifferent wolves cruising a buffalo herd.

The time the salmon spend in the bay is a time of metamorphosis. Florid spawning colors replace their sea-run chromium brightness, and their once-sleek bodies become grotesque. Male pinks develop the hunchbacked profile that gives them their common name—humpy. Male chums, their sides splotched with calico patterns, grow big, wickedly hooked teeth. That the spawning run inevitably ends in death is one thing, but it's always seemed to me gratuitously cruel on nature's part that these once-beautiful animals should go to their demise monumentally ugly.

On the other hand, pretty is as pretty does. Neither the pinks nor the chums are such spectacular fighters as their coho cousins, but a big male chum is no sluggard, especially one in which the irritability and defensiveness of spawning time is well advanced. Swim some outrageous pink-and-silver or orange-and-silver fly past him, and he's likely to hit it with a slashing strike. Even though the subsequent struggle won't involve much leaping or blazing runs, it won't soon end, either. With a rod of sufficient spine you can turn him, but you can't stop him dead, at least not at first. Both of my 9-weight rods—a Scott and an Orvis PM-10— are extremely powerful; still, quite a few big chums got well into the backing and stayed there for a good while before I could make much headway toward bringing them in.

Pretty is as pretty eats, too. I won't belabor the point, but what J. W. can do with a freshly caught pink salmon, slathered with Hollandaise sauce, sprinkled with lemon juice and dill weed, and cooked over charcoal, is as tasty as any sin I've yet to find.

With arms and appetite thus well exercised, I might have been content to spend the entire week in the bay working over the salmon, but at lunchtime the second day J. W. suggested we hike upriver and see about raising some fish on lighter tackle. We did, and I haven't been quite the same since. It also started a chain of events that turned a fishing trip into an adventure.

As the first step, I fell in love—and that happened when the first arctic char nailed the chenille salmon egg I drifted through a narrow riffle a mile or so upstream from the bay.

Salvelinus alpinus is related to brook trout, lake trout, bull trout, Dolly Varden, and myriad other species and subspecies of fish worldwide. It's only found in far-northern waters; in fact, some of the chars range farther north than any other salmonid, which means that finding them requires some goodly travel. I don't know about most of the others, but I can tell you that getting hooked up with arctic char is worth every effort it takes.

They are elegant fish, silver-bellied and golden-finned, steel gray on top, their sides speckled with dots of pastel pink. When they spawn, their bellies and lower fins turn bright red-orange. In August, however, they're more concerned about the salmon's spawning than their own, so keyed on snatching eggs dropped prematurely or washed out of the redds that a box of egg patterns on No. 8 hooks is all the arsenal you need.

The take might be a quick sip-and-spit that's easy to miss if you're fishing by feel alone, or it can be a lusty gulp in which the fish virtually impales itself. Either way, if you can set the hook you're in for a fight.

Char are not as acrobatic as rainbows, but they do jump, sometimes repeatedly. Their real sportiness, though, comes from a combination of strength and determination. Spending their whole lives in fast-moving water makes them astonishingly muscular, and their little brains are wired to simply never give up. They make short runs this way and that, using the current to advantage; stop and shake their heads like terriers dispatching rats; relocate, tug, and jerk; and generally begrudge every inch of line you attempt to gain.

That evening, J. W. polled the delegation's interest in a side trip. There is, it seems, a pretty little river a couple of mountains over, and Wayne, the camp pilot, could fly us there tomorrow along with gear for a spike camp and provisions for a couple of days' fishing and exploring . . . .

A char river? Yeah, better than this one. The motion passed by acclamation.

It took a couple of trips for the tiny plane, but by midday we and the gear were about forty miles from Nakalilok, on an old volcanic ash bed that is a first-rate natural landing strip. Some more trips on foot got everything to a mile-distant alder grove a few hundred yards from the river. There, Dawn set up her portable camp kitchen while the rest of us pitched the tents, hoisted a rain fly, dug a fire pit, laid in a stack of dead wood for fuel, and jugged up a supply of water from a sweet spring down near the river. By mid-afternoon the work was done and the river was calling.

Running swift and clear and cold over a freestone bottom, it's seldom more than knee-deep and mostly narrow enough to spit across. And it teems with fish. I wasn't keeping count, but J. W. says I landed and released eleven char in the first hour, with at least half again that many as temporary hook-ups. Stan and Pete did just as well. Although arctic char can reach twenty pounds or better, these all looked to be somewhere between two and four pounds—tough, hard-bodied, tenacious. It was by any definition a splendid, though short, afternoon.

Next morning we set out early, intending to work our way upstream till midday, kill a couple of fish for a shore lunch, and then mosey back down to camp, fishing as we went. At the first deep pool, just under a steep bluff at the head of a long riffle, the first bear of the day left off his own fishing to go gallumphing away through the alders at our approach. That same hole yielded the first serious char of the day, an eighteen-inch slugger that gave me and my Thomas & Thomas 5-weight a good working over before tearing out the hook in a final surge.

The farther we went, fishing the riffles and bypassing the runs of relatively smooth water in between, the more local secrets the valley revealed. Eagles soared overhead in the clear, bright blue sky and perched on rocky outcrops to watch us, unalarmed. A pair of tundra swans flew by, so low I could hear the wind from their wings. Bears appeared and disappeared far upstream. J. W. found a set of fourteen-inch footprints, left by one very big dude as peninsula bears go, and we came across a single wolf track larger than my fly reel. The wilderness is uninhabited only in the human sense of the word.

My roster of fish caught and released was satisfying enough, but there was one goal not yet fulfilled by lunchtime: I wanted a char as large or larger than the twenty-incher I'd landed in the river at Nakalilok. Just one, just for the experience.

Experience usually is what you get when you don't get what you want, but if there were no such thing as optimism, there wouldn't be any such thing as fishing. So when we came upon a piece of water where a little feeder stream flows into the river, I tied on a fresh egg-pattern, shot out enough line for a long drift, and dropped it just inside the mouth of the stream, figuring that the current would swing it down along the seam where the two waters meet. For once I was right, and when the line went taut it felt as if I'd snagged a rock. Then the rock took off for the opposite shore. At first even a small char can feel like a big one, but by then I'd caught enough of them to know the difference. The little T&T rainbowed under the strain.

Being hooked up to a big fish you don't intend to kill is a juggling act, an attempt to balance essentially opposite intentions. You want to land it, because that's the fisherman's way of counting coup, but you don't want to exhaust it to the point where its ability to recover is impaired. The fish, of course, is no help at all, especially one as hell-bent on resistance as a char.

So we strove together, trading and reclaiming line, gambling liberties until the fish finally eased its grudge long enough to be unhooked and photographed. We had no tape, but it was longer than the twenty-inch barrel of J. W.'s shotgun by about six inches—altogether suitable as the Big One for this trip.

As it turned out, Nature was about to contribute a Big One of her own. The plan was that Wayne would fly in next day and pick us up. Because the landing strip at the main camp is the tidal flat, it was an exercise like the Reverend Maclean's approach to casting: it had to be performed between ten o'clock and two o'clock in a rhythm dictated by the tides.

Morning came up socked with fog and a few drizzly spatters of rain. As flying weather it was chancy at best, but by ten we had the camp broken, all the gear hauled down to the ash bed, and a temporary rain fly draped over a clump of alders. To pass the time, J. W. and Pete and I hiked down to the lower stretch of the river, where I caught a nice sea-run Dolly Varden and a snag that ate about two feet of a twelve-dollar braided leader. The rain came and went; the fog stayed put. Then the rain did, too.

Back at the strip we lounged under the dripping fly watching a young caribou bull that wandered up within a few yards to hang around grazing moss and giving us curious glances. Two o'clock, and with a collective sigh we trudged our stuff back up to the campsite, repitched the tents and the fly, and, as it was clear that this cauldron of meteorological soup could simmer for a good while, we took stock of the necessities.

Food: A few odds and ends left from what we brought, and a river full of fish nearby. No problem.

Water: One spring, recharging itself by the minute. Perfect.

Fuel: Plenty of dead alder. Great.

Accommodations: Snug tents, sleeping bags only mildly damp from the humidity. Fine.

Clothing: A bit gamey but serviceable, and fleece undersuits to keep us plenty warm. Okay.

Whiskey: Two empty bottles. Grim.

Pipe Tobacco: About four bowls-full. A potential calamity but at least one that would affect only me. I thought about the half-pound waiting in my base-camp tent and started wondering how long it takes to walk forty miles over two mountain ranges.

Now, I don't know if you've ever been stranded in the wilderness, but I have, and I can tell you that the people you're with are the key to everything. One panic-monger, one whiner, one bad attitude, and the whole thing goes to hell. It's as simple as that. But in the right company it's a grand adventure. Give me J. W. and Dawn Smith, Stan Graff, and Pete Tabisz, and you can drop me on top of K-2 in my underwear with a broken compass and a Hershey bar. I'll be a happy lad.

Dawn set about organizing her kitchen, J. W. and Pete and I headed for the river, and Stan went off to glean half a cookpot of the tiny, honey-sweet tundra blueberries that were at the peak of ripeness.

So dinner was a feast you couldn't buy at Maxim's or Perino's or anywhere for any price—three hard-fleshed, fresh-caught arctic char broiled slowly over an alder-wood fire, odds and ends on the side, and for dessert, tundra blueberries drenched in cream whipped up from powdered milk and water from a wild Alaskan spring. Afterwards I splurged by smoking a whole bowl of tobacco; an ounce of peaty-tasting Scotch to sip with it probably would've sent me straight to the grave wearing an indelible smile. I've never felt better under such coarse circumstances.

Sunrise was cloaked in a soft, steady rain. J. W. and I slogged and stumbled down to the river to catch breakfast and lunch, and when we reached the two-foot bank where grass gives way to the riverside rocks, we looked out to find a bear fishing in the riffle where we'd planned to start. Not a big bear but a big bear in the making—a teenager really, maybe six hundred pounds, but long-legged in the way that young brown bears show what they'll be when they finally get their growth.

We stopped. He went on slapping the water without a clue he was being watched. We waited. He worked downstream, and then caught our scent. His nose went up, he spun our way and came loping to us. He slowed at sixty yards, stopped at forty, turned this way and that probing air currents, and finally sat down like an enormous puppy, sniffing the wind.

J. W. and I looked at each other and sighed. He unslung his shotgun; I unsnapped the safety-strap to free my .44 Magnum.

"He's never seen people before, so he's gonna do this again sometime and either hurt somebody or get himself shot. Let's scare him off." I nodded. J. W. shucked at his sturdy pump gun. The slide refused to budge.

"Jeez. It's kinda rusty, after all this rain," he said.

Oh, great. What a comfort to know that my faithful guide

was ever ready to protect life and limb. The bear continued to watch us, cocking his head to one side and then the other. J. W. hauled on his shotgun slide till his face turned red with effort. Finally, just as the bear stood up, came the reassuring *schluck-chuk* of a chambering round.

"On three," J. W. said. "One, two . . ."

Even in the muffle of heavy, humid atmosphere, the combined roars of a 12-gauge and a .44 fired into the air are impressive. The bear went about three feet straight up and took off humping for the river. J. W. leaped down, scooping rocks.

"Chase him! So he won't forget!"

I won't forget it, either—chasing a bear across a hundred yards of gravel bar, pitching stones and yelling at the top of my lungs. Thankfully he kept on going across the river and paused in the sheltering alders to give a backward glance over his shoulder. More flung stones and shouting sent him on his way.

He reappeared after a while, crossing far upstream with wary glances in our direction. After that we didn't see him again.

But a couple of hours later Wayne's little fabric-covered plane came riding the bumpy thermals over the mountain saddle in the east, and we made base camp in time for a long drink, a hot shower, a good dinner, and time to think about adventuring. Tomorrow we'd start the long journey out, and home.

Part II

Heading South

- *Arkansas*
- *Texas*
- *Mexico*
- *Brazil*
- *Argentina*

Green Heads, Green Timber

T HEY CALL IT the Chicago Hole, and if you saw it in spring or summer, you'd wonder why anyone would bother giving it a name. After all, one opening in the woods looks much like another, even one with a big oak tree in the center. If you hung around a while, you might notice that some trees around the perimeter stand in bowl-like depressions about a yard wide. But that, too, you can find elsewhere, and besides, there's really nothing to see that tells you why.

Come back in the fall, though—say, November or December—and the Chicago Hole is a different place. For one thing, you'll get there by boat or only after a long, slow, sloshy walk, because the woods now stand in two feet of water. See it then, and the Chicago Hole is more than just a clearing in the timber. It looks like a David Maass painting. In fact, it *is* a David Maass painting, and *Green Timber—Mallards* so faithfully holds the spirit of the place that actually being there creates a feeling that life and art have gone on a spree of mutual imitation. All the more so, I suspect, because the first time I saw the Chicago Hole, Dave Maass was there, as well, along with his stepson, Paul, and our mutual friend and host, Larry Grisham,

Good art is a map and a doorway through which we can revisit something of our own experience. It can also, I discover, be a pathway toward reshaping experience. In this case, Dave gave me the map and then, along with Larry and Paul, showed me the territory as well. Taken together, it formed the missing piece to an old puzzle.

I have hunted ducks much of my life and have had the good fortune to do so from Canada to the Louisiana coastal marsh, from Mexico to the vast, grassy riverine wilderness of Argentina. I love the birds, and I love the environments where you find them; I've deeply enjoyed the companionship and the shooting, the effort and reward. Yet ducks have never held the central place in my life as a hunter. If they did, it would be a different life. My Brittany would be a Labrador. My guns would be heavier, and so would most of the cartridges on the storeroom shelves. I'd own about a dozen sets of waders and hip boots but only one shooting vest, instead of the other way around, and I might even own something patterned in camouflage. No doubt I'd have more duck calls than the one 1930s-vintage Olt that belonged to my father.

For me, the difference between hunting ducks and hunting upland birds has always been the difference between having an old, much-valued friend and being in love. Which means it's a difference difficult, if not impossible, to explain except to say that something is present in the one that's missing from the other. Or was until I got a taste of hunting in the green timber.

Actually, it's brown timber, the color of dead leaves still clinging to the oaks. And gray timber, with tree trunks standing out like the slashes of a charcoal sketch. But these are living woods, full of potential, full of vitality gone dormant for a while. And full of ducks.

You'll find such woods scattered throughout the southern Midwest, bits and pieces of it from Texas to Mississippi, southeastern Missouri, west Tennessee, here and there. But the heart of green-timber duck shooting lies in Arkansas, right at the neck where the Mississippi Flyway funnels down, in the flat lowlands where woods and rice fields intersperse. It may be the only place in the world where modern agriculture actually creates wildlife habitat on a massive scale.

Both rice and ducks require standing water, and the rice fields themselves are important feeding grounds. But as the rice-growing industry has evolved, means of holding water in ready supply have evolved along with it, which in turn create other environments for wildfowl. In reservoirs where timber is flooded year-round, the woods die and gradually open. Ducks use these dead reservoirs, as they're called, as resting areas. Green timber, where water for the rice fields is stored during the winter and drained off each spring, offers everything—safe resting space with a mast crop underneath. It's puddle-duck heaven, and they pile in by the thousands.

I lived less than a day's drive from all this for nearly fifteen years without once giving it a try—there were invitations I could not accept, for one reason or another, and in a couple of instances, firmed-up plans that vagaries of weather sent awry at the last minute. Which came with some regret but not with bitter disappointment; it wasn't, after all, as if chance and nature were gypping me out of hunting quail or grouse or woodcock or pheasant or . . . well, you get the idea.

Then Dave Maass put the green-timber bug in my ear. We were in the early stages of collaboration on an art book, and the more we talked about the paintings he's done of Arkansas settings, the more I began to wonder if I hadn't missed out on something.

I held up a transparency of *Green Timber—Mallards* and said, "This is really how it looks from the blind, with the foreground birds this close?"

"Nope," Dave said. "That's how it looks when you're standing next to a tree and they fly into your lap. There's no blind."

"No blind?"

"No blind. It's a great experience."

A year later, Larry Grisham told me the same thing, and said, "You need to try this. Come down to my duck club the weekend after Thanksgiving, when Dave and Paul are here, and I'll show you something I think you'll like."

It starts, as much duck hunting does, with strong coffee before sunrise, a bit of driving, suiting up in waders, and a boat ride in the dark. The difference begins to show when you realize you're heading into the woods and not onto an open marsh.

The world was just turning from black to charcoal gray when the softly chugging outboards shut down and we eased over the side, uncased our guns, and pulled a tarp over the boat. I followed the others, deeper shadows against the gray, another fifty yards into the woods. At the edge of a roomy opening, Dave and Paul chose their stands, and Larry led me a few yards farther on.

"Just get up next to a tree," he said, "and stand close. Stay on the south side; the birds'll come in from the north."

"I hate to tell you, old chum, but right this moment, I wouldn't know south from up." Clouds overcast the sky, so that the first, faint morning light seemed to come from everywhere at once, and my sense of direction had gone off-kilter after the first minute in the boat.

Larry Grisham has a grin you can hear in his voice. "This side," he said, guiding me toward a thick oak. The ground suddenly slanted down toward the base of the tree.

"The water'll get a little deeper right there," Larry said. "A lot of duck hunters have stood next to these trees."

The second boat had come in just behind us, and I could hear other hunters moving into place across the way. I shifted a handful of No. 4 steel loads from my coat pocket to the chest pouch in my waders, fished out my pipe, put a match to it, and leaned against the tree to wait.

The first ducks were just a whispery slither of wings in the gloom, followed shortly by two faint splashes in what I now knew to be the north end of the pool.

Sunrise is a perennial feat of magic; I can always recognize its stages but never follow its progress. I simply was looking into twilit shadow one moment, into Dave's painting the next. All the hunting pools in these woods have names. As best I remember, the Chicago Hole is so called because some hunters from Chicago once held the lease here, but by any name, I knew instantly where I was. Whether by accident or design, the view from where Larry put me was the same view you see in *Green Timber—Mallards*, farther back but exactly the same angle. The big oak in the center seemed as familiar as an old friend's face, and so, presently, did the ducks.

The callers spotted them first, circling above the trees, and started their serenade. Others sloshed their boots back and forth in the water, sending out ripples that set the decoys bobbing. When they made up their minds, the birds dropped straight down, sideslipping like leaves. Some went directly onto the water; others swung out for a low-level pass around the pool, and a couple of those smacked the surface just as the first echoes of gunfire batted back among the trees.

The rules here, as in every good club, are straightforward: Shoot only your own ducks and make sure they're greenheads— which is both an admirable rule and one that imposes no hardship. Teal zip through now and then, sometimes high enough to afford a safe shot, and the occasional oddball shows up, too, like the black duck Dave shot that morning. Mostly, though, it's mallards, in big flocks and little flocks, in singles and pairs, on the water, in the air, mallards all around. You can pick your shots according to whatever it is about duck hunting that means most to you—high birds, difficult angles, certain postures of flight, freeze-frame images you might carry for years in your mind and heart.

The shooting is grand, the watching better yet. In open

water, you don't get much sense of how maneuverable these big birds really are, and it's not hard to imagine one crashing through the treetops bluntly as a bowling ball. But of course they don't. They thread their way, graceful as dancers, wings alternately cupped and thrown back, feet down, necks craned forward, turning this way and that. Startle them, and they leap off the water in a splash or simply reverse engines and beeline in a powerful climb back toward the sky. It's like having a front-row seat while a football team performs some exquisite ballet. Once in a while, you find yourself onstage as well, and that's where green timber hunting shines.

Next morning, Larry and I split off from the others to try our hand alone in a little pool a few hundred yards from the Chicago Hole. Dave and Paul had left the evening before, bound for Memphis and on to Minneapolis. As we saw them off, Dave said he was happy I'd enjoyed the morning shoot and added, "Sometimes, when everything's just right, this green timber isn't like anything you ever saw."

Which seemed a bit cryptic, because I thought I'd already discovered that. But as it turned out, I wasn't through discovering just yet.

"I want to see if we can get a big flock to come in," Larry said as we covered the boat and made our slow, shuffling way across the narrow pool. "I'm going to stand back here by the big trees; you take that little clump of saplings out toward the middle."

The sky was just fading to the color of wood ash when I heard their wings. Larry started calling and splashing. I leaned slowly back and looked up at the one sector of sky I could see without turning my head. The flock streamed past, just over the trees, swung around behind, came into view again. Forty birds, my first thought, became sixty the second time around. I revised the number, upwards, again on the third pass and refused to go on guessing. I've seen flocks of ducks that'd run into thousands, but I wasn't about to let myself believe that even seventy-five mallards were going to drop into this little hole all at once.

So, I don't know how many there were, only that the whole bunch shifted like a single organism and followed their leader obliquely down through a notch in the trees above me. Had I been sitting, they'd have come literally into my lap. As it was, they seemed to fly right into my face, streaming down and down and down in an endless, wavering line, each bird following the same undulating course, a cascade of ducks pouring in, breaking up just overhead and settling like chunky, buoyant leaves all around me. One hen hovered so close I could feel the wind off her wings and expected to feel any moment a double-handed slap on both sides of my head. If I hadn't been too awestruck to move, I might have reached out and grabbed her at less than arm's length before she exercised female prerogative, changed her mind, and landed a yard to my left.

The deluge couldn't have lasted more than ten or fifteen seconds, real time, but when it's raining ducks there is no such thing as real time. But finally it ended, leaving me surrounded by a splashing, muttering carpet of birds, dipping their heads, shaking their tails, paddling past my knees.

You know the kind of dream in which motion slows down while time speeds up? That's how it felt, trying to look everywhere and study everything without actually moving anything but my eyes. It's a bizarre sensation when you're wide awake, and I'm not sure I've been quite that wide-awake since. It was like attempting to memorize a complexly orchestrated piece of music the first time you hear it.

And then one of them took a notion that something wasn't right. There was a whoosh and a roar and a great applause of wings, and they were gone. That probably took five seconds, real time.

Larry's Arkansas drawl drifted out from behind me, into the sudden silence. "You here to shoot ducks or what?"

"I was waiting for you."

"And spoil the show? Not on your life. Well, maybe some more'll come in."

Some more did come in, and we did it the same way and shot two apiece, and it was as anticlimactic as pulling off a leaf after a hurricane. Between the little flights, I asked Larry, who hunts these woods every day of the season, "How many birds were in that flock?"

"Least a hundred. Maybe a few more."

It felt like a thousand. It felt like a covey of quail or an explosion of pheasants or the fine roar of a grouse. It felt like the missing piece.

It felt connected—no blind, no dissembling, no sense of skulking in ambush, nothing between me and the ducks. That felt right, felt like being in love.

Quail in the Thorned Land

SOUTH OF SAN ANTONIO, the big country begins to narrow between the Gulf and the Rio Grande. Or so it shows on the map, shaped by two waters and veined with twisty rivers. But on the land itself, water and confinement hold little sway. It is a festival of sky and light and space, as if the territory refuses to recognize the diminishing boundaries of its map.

In the west, the Brasadera—the black-brush country—flows mile after mile toward Mexico. Gulfward lies open grassland dotted with oak and manzanilla growing in isolated clumps called "mottes" by the locals. It is by turns a landscape stark and hard-bitten, delicate and lush, home to the rattlesnake and javelina, whitetail and razorback, jackrabbit, turkey, bobcat, and cougar.

And quail. It's a far cry in looks from Midwestern grain-fields or the pine woods and broomsedge of the South, but this southern spur of Texas, shaped like the tip of a stout blade, is quail country to steal a hunter's heart.

As game birds go, quail are my oldest friends. I suspect I've traveled more linear miles in behalf of pheasants, but along the contours of the heart, which is the mileage that really counts, quail have taken me farther than any. Put me down in some quaily place with a few dogs and good friends, and you will find me a happy man. Make it a place I've never been before, let me explore it with those who know it well, and you will find me an extremely happy man. Add in the astonishing diversity of both land and game you'll find in south Texas, and the feeling borders on delirium.

In all the knocking around I've done to spend time in the company of quail, south Texas took a long time getting onto the itinerary. I don't know why, especially since the shooting there borders on legendary. But the older I get, the more convinced I am that the really good things come along only when the time is right to appreciate them. So I was forty years into my life as a quail hunter when I finally got there.

"The thing about Herradura," David Gregory said, "is you'll find as many blue quail as bobwhites." We were rolling out of San Antonio just on the trailing edge of sunrise, southbound for Cotulla and the cutoff leading east into what is mostly blank space on the map. In fact, except for Interstate 35 and a few villages scattered along it, the map shows precisely seven highways and two towns in all of La Salle County, an area of just over 1,500 square miles. My kind of place. Knowing from experience that Brother Gregory does not overestimate the quality of the shooting he books, I figured Herradura Ranch would be my kind of place, too.

And then there were the blue quail he talked about. In the field guides, they are scaled quail; in local parlance, cottontops; in scientific circles, *Callipepla squamata*; in my hunting life to that point, merely a wraith. I'd had some momentary brushes with them in Mexico, first in Nuevo Leon and later in Sonora, but only so brief as a flush and a couple of wild, fruitless shots. According to one guide to North American birds, obviously not written by a quail hunter, blues are gregarious and therefore usually found in flocks; as a rule, moreover, a blue quail "seldom flies, preferring to run."

In the rhetoric classes I used to teach, we called this "understatement." In practice, when you're on the ground with a covey close by, you'd call it any number of things, most of which are unfit for tender ears. One leathery old south-Texas hunter told me, "Best way to handle a cottontop is shoot 'im on the ground, and then go stomp the little bastard flat before he gets up and runs off."

The ways they interact with the environments where they live are key factors in determining which birds are game and which birds aren't. For some, the environment is a factor all its own. Woodcock hunting is that way, and so is the business of ruffed grouse. Their habitat can be frustrating. So can blue quail habitat, but as if to add even a bit more edge to the sport, it can also kill you.

Unlike bobwhites, who are considerate enough to live in places reasonably comfortable to a hunter, blue quail hang out in the brush, and if you want to make medicine with them, you have to hang out there as well. Now, in most places, "brush" can be anything from doghair popple to an understory thick with shrubs, vines, and creepers. It can be unpleasant, especially if it owns a quotient of blackberry, but it seldom is truly miserable. In south Texas, however, as in Mexico, "brush" means black brush, and the only black brush pleasant enough to be miserable is a patch that's been chopped, burned, bulldozed, and buried.

Black brush is vegetation with character and a streak of villainy. Mesquite and huisache make up the heart of it, but the full depth of its character (and most of the villainy) comes from an incredible variety of smaller, thorn-bearing plants, each in its way capable of drawing blood, inflicting pain, or both. In the black brush lurk prickly pear and Spanish dagger, devil's head and wild currant, and a whole array of things known mostly by their Spanish names—*coma* and *brasil* and *clepino*, *retama*, *retama chino*, *junco*, *granjeno*, and most vicious of all, *tasajilla*. *Tasajilla* is sometimes called rat-tailed cactus, which comes close enough to describing the slender green branches, but words can scarcely capture its long, prickly spines. They're so sharp that even one feels like a jolt of electricity and so numerous that the whole plant seems to swarm at the merest touch—which is why *tasajilla* is also called jumping cactus.

At the edges where it meets the grassland, the black brush is open enough to stroll through without great difficulty. Leave the edges, though, and it's a different world. J. Frank Dobie, the great Texas historian and writer born in the Brasadera, once described black brush as "too thick to cuss a cat in," which is about right. But it's wonderful game cover and definitely not too thick to cuss a quail in. Down at ground level there's plenty of running room, and the quail, blues especially, use it to full advantage.

Given all this and a bird that would rather use its legs than its wings, you might wonder why anyone in his right mind would bother. Actually, no one would, or at least no more than once, if the only way to hunt were simply to strike off cross-country, flogging brush that's capable of flogging you right back even when you're wearing chaps tough enough to be almost bulletproof. The country's too big for that sort of thing anyway; at 15,000 acres, Herradura is a modest-sized spread by local standards.

So you hunt from vehicles, in keeping with the fine old quail-shooting tradition practiced all across the South. In Georgia or Tennessee or Mississippi, this would be a rubber-tired democrat wagon and matched team of mules; in Texas it's a pickup custom-fitted with high seats, gun scabbards, and dog boxes.

And you hunt the edges—the ranch roads and the *senderos*, which is the local name for any clearing, natural or man-made. At Herradura, the ongoing management plan has created a vast network of *senderos* through the brush, providing the multiple benefits of access for hunting, more places for the birds to dust and feed, and in general more of the sort of edge habitat quail love so well. To say that it's been successful is to understate the case. I suppose you could keep count of the coveys, though on a typical day you'd need more than both hands and both feet to do so, and at that level of quail hunting numbers hardly matter.

At any level, quail hunting is a triad, a seamless weave of hunter, bird, and dog. All upland bird hunting is that way to me. I know it's possible to hunt quail without a dog, because I've done it, but it's only a partial equation, missing some vital component, incomplete. Having been a lifelong foot hunter, I can't think of many pleasures more complete than rambling the countryside to the sound of dog bells—unless perhaps it's riding perched on a high-seat or bumper rig, slowly cruising a dusty ranch road, flanked by a brace of dogs coursing the grass and the brushy edge. If I were inclined to submit my carcass to a funeral procession, that's the kind of hearse and cortege I'd want.

You'll hear it said that no dog but an English pointer is worth a hoot in the Texas brush; that setters are too thin-skinned, too delicate, too long-coated or short-winded, or too something-else to function in the heat and the cactus. The problem is, no one has bothered to tell this to David Schuster's setters, so they go out day after day, cover the ground, find coveys and point singles as if they didn't know any better. David, who is the manager at Herradura and a dog man of the first water, keeps a few pointers in his kennel as well—most notably a big, brush-scarred old campaigner named Hank. This dog paces himself like a marathon runner and seems to know every trick a blue or a bob ever thought of pulling—but the setters are the stars of the show.

Dogs wear down quickly in this warm country, even in January. Two brace is the minimum staff; three's better, worked on half-hour rotations with a long drink and an hour's rest between. For a handler, it's a continuous balancing act, trying to give the dogs full opportunity to show their stuff while at the same time conserving their energy.

For a hunter, shooting over the Herradura dogs is a delight. In the course of two full days, one young dog got over-antsy with a covey of bobwhite just one time. You can't ask for better dog work than that—nor, what with covey after covey of bobs on the broad prairies, for better opportunities to enjoy it.

Handling blue quail is no mean feat for a pointing dog, because the little guys just won't sit still. If you can get them to flush and scatter a bit, the singles and pairs are more inclined to hold, but the classic scenario of easing in past the dogs and putting up a covey just doesn't happen with blues. Instead, it turns into a footrace the moment the dog strikes a point. If you don't push them hard, they simply run off, and if they do flush, you won't know exactly where they'll come from—except it won't be underfoot. As all this happens in the brush, trying to move fast through a world of thorns with one eye cocked for birds and the other searching for the next safe step gets to be a complicated little exercise, sort of like chasing bees while wading through porcupines.

Having thought about it since, I wonder if a man couldn't do himself a treat by hunting blues with two dogs, one of pointing breed and the other a small, nimble, well-schooled flusher to circle in and make 'em fly. I don't know whether anyone has tried this, but if you do, I'd be interested to know how it works.

Once in a while, in just the right place, blue quail can turn from demons to darlings, and after dragging us through the brush to make sure we paid our dues, David Schuster led us to the gate of heaven.

Not that it looked very heavenly—a fencerow-wide strip of scrub and cactus with a hundred yards or more of grass, sorghum, and wildlife plantings on one side and a narrow, grassy *sendero* on the other, leading off to the brush. As a piece of landscape, you wouldn't give it a second look, and even then you wouldn't necessarily recognize it as a splendid example of habitat management. But it is. The blue quail move out of the brush to feed and use the fencerow strip for cover; flush them and they head back for the brush, crossing the *sendero*.

We were just three guns, David and Theresa Gregory and I. David took the far side of the fencerow, leaving the *sendero*—and, bless him, the best of the shooting—to Theresa and me. I moved out toward the edge of the brush to give Theresa first crack at the flushes, in part because I was raised on the concept of ladies first and partly because Theresa gets such a charge out of quail hunting that watching her is as much fun as the hunting itself.

I couldn't begin to tell you how many birds were in that little strip. Hundreds, easily. Blues being blues, they went sprinting down the row, flushing far ahead in knots of ten or a dozen, winging out across the *sendero* and pitching into the brush. I doubt we shot at even one percent of the birds we saw, but we got plenty of shooting nonetheless, because enough of them sprang up inside the gun, as the English say, to keep us busy. The dogs kept pointing and repositioning in a steady buzz of wings and the *whomp* of Theresa's 20-bore double.

It's the only time in my life I ever pass-shot quail. By the time they got out where I was, they were hammering on at top speed, crossing left to right, some still climbing, others slanting toward the brush. It was like a driven-partridge shoot turned ninety degrees, and it was wonderful.

The fencerow and *sendero* stretch on for at least a mile. The farther we went, the more it seemed that every blue quail on this end of the ranch must surely be in there. But then, going over to pick up a dead bird near the brush, I spooked up a big covey that no doubt had paused on its way to the cover strip to let us pass by. There was no telling how many had already moved in behind us. I'm sure we could've had another good round of shooting had we chosen to work the same cover going back.

But it was late in the day, and we were near enough to filling our daily limits that a few more birds wouldn't matter. David Schuster had brought the truck around to pick us up, and there was water for the dogs and cold drinks that came out of the cooler with chips of ice sliding off the cans. My knees were just to the point of being pleasantly achy.

But first we had to have the daily lesson to prove that the only ultimately predictable thing about quail is their unpredictability. The fencerow ends with one low bush growing in a thick patch of grass no larger than a washtub. And while the four of us stood there talking, not twenty feet away, one of the little setters came loping by, swung around as if lassoed by the nose, and locked up solid on that swatch of grass.

We looked at this, then at one another, and came to an instant consensus: Surely a blue wouldn't sit there so long with all of us so near. Surely. But something clearly was there, so I walked over and kicked the bush. Exit one blue quail brushwards, in a powerful hurry. It's one of the pair I brought home for the taxidermist.

There is a certain moment in a quail-hunting day when time comes to a halt. It lies on the cusp between the hard-edged memory of wings and the anticipation of a warm shower and the cold, sharp taste of whiskey. It sounds like the sigh of a tired dog nestled in thick straw, and in south Texas it is the color of darkening land under a sky washed in outlandish pastels.

I was leaving Herradura next day, so I rode the high seat to get a last, long look. As we rolled slowly down the ranch road toward the highway, the moment of suspended time broke and the brush country turned toward night. A pyrrhuloxia, the little Southwestern songbird that looks like a cardinal that had a parakeet for one of its grandparents, darted in front of us, heading for a roost in some mesquite or *huisache*. The javelinas were beginning to stir, mincing out of the brush on their impossibly tiny feet, stiff-necked and ill-tempered. I had earlier found the skull and jawbone of one of their kin, bleached white and still bearing its quartet of sharp two-inch tusks. Now, wired together and looking appropriately ferocious on the sitting-room mantel, it reminds me of the day and the country and quail among the thorns.

Quail at La Rucia

THE ONLY THING BETTER than exploring new country is exploring new country with someone who knows it well.

I said something like that to Herb Booth as we rolled along the asphalt ribbon of highway with Herradura Ranch and a typically outrageous south-Texas sunset at our backs. Herb, who's been poking around the heel of Texas behind successive generations of his shorthair quail dogs for better than twenty years, said something in reply, and then we both saw the same thing at the same time.

At a quarter-mile distance, it was just a dark blob. I thought it must be a javelina that had wandered out to where the center-line of Highway 97 would be if Highway 97 were painted with stripes. After all, we'd already passed a dozen or so of the grumpy, pig-like little animals browsing the "borrow pits" (the Texas term for roadside ditches). Herb thought so, too, and let off the throttle to be ready for evasive action no matter which way it decided to go. We rolled closer and closer, shedding speed, until at about thirty yards the blob took shape.

It wasn't a javelina at all. It was a bobcat, as big a bobcat as I've ever seen, hunkered down on the highway licking up the remains of some tire-flattened creature. His eyes looked the size of teacups, his paws as big as my hands.

He took one last slurp of Armadillo Goodyear, or whatever the roadkill du jour happened to be; uncoiled in a long, graceful leap across the east-bound lane; bounded the wide, grassy borrow pit; slipped the fence; and disappeared into the gloom of the black brush.

We were almost stopped by then. Herb downshifted and let in the clutch.

"Oh my, I do love this country," he said.

At that point, my tenure there was minuscule compared with his, but I knew the feeling exactly. Take a bird hunter and lover of wild places out of the bone-chilling damp of a Missouri January, plop him down in an immense, temperate, starkly beautiful landscape teeming with quail, toss in some good dogs and some old friends to bind it all together, and what's not to love?

I'd been there less than a week, and already south Texas was stealing my heart. Our chance meeting with the bobcat, an animal normally shy as a shadow, seemed just one more instance of the big country revealing its gifts.

Not that it was wholly unfamiliar, even on first look. I'd seen it before, in the work of artists who are themselves captivated by its infinite variety of shape and color and contrast—and particularly in the work of two who've made this place their special turf. In John Cowan and Herb Booth, south Texas has found its clearest voice, its master interpreters. If there's anything to modify my belief that the best way of exploring new country is in the company of one who knows it well, I could only add: especially if he's an artist. Then, it's like finding yourself in a territory whose map you've memorized, a place all at once familiar and new, intimate and strange.

I'd already left enough blood and odd bits of my hide on its claws and thorns to feel a certain intimacy with the black brush, and I was looking forward to seeing the grasslands that lie east and south, along the Gulf. Here are vast ranches established more than a hundred years ago by such men as Abel "Shanghai" Pierce and Captain Richard King, a steamboat man who began with

15,000 acres on Santa Gertrudis Creek in 1853 and from there proceeded to build a ranch that eventually came to be almost twice the size of Rhode Island and even a bit larger than Delaware.

At about the same time, Captain A. C. Jones started buying land in Brooks County, to the south. Although his holdings never quite matched the scope of King's, the Jones Ranch was no modest little spread even by Texas standards. What remains in family ownership today is still a substantial piece of country, and it was there that Herb and I were bound, to the 15,000-acre portion known as La Rucia.

Once over the county line, we passed through Falfurrias heading south, on to Encino, and yet a few miles farther to Rachal, where we turned west—thus visiting precisely three-quarters of the towns in the whole county in less than half an hour. We could have made it a grand slam with a three-mile detour from Falfurrias to Flowella. Apart from these towns, one federal highway, and two roads paved by the state of Texas, the *Rand McNally Road Atlas* shows Brooks County as pure white space.

Seen firsthand, there is space, indeed—mile after mile of bluestem grass flowing knee-high among mottes of scrub oak and mesquite brush. In the broad view, it's mostly the color of a buckskin horse, but if you take a closer look you soon realize that an artist would paint this landscape with almost exactly the same palette of colors he'd use to render the plumage of a bobwhite quail.

Which is no accident, especially at La Rucia.

This is classic cattle country, which is why the pioneering ranchers settled here in the first place, but on La Rucia the grazing kine are a means rather than an end. There, cattle are a management tool, run only in such numbers as will keep the grasslands in optimal condition to support an abundance of quail. The natural wealth of seed-bearing plants, moisture-bearing greens, insects, and protective cover does the rest.

Jones family scion Bob Ellsworth has been managing the

ranch this way since the late 1980s, building a population of birds that probably still hasn't peaked.

"La Rucia's always been especially good for birds," Bob said, weaving the hunting truck slowly among the oak mottes. Ahead, two lean, white shapes flowed back and forth through the coppery grass. "We've been selling hunting only since 1988; before that, it was the family's favorite place to hunt, and I intend to keep the family atmosphere intact, sell only a few trips each year for small parties."

As it turned out, we were a party of six, and if not a family in the strictest sense, then certainly one in the way that all who truly love the life of birds and dogs and lightweight guns are kin. And old friends to boot—besides Herb and me, Jon Hollinger, Bob Winn and his two sons came in from Colorado. I've spent good days afield with all of them, before and since, and if the red gods see fit to give me more to come, I'll count myself a lucky man.

Some of the dogs were old friends, too—of mine, if not each other. Jon brought his four-year-old shorthair, the lovely Kate, with whom I've hunted a goodly variety of birds in a goodly number of places and for whom I have as much affection as if she were my own. Belonging as she does to a professional outfitter who hunts more than a hundred days every season, Katie's experienced well beyond her years, and she combines it with the sweet nature of her breed.

And so, for that matter, do Herb's shorthairs, a team of cousins named Penny and Kate, who are descended from the first dog Herb Booth ever saw point a quail. Keeping a canine gene pool viable for twenty-odd years is of itself no unusual feat, but keeping the level of quality high is another thing altogether. That takes some effort and thought. I don't know all the details of how Herb has accomplished it, but you only have to spend a day behind Penny and Kate to see that it's worked.

To avoid any confusion from working together two dogs of

the same name (though it's generally more confusing for the hunters than the dogs), we split up for each half-day hunt and teamed the shorthairs with dogs from the La Rucia kennel. Probably because they were the first dogs I ever followed for quail, I get a special kick out of hunting bobwhites over good English pointers. I love their tough, lean grace and hard-driving style—especially if I don't have to depend on my own aging legs to keep up their pace. In big, open country on horseback, wagon, or hunting truck, my heart sings a special song for pointers.

And pointers are the stars of La Rucia's kennel. Old, young, large, or small, they are athletes every one, hard-muscled and canny in the ways of quail. The only notable exception was Fritz, an ancient shorthair whose rheumy eyes had the look of a dog who'd seen it all and remembered everything that was useful to know. A dignified old gentleman, Fritz scorned the headlong rush of the younger dogs. Put him down, and he simply strolled off as if he knew exactly where the covey would be. More often than not, he was right. Then it was point, hold for the flush and shot, nail down two or three singles, amble back to the truck, hop up by the high seat to get a good view, and ride with us to where the next covey waited.

I'm told it was Fritz's last season, that he's since gone to his reward. In his case, I imagine that would be some place that looks a lot like south Texas, some place where the grass is lush, where every oak motte harbors a covey of birds, and where the life of a dog is not so unjustly short.

Come to think of it, I wouldn't complain if that were my reward as well, and if I had my druthers, it would be a collage of all the places where quail and I have spent time together and where all the dogs and friends who've shared it could come to visit. In form and content, each day would go something like the last La Rucia afternoon.

Bob had commissioned Herb to do a painting of him and

his sons hunting together, so the four of them went off to one part of the ranch to shoot birds and photographs, while Jonny and I commandeered a truck and headed for another.

We roamed and rambled without any particular plan, following our noses from windmill to brush, down one *sendero* to another, from motte to motte, covey to covey, while the sun slanted lower in the southwestern sky. Had you asked me at any point where I was, I couldn't have been much more specific than county and state, and it didn't matter in the least. It never does when you're right where you want to be.

We put young Katie down for one last turn among the lengthening shadows, and before we'd crawled the truck a hundred yards, she was gone. For the Queen of Colorado, that means just one thing. The question was where? We could see about ten oak mottes, any one of which was as likely as another.

We circled one, then another, and yet one more.

Jon stopped the truck, and I climbed up to the high seat for a better view. Around another motte, and another. No Kate, no rigid, brown-patched white form showing horizontal lines among the vertical grass. A few more mottes and we were back where we started. Nearly half an hour had passed.

Agreeing that wherever she was couldn't be far, we uncased our guns and decided to search on foot, starting with the nearest motte. Jonny took the left side and I the right, and I hadn't gone twenty feet when I heard him say, "Hey. Come around and look at this."

And there was Katie, her stubby tail pointing at the sky, head up, mesmerized in a column of scent. Without moving even her eyes, she gave a tiny, eloquent sigh. How do you apologize to a dog for being nothing more than a man?

Jon and I looked at each other, grinned, and within a dozen steps exploded a covey that went off like a world of bees. She was already partway back with the first one when Jonny cracked open his little 28-gauge and caught the empties. By the time she laid the fourth in his hand, we were both standing with open, empty guns.

Hunt long enough with someone whose soul is a counterpart to your own, and you make mutual decisions without resorting to words. Kate, herself no slouch at reading signs, tagged along behind as we walked back to the truck, wading the tall, golden Texas grass.

Somewhere in the distance, a quail asked softly after the whereabouts of its covey-mates.

Quail at the Seventy-Four

$\mathbb{B}$Y EARLY NOVEMBER, South Texas is usually dressed in the same pale autumn colors as a bobwhite hen—buff and brown, touches of russet and gray. Some memories of summer green still linger in the grass, but for the most part the landscape is a muted palette painted sparse across a sandy ground.

It's quail time, when the birds draw in from thinning summer range, seeking the reliable brush, and the dogs can stretch their legs in big horizons. Just then, there's no place quite like Texas.

But some years the weather gods are perverse; they bake the countryside brick-hard all summer and then unloose torrents of early fall rain, springing shoots and sprouts and sowing green everywhere you turn your eyes. There's no place quite like Texas at quail time in those years, either, unless it's Amazonas or the Mekong Delta.

With plenty of cover just about everywhere, the birds can be just about anywhere, and on a ranch the size of the Seventy-Four, that lends a definite complexion to the hunting.

The Seventy-Four is so named because that's how big it was originally—74,000 acres sprawled across the southern part of Atascosa County. The vagaries of time and fortune have reduced its boundaries somewhat, though at 27,500 acres you'd hardly think of it as a shadow of its former self. And when my friends

David and Theresa Gregory took me there to hunt the wily quail, virtually all of it was green as envy.

Rick Hodges, who manages the hunting there, summed up the prospects in one sentence: "The birds are here, but they sure haven't been easy to find."

Theresa looked at me with one of her ear-to-ear smiles.

"This is gonna be fun," she said, and meant it.

Let me tell you a bit about Theresa. If there were no such things as bobwhite quail, pointing dogs, and the quarter of the year that runs from November to March, there would still be a Theresa but not the one I know. Put her on the ground with her 20-bore side-by-side, a dog to follow, and a covey of quail somewhere in the same county, and she is a supremely happy woman.

We've hunted birds together over some sizeable chunks of Texas and Mexico, in places so woolly that even the guides chickened out, and any time she needs a partner, she'll find me at the head of the line. I don't know anyone who puts more love, energy, respect, and good humor into bird hunting, nor anyone who takes more sheer delight in combing the boonies on the chance of finding a quail. Just seeing the sparkle and snap in those dark Basque eyes when she pulls down a darting bob or cottontop is all I need to remind me why I've spent forty years doing the same thing myself.

We take David with us, of course, because he's good company and a good shot, takes great photographs, and doesn't get upset when his wife bags more birds than he does, which she is apt to do on occasion.

Next morning, one of those deceptively cool, foggy south-Texas sunrise hours when the air seems lit from every direction at once, Theresa climbed up onto the quail truck's high seat, slid over to make room for David, gave me a squeeze on the arm, and said, "C'mon, you two, let's find some quail."

Now, locating little groups of five-ounce birds scattered over an area just under ninety square miles might seem a daunting task, but we were not without resources, the best of which lay directly beneath us, in the dog boxes.

Harlan Winter runs a motley string of charges. On any given day his truck will harbor pointers, English setters, shorthairs, Brittanies, red setters, a Labrador, a Boykin spaniel, and Lord knows what else. After a while I started looking for Drathaars and Pudelpointers, just on the premise that any breed ever born to work a bird was likely to be in there somewhere. I didn't see any, but what I did see was impressive in both variety and enthusiasm.

Harlan is a sculptor in bronze and a dog trainer and handler beyond reproach, living proof that if you put a dog with any instinct for birds into the hands of a patient man who understands the canine psyche, you'll come out with a dog that hunts. Give them a place to look and some time to work, and Harlan's dogs will find the game.

Even at that, it took some doing. The Seventy-Four is white-brush country, lying just north of the invisible line that divides the Brasadera, the black brush, from the civilized world. In the Brasadera, everything that grows is capable of drawing blood, be it mesquite, manzanilla, catclaw, prickly pear, *tasajilla*, or a hundred others all armed to the teeth. The white brush is softer stuff, its various twigs and branches more pliable and essentially far less thorny. But it can be thick, and that's where most of the birds were, socked down in the heavy brush where the overstory offers a screen against hawks and patches of shade against the sun.

In there, hunting bobwhites is much like hunting ruffed grouse in miniature. They give you sound-flushes and fleeting glimpses. If you can actually see one or two from a covey, you'd better be ready—it's a quick shot or no shot at all, and every bird in the bag is a trophy.

By lunchtime we had about fifteen trophies among us, each one earned by dint of persistent dog work and a willingness to get down and flog through the tules. Theresa, who'd spent as much time in the worst of it as anyone, still looked as cool and crisp as a catalog model. David and I more resembled leftovers from a fire sale—but if there's a better reason for getting sweaty and bedraggled than six or eight coveys of south-Texas quail, I can't imagine what it might be.

It's hot country at midday, even in November, and the ritual of Texas hunting calls for a cold beer, a cool shower, lunch, and a siesta. Just because you're dealing with roughneck birds doesn't mean you can't be civilized about it.

Afternoons tend to fall along more classic lines, especially as the shadows gain some reach and the birds move out of the brush to get their little bellies full and find an open spot to circle their wagons for the night.

"Normally we could go right to them," Harlan said as he sprayed the first brace of dogs with cool water before letting them dive off the tailgate and get to work. "But now there're so many places for them to roost, we'll have to cover some ground."

Actually, it's the dogs that cover the ground, big-chested pointers and wiry setters sweeping wide loops through the grass while the hunters follow along in the truck. To my eye there's no prettier view of Texas grassland than the one you get from the high seat, watching two white specks cast this way and that in the distance, nor any sight more pleasing than to see one and then the other freeze on a dead run, immobile as a pair of marble carvings.

Then you ease up in the truck, climb down, slide your gun out of the scabbard, drop in a couple of cartridges and move for a few moments through an exquisite suspension of time, until fifteen or twenty little brown bombs go blazing up in a flurry of wings and gunfire. It's always the same, always somehow new.

Once in a while the birds add a certain twist. It may be white-brush country, but it's not without its thorny spots. One of the dogs nailed down next to an isolated patch of brush the size of a minivan, armed with more spines than a sackful of porcupines.

We could hear the birds in the middle of it making soft little chirps, nervous but smart enough to know they'd be better off staying put.

"Time for the specialist," Harlan said, opening one of the dog boxes. Out boiled about twenty pounds of pure energy dressed in dark-brown fur.

If you've never seen a good Boykin spaniel do its thing, you've missed a treat. They do nothing by half-measures, especially flushing. This little guy buzzed around for a moment, caught the scent, and tore into the brush like a Skil saw on feet. Instantly, birds started springing out in singles and pairs as if fired from a slingshot. The depths of the brush sounded like a lawnmower with its governor gone. The whole thing hit my funny bone so hard I forgot to fire the second barrel. I was still laughing when the last bird left and the Boykin came roaring out, looking for something to retrieve. When he had them all, Harlan called him back to the truck.

"The other guides call him the Tasmanian Devil," he said. Made sense to me.

And once in a while nature adds a thrill of her own. Texas is not generally as strewn with serpents as some of the stories you're apt to hear, but it is snaky country. You simply wear stout leather boots, snake-gaiters, and don't worry about it; a quail hunter is more likely to get hit by a falling meteor than even see a diamondback. A quail dog, on the other hand, is a different story, and every handler worth his salt takes pains to periodically snake-proof his dogs. It's done with a captive snake and a shock collar, and it works. Fortunately.

We'd set off for a turn through a patch of thorn-brush that had been roll-chopped the previous winter. A big shorthair named Lars was working well out in front when he suddenly launched straight up in a combination back flip and sideways roll that was about as athletic a maneuver as I've ever seen a dog perform. There was no need to wonder why. Harlan called him in and looked him over.

"I just de-snaked him two days ago," he said.

"Good thing, 'cause that one must've been close."

From the near distance we could hear a dry, angry buzz.

"Damn those things," Harlan said, unholstering the single-shot .410 he carries for such occasions.

Slowly we worked toward the sound, closing in, looking carefully. Harlan found it first, drew a bead, and removed the better part of its head. We carried it back to the truck and laid it out on the dusty road. A rough measurement showed just under five feet. We cut off the rattles and gave them to Theresa.

My favorite birds of the day are always in the sundown covey. Maybe it's because I love moments on the cusp, but nothing touches my heart like sunrise and sunset, those times when something is about to end and something else begin.

It was a sizeable bevy, already getting tucked in for the night, and we wouldn't have disturbed them if the shorthair hadn't caught their scent and locked up so nicely that we hadn't the heart not to salute his work.

Trying to balance a good dog's training against a fondness for the game, we each fired only once. He scoured around and found all three, brought them to hand, looking pleased with himself.

Harlan asked if we wanted to pursue the scatters in the fading light. Each of us answered for another, all at the same time.

"Theresa's getting tired . . ."

"David's had enough . . ."

"Michael's knees are . . ."

"What a day," I said to nobody in particular as we cruised slowly toward the distant lights of the lodge.

"Yeah, and you know what, Silverhair?" Theresa said, borrowing David's pet nickname for me. "We get to do it all over again tomorrow."

Now there's a thought worth waking up to.

Treasures of the Sierra Madre

I<small>N</small> M<small>EXICO</small>, every mountain range is called Sierra Madre, the Mother Mountains. They're young as mountain ranges go, jagged and stony at the centers, falling away into steep-sided foothills that spread out like slowly smoothing folds of the great mother's skirts.

In the east, where the hills face one another across broad valleys as the Sierra Madre Oriental slope down toward the Rio Grande Valley and the desert flatland of southwest Texas, the brush country stretches for miles. Here and there it's patched with pastureland and a few swatches where row crops struggle against an arid climate. In early January, it's all dressed in subtle shades of brown and grayish green, making it a landscape of stark, austere beauty, both from the air, slanting in toward Monterrey, and from Highway 85, which runs north through the foothills and into the wide valleys beyond.

Even up close, the endless brush has a barren look about it—country, you'd guess, for armadillo and roadrunner, sidewinder, horned toad, and not much else. You could scarcely guess more wrongly, though, because this country supports game in astonishing diversity and abundance.

Climate and land use are key factors. This is warm, dry country that attracts migratory birds by the zillion. It's arid enough to suit those species that like dry weather, and yet there's sufficient annual rainfall to support good vegetative habitat for the upland birds, visitors and natives alike, and enough wetland to keep the waterfowl happy. It isn't good agricultural land to begin with, and what little farming there is lacks the intensity and efficiency that usually spells bad news for game populations.

It certainly is no secret that Mexico offers some of the finest wing shooting in North America; the surprise, to me, anyway, came in the variety of species. In the state of Nuevo León, you can find bird hunting in smorgasbord proportions. Operating from Hacienda Paloma Blanca, near the village of Sabinas Hidalgo, we shot geese, ducks, mourning doves, and bobwhite quail, all in four days' time. A bit earlier in the year, we could have added white-wings, and had we taken an extra day to hunt the mountain slopes and foothills, we could have shot scaled quail, as well.

Both Robert Brand, an amiable Texan who owns Paloma Blanca, and his son Robert Jr., who manages the operation, called it the off-season. If that's true, I'm not sure I could stand it at the peak.

I have no idea how many hundreds of white-fronted geese came in to the little pastureland lake we hunted the first morning, but it was enough. The Paloma Blanca guides had watched them all season long, keeping track of their daily flights from feeding grounds to one or another of the few small lakes scattered around the countryside. They chose the lake to hunt based on where the birds had gone during the two or three days before. By the time we arrived from the hacienda at mid-morning, the blinds were in place—foot pits dug and surrounded by freshly cut willow branches.

I shared a double blind with Don Livingstone and his dog, a big Labrador, friendly as a pup, who had come out of his traveling crate at the airport ready to fetch anything in sight. Mike Okray, the outfitter who put the whole trip together, had a blind of his own a hundred yards or so down the lake. On the far shore, Carl McIntosh had his/camera and microphones ready to record footage for a hunting video. (Ours is not an uncommon name, and as nearly as Carl and I could decide, any ancestors we might share must have stayed in Scotland.)

As it turned out, the guides had both the geese's itinerary and their timetable figured perfectly. This pond at ten o'clock, Willie said. The first specklebelly arrived five minutes early and splashed in near the far shore. The first skeins were overhead by a quarter past, swinging down in wide circles and talking all the while.

The plan was to let the vanguard flights come in without any shooting, both to give Carl some videotape and to avoid spooking the main flock, which would follow a few minutes after. I don't know about the other blinds, but with line after line of geese planing past just a few yards up, the atmosphere in ours got pretty thick. Don's dog kept rolling his eyes upward, then glancing toward us, his face growing more quizzical by the minute. Don and I just watched each other's blood pressure climb.

And then something spooked them all. Those on the water came up with a roar of wings, and a couple of hundred voices joined in one great, clamorous shout. If there's any moment in goose hunting more stirring, I don't know it. The birds over our blind at that moment started to turn and climb. I heard Don's gun next to me, and then the world contracted into a narrow picture of my own barrels pulling along the line of an outstretched neck, past the bill and into the sky. Next instant, the big wings went akimbo, and the bird heeled over in a loose-necked, downward plunge.

I've hunted with people who have the presence of mind to shoot doubles on geese, but I'm not one of them. The sight of a falling goose is just too captivating to look away from. Even if I do wake up in time for another shot, it's invariably an aimless poke, productive of nothing but a few pennies more profit for whoever made the shells. Which is fair enough. One goose at a time is as much as my heart could handle.

Whatever sent the first birds packing evidently didn't bother the rest. Twenty minutes later, their wavering, barking lines stitched the sky all the way from the northern horizon to the lake, and birds piled onto the water until the dense, shifting mass of them nearly covered the surface from shore to shore. To give Carl the best opportunities for pictures, we fired only at the last flights in, hoping to also get some shooting when the whole crowd left. Geese being geese, and with only two shooting blinds on the lake perimeter, it didn't work out that way, but Don and I took one more bird apiece and called it enough. The places in the world where you can see that many geese in a single morning are only a handful compared with the places where you can't.

Next morning, the geese took their turn at guessing where *we'*d be—a different ranch-country pond, settled into freshly dug pits camouflaged with brush. An hour after the birds should've shown up, Willie went off in the van on a recon mission. He came back to report them at another pond about three miles away. Willie has an eloquently wry little smile: "Geese."

In such relatively water-poor country, ducks are more predictable. Every little pothole seems to hold a few, and the big lakes hold a lot. We first hunted a large reservoir, then a somewhat smaller lake. At both, we hunted from shore, wearing burlap serapes and using natural vegetation, shoreline rocks, or, in my case, standing dead trees for a measure of camouflage. The guides had put out a scattering of decoys at likely places.

Which ducks you see in Mexico depends upon where you hunt, since the country represents wintering grounds for both the central and Pacific flyways. In some places, Central and South American species predominate, and in others, the species are mixed. Those we found in Nuevo León were almost exclusively North American, Central Flyway birds and, on the big reservoir especially, of remarkable variety—divers on the open water, puddle ducks in the bays and inlets: teal, widgeon, shovelers, gadwalls, pintail, bluebills, even a few redheads and canvasback.

Here, a hunter comes face to face with his own conscience, because Mexican law imposes no restriction on what species you can shoot and few limitations on the daily bag. We all know that habitat destruction and unusually dry weather in the breeding grounds have sent North American populations plummeting over the past few years, and all I can suggest is that you approach duck shooting in Mexico according to your best personal feeling. For my own part, I found it perfectly satisfying to take a few birds of the most abundant species and to simply watch the rest.

In fact, the shot I'll remember best is one I didn't take—swinging an unloaded gun at a magnificent bull canvasback barreling past, seeing in memory the long-ago days when Dad and I shot our share of cans out of huge flocks that plied the river near home. Sending this one off with wishes for a long and fruitful life made those memories sweeter still.

If certain members of the Family Anatidae are struggling to survive in North America, those of the Family Columbidae are not, and Mexico arguably provides the finest dove shooting on the continent. This hot, dry climate could hardly be better suited to whitewings and mourning doves, both as breeding and wintering grounds. In some ways, it's equivalent to the duck factory of the Canadian prairies—and to all appearances, considerably more durable. Land-use changes that might disrupt the doves' three- or four-brood annual production are hard to imagine for this country.

In Nuevo León, September is the peak of the shooting season. The local whitewings have all moved south by January. Some of the mourning doves probably have, too, since the weather can turn rainy and chilly at that time of year. I don't know what portion of the population was still around when we were there, but I do know that, once again, it was enough.

We'd discovered the rain and chill that morning, hunting ducks. The rain moved out by lunchtime, and mid-afternoon came on warm under a clearing sky. Robert and Willie agreed that we ought to find some doves at the same pond where the whitefronts had fooled us the day before.

It looked like a classic stand for late-day doves by anybody's definition—a few yards of grass and sparse, woody shrubs between the pond margin and a vast patch of stunted thorn trees and brush that probably was every bit as impenetrable as it looked. And with Carl and his camera tucked away in a safe spot, we gunned it in classic Mexican style, the three of us spaced thirty yards or so apart, each supplied with a bag of cartridges, a few bottles of soda, and bird boys for marking and retrieving.

Peto, a handsome young chap of ten or eleven with a mop of tousled hair and a quick, gleaming grin, came with me, and over the next couple of hours we each used our grasp of the other's language to the fullest. I know a bit more Spanish than *mas cartuchos, por favor* ("more cartridges," please), *derecho* ("right"), *izquierda* ("left"), *atrás* ("back"), and *gracias* ("thank you"), but not much more. For his part, Peto tended to combine his English vocabulary into two words: "Meestr, beehinyu!"

He got plenty of opportunity for practice. They came in scattered flurries at first, little groups of three or four raking fast and smooth over the brush, doing all the twisty aerobatics of their kind the instant we moved or fired a shot. The big flocks came later, how many at a time I couldn't begin to guess. Every few minutes, the sky would seem to fill with doves, darting and diving in so many directions at once that you could almost go dizzy watching.

I can't say I shot my gun barrels too hot to hold, but after the birds made their first chaotic rushes, I was glad to be wearing a glove on my left hand. At one point, I took four in a row by loading only the right barrel of my 16-gauge Smith; I could see the shots coming, and there just wasn't time to drop in two shells. A dog may be man's best friend, but when the birds are flying that way, ejectors come in a close second.

We quit when the gathering dusk made finding downed birds difficult, leaving the doves some time to have their evening drink. With guns and gear stowed away in the van, we had an evening drink of our own and watched them stream back and forth, still flying, until we could no longer see them in the evening dark.

Next day, it was quail. Much as I love the thrill of wildfowl and the demanding frenzy of a really good dove shoot, few birds touch my heart as quail do. We go way back, bobwhite and I, back to where I first learned the ways of guns and dogs in the company of my father and Gentleman Bob. Since then, I've spent a lot of good days with quail in a lot of good places.

In terms of quail hunting, Mexico is a decidedly good place—not the friendliest of environments, at times, but a good place nonetheless. Quail prosper in the warm, dry atmosphere, and the brush country is sufficiently rich in cover, in seed-bearing vegetation, and an annual growth of leafy green plants to provide bobwhite with everything he needs to make a good living.

Hunting quail in the ranch land isn't much different from hunting quail at home. The grass there doesn't grow as densely as the thrice-cursed fescue that now covers much of the United States, and you can find any number of birds in the pastures, brushy fencerows, and draws that lace the landscape. It's good country for big-running dogs.

Hunting the chaparral, however, isn't anything like home, unless you live in the Texas brush country, and even much of that is tame as a city park compared with the Mexican bush. The thing is, brush is a generic term, and in Mexico it denotes a biome comprising several dozen varieties of shrub, succulent, grass, and broadleaf plant, almost every one of which is armed with a murderous array of spikes, spines, thorns, hooks, needles, saw-toothed edges, and other botanical weaponry. Generally speaking, anything that grows there is capable of drawing blood or inflicting discomfort far out of proportion to its peaceful appearance. The quail love it, and once I learned a few of the rules, I loved it, too.

On the last morning, we simply walked off the hacienda grounds and into a three-hour period when we were continually working quail, either coveys or singles. One reason why the birds survive so well in the bush is that very little of the thorn and hardship grows down to their level. The vegetative miseries reach from perhaps chest height or better on an average man, down to maybe a foot off the ground; below that, it's a remarkably open little world, dotted with frequent clumps of cholla and prickly pear and other needle-bearing stuff but otherwise essentially bare sand mixed with gravel-sized rock. Thus screened above and given plenty of room to maneuver, quail are as safe and mobile as quail can be.

Naturally, they exploit it to the hilt. In the bush, unlike the grassland we'd hunted the afternoon before, we never had a walk-up covey flush over a point. The birds simply wouldn't hold, so at the first sign of birdy behavior from a dog, one of us or one of the guides took off in a long, looping circle, hoping to head them off and either pin them for a moment or simply push them into a wild flush. After that, the hunting gets more familiar, because singles and pairs are much more inclined to sit tight under a point.

Which is a mixed blessing, since some of the places they choose to sit in are places where you wouldn't want to stick your foot even if it were shod in a cast-iron boot. The punishments for carelessness are swift and severe. Early on, I walked up to a point, watching the air ahead of the dog, as usual, and merely brushed against something that bit back, instantly and about as painfully as I've ever been stuck. I did flush and shoot the quail, but it hadn't even reached the ground before I had my reading glasses on and my pant leg up, picking hair-like needles out of my knee and feeling ever so grateful that I hadn't blundered straight into the damn thing, whatever it was, since nylon-faced brush pants clearly weren't much protection. After that, I learned to keep one eye on the game and the other just ahead of my next step.

Like all wild bobwhites in southerly latitudes, Mexican quail are small. They also fly like bees, which makes them supremely sporty. Their size and quickness puts a premium on concentration and good shooting technique. There's nothing to feel bad about if you miss, and plenty to feel good about if you don't. Given the combination of environment and qualities of the game, this is quail hunting you won't soon forget.

Actually, Mexican hunting in general can be a lovely treat, regardless of the game. In some ways, it's like stepping back in time, back to when our own wealth of game was richer and more widespread. This is good, wild country, the Sierra Madre. It demands some effort but in turn offers up treasures to gladden any hunter's heart.

The Legend of
Barba Blanca

Mexico's Yaqui Valley is a land steeped in legend—
ancient stories handed down among a hundred generations of
Indians, passed on through descendants of the Spanish conquis-
tadors who arrived some four hundred years ago, kept alive by the
country folk.

In certain parts of the lower valley, the farm workers tell of
Barba Blanca, he of the magic eye and mighty gun, who simply
appeared one day at the end of harvest time, when the swift gray
birds swarm out of the wilderness to glean the grainfields. They
speak of how he reaches to the sky for birds flying fast as the
wind. When rain makes a rare visit to the valley, they listen at
night to the thunder booming among the wild mountains in the
east, and they say, "It is Barba Blanca, shooting the stars . . . ."

It isn't every day that a new legend ascends to the pantheon
of myth, rarer still that the tale can be captured in print. Besides,
it was one of those shooting trips in which form and content
shaped each other into something greater than the sum of parts.
Even the cast fits a classic mold—the Dark-Haired Lady, the
Hero, the Loyal Counselor, the Knave.

Auspicious beginnings. Late one summer, a phone call from
Chuck Wechsler, editor of *Sporting Classics*: "I want you to go to
Mexico in late January for a story on shooting mourning doves

and whitewings, and some ducks as well. It's set up with Rod &
Gun Resources. By the way, I'm going, too . . ."

I started to say how much that pleased me, since I enjoy
Brother Wechsler's company immensely, but he went on.

". . . because that way I know I'll get good photographs. I
might even give you a few pointers on dove shooting."

Oh.

Actually, it wasn't quite as churlish as it sounds. Chuck and
I have had this conversation before; I can seriously hunt and prepare a story, or I can seriously shoot photos, but I can't do both at
the same time. And I'm better at hunting and writing, so I don't at
all mind leaving photos to someone else. The dove-shooting
snidery also has some minuscule basis in fact; I once gave Chuck a
formal shooting lesson, and in demonstrating some suggestions
on how he might improve his technique, I missed the first four
targets I called for. You'd think he'd have the good grace to forget
about that after all this time.

With two principals in place, enter the Dark-Haired Lady.
My wife, Susan, loves Mexico about as much as she hates cold
weather. At the end of December, a freakish barrage of storms
bearing rain, sleet, and snow laid seven inches of solid ice on the
countryside at home, and it stayed on for three weeks. "Buy me a
plane ticket," quoth she. "I'm going, too."

Okay. Susan likes to hang out with bird hunters, and she's a
good traveling companion; I was about to escape the Missouri ice
cap during the gut of winter for four days of comradely bird
shooting in the Sonoran Desert. It doesn't get any better.

Except when it does. Aero Mexico landed us at Guaymas,
there to be greeted by one J. W. Smith, co-owner of Rod & Gun
Resources. Enter the Loyal Counselor. I've been lucky and have
never found myself on a trip with an outfitting agent who wasn't a
thoroughly likeable sort, but Mr. J. W. Smith is an exception
among exceptions. He knows his job inside out, knows equally

well the places where he books his clients, organizes beautifully, and is generous and patient, amiable and laid-back; all told, this is a man to ride the trail with, any day.

Fourteen other shooters arrived on the same plane, accompanied by an outfitter from Louisiana and bound for the same place we were—Ciudad Obregon, an hour south, where Francisco Ruiz headquarters his guide service.

He's better known as Gabino, his lifelong nickname, which I'm told is Mexican slang for "the big one." I can well believe it. Besides being an imposing figure of a young man, he's a veterinary graduate who soon gave over the practice of animal medicine in favor of hunting and guiding for doves and ducks. "Working in clinics and barns was boring," Gabino told me, flashing a smile. "This is fun!" I can well believe that, too. Nobody would put such enormous energy into a job he didn't love. I have no idea when he sleeps. During the off-season, apparently.

Chuck and J. W. and I had already agreed that we wanted most of our shooting at doves, with only a single afternoon in the marshes to watch ducks and shoot what few our collective conscience would allow. Besides, the dove shooting in the Yaqui Valley is itself the stuff of legends. Even though it's part of the Sonoran Desert, the valley has been farmland since the Yaqui Indians owned it. Now, nourished by irrigation from the Yaqui and other rivers, it's one of the three or four most productive valleys in the world. These vast fields of vegetables, fiber, and grain, surrounded by an even vaster wilderness of mesquite and chaparral, provide everything doves could possibly want for habitat—and the birds respond with some impressive production of their own.

I love dove and pigeon shooting for several reasons. One, of course, is the shooting itself; to my mind, the various members of the Family Columbidae offer the sportiest, most demanding gunning there is. They'd be almost impossible if you really had to hunt them. Fortunately, all you have to do is figure out where they're going to be at a given time and let them come to you—either circling in to food or water, or simply passing through like feathered bullets that seem to ricochet crazily off the air itself.

This makes dove shooting a supremely sociable sport. I enjoy few things better than spending a few hours around a feeding ground or on a pass in the company of friends, applauding the good shots and chaffing one another for allowing such little birds to make us look like such colossal fools. I have a notion that doves, like our most comfortable friends, were put here to keep us from taking ourselves too seriously.

Which in turn breeds a superb creativity. If you think skeet and trap shooters are the masters of inventing excuses for not putting the shot where the target is, you haven't hung around many dove shooters. They could put Shakespeare to shame. I've heard some dandy alibis, even come up with a few myself, but I must say, Mr. Wechsler outdid them all. And with an absolutely brilliant strategy as well, because he managed to establish an indisputable loophole of amnesty hours before anyone fired a shot.

Midnight, before the first day of shooting. A tap on our door. Who's there? "It's Chuck. Do you know where J. W. is?" Next door. Two minutes later, another tap.

Chuck? "Yeah, can I come in?" Of course.

He looked pained, clearly worried. "I need to find Jones." Jones was one of four physicians hunting with the other group. Why? "I'm having chest pains, right here," pointing to his lower sternum. Mother Susan leapt into action: "Sit down. I'll get Jay-Dub."

"I want to see Jones," Chuck said. By this time, Susan is down the way, knocking on J. W.'s door.

"I think one of the other doctors can help you better," I said.

"No. I wanna see Jones."

"Chuck, Jones is a gynecologist."

"Oh."

Susan was back, having got most of the guests at the Hotel Valle del Yaqui on their feet, and was on the phone with the desk clerk to finish the job. J. W. came in.

"There's a good hospital just down the street," he said. "Let's take you there." (Knowing where to find emergency medical care, especially in a foreign country, is one mark of a first-rate outfitter. It's also something you should always check on before you book a trip.)

"Let's see if we can find one of the doctors here first," Chuck said.

"I found one," Susan said, hanging up the phone. "He's on his way down." Chuck gave her a quizzical look.

"He's a GP. We also have a radiologist on board. And two gynecologists. Looks like I'm in better shape on this trip than you guys."

It's funny enough in retrospect, but it was a scary little episode at the time. The good doctor George Miller found no signs of a cardiac event and reckoned, rightly, that it was an incipient hiatal hernia, which allows some stomach acid to escape. It also hurts like bloody hell. I know; the same sort of acid backlash once landed me in an emergency room at three o'clock in the morning. Antacid tablets eased the pain enough for Chuck to get some sleep, but nobody was exactly bushy-tailed when Gabino rattled us out at six for the first go at doves.

Actually, the morning brought several firsts. I'd never shot whitewings before, and I was keen to try them. Having done so, I'm even keener to try them again.

They're bigger than mourning doves and don't seem to fly so erratically, but they make up for it with sheer speed.

Case in point: By mid-morning the first day, I'd shot a few whitewings coming in to feed on the cut corn behind my stand and was beginning to wonder what all the fuss was about. Doves looping into a field don't fly as fast as doves bound for someplace farther off, and I was finding the straighter-flying and slower-flapping whitewings to be easier marks than the mourning doves that had come in earlier. Then I noticed a pair coming toward me, maybe forty feet up, flying in perfect tandem. As an opportunity for a right-and-left double, it was money in the bank. At about thirty yards, I started to move the gun, and something spooked the birds.

They didn't alter course by an inch, just kicked in the after-burners, zoomed over my head and were out of range before I could turn around and even consider a going-away shot. Impressive.

The Dark-Haired Lady had a first, too. I sat down to ease my knees, and Susan said, "This looks fun. Let me have your gun for a while." No slouch as a target shooter, she'd never fired at a live bird before. But she took my 20-gauge, stood up and smoked a right-to-left crossing mourning dove with the first shot. "This *is* fun. Wish I'd brought my gun."

She took a couple more turns and, before the morning was over, accounted for three more birds—not quite as handily as the first, but to reveal the number of cartridges she fired in the process would be ungallant of me.

On the other hand, another member of the party was doing even worse. Not to mention names, but one whose initials are Charles E. Wechsler came straggling in looking sheepish. I asked after his success.

"Oh, okay," he said. "You?"

"How many, Susan?"

"Thirty-seven for you and four for me."

"I'm really having trouble getting used to this new gun," Chuck said, holding up a 28-gauge version of Browning's excellent Model 12 pump gun. I looked at Chuck's bird boy, who appeared to be holding the entire morning's bag in one hand. "Doesn't look like Alexandro's worked up much of a sweat."

"Well, no," Chuck said. "Actually, I think he fell asleep once or twice."

"The action's slowing down here," I said. "But maybe you could still give me those pointers you mentioned."

Mr. Wechsler looked aggrieved. "Is that any way to talk to a man who was up half the night almost having a heart attack?" To Susan: "How can you put up with him?"

Susan said, "Guess what, Chuck: I hit the first dove I ever shot at, just a while ago. Then I hit three more."

"Aw, jeez," Mr. Wechsler said.

Now, lest you start feeling too sorry for the poor chap, you should know that Chuck started shooting better that very morning and later gave me a thorough lacing on a couple of dove shoots—to say nothing of the ducks.

Ducks are Francisco Ruiz's great love, both as a hunter and as a guide, and the duck marsh he's created in the Yaqui Valley is a thing to behold. It amounts to several thousand acres of flooded desert; I know "flooded desert" sounds like a contradiction in terms, but that's exactly what it is—brackish water diverted from the Sea of Cortez onto hardpan. It varies from a few inches to knee-deep or a bit more, and the puddle ducks love it. Gabino has built a series of platform blinds accessible by airboat, keeps the camouflage and decoy spreads in fine trim, and altogether offers duck shooting of a quality hard to find anywhere in North America.

As I said earlier, Chuck and I agreed that we had no taste for shooting a boatload of ducks, and none for pintails at all. The Yaqui Valley is prime wintering ground, but pintail populations have suffered dreadfully in recent years. We would, we decided, be perfectly content to take a few teal and shovelers and whatever other relatively plentiful species happened by, and simply to watch the rest.

It's hard to say which turned out the better. Teal and shovelers are abundant in that corner of the world, and the teal especially are as sporty there as everywhere else. Gabino apparently shifts his hunters among enough locations that none of his blinds gets overshot; certainly, we didn't seem to be dealing with decoy- or blind-shy birds. All we had to do was sit still, and they homed in the way ducks do in a hunter's dreams.

So the shooting was superb, but I believe I enjoyed the watching more, especially the pintails. A bull sprig in winter plumage is to me the most elegantly beautiful duck in the world, and to see them, as we did, circling just overhead, limned in the glow of late-afternoon sun, is a picture that goes straight to your soul.

So is a great flock of ducks coming up against the sky on a far-off horizon, rising like smoke, breaking up into smaller groups, spreading out above the pale, shimmering water. Even those that didn't come our way were as welcome a sight as those that did.

Teal are nimble, wonderfully speedy little customers that put you on the edge of your skill, and Chuck, I must confess, won the gold medal at ducks. He also won a bit of revenge in the process. It started with a lone greenwing barreling past my side of the blind. I stood up to shoot, the bird flared, caught the breeze, and hung nearly motionless for an instant, the same instant, unfortunately, that my shot charge passed about four feet ahead of its bill. Next instant, I shot four feet behind.

"Is this another one of your shooting lessons?" Chuck said. "That duck was just *hanging* there!" Just then, a little knot of teal buzzed by on his side, and he took as sweet a double as you'll ever see—two shots, two ducks on the water, just like that.

He ejected the empties from his gun and turned to Susan, who was sitting between us. "Now, it's called 'wing shooting' be- cause the birds are actually *moving* when you fire at them . . . ."

If you asked, he'd also tell you about the morning when he shot many more whitewings than I did, and he'd be right—but he was hunkered in brush with bare trees full of doves a hundred yards behind him (live decoys, in other words), while I stood in the open and took the stragglers. But my word, what stragglers they were.

My favorite shot at doves is the high incomer, the higher the better. I certainly don't hit every one, but no other shot is quite as satisfying to make. That morning, the low fliers kept their distance, because they could see me perfectly well, but there were enough birds confident in their altitude that I had a lovely time of it. And that's the day the legend of Barba Blanca was born.

I was set up in a corner, a few yards out from the thick wall of brush and trees surrounding the field. About mid-morning, a Mexican family appeared, two adults and about eight children of varying height, clearly out to glean a meal from unretrieved doves. If one of the bird boys came out of the bush empty-handed, all the kids dived in. One of the sons carried a rusty old single-barrel and took an occasional potshot at a dove in a tree. Occasionally, he hit one. They made their way to my corner and stood for a long while. After I'd killed three or four good, high birds, they moved through the brush behind me and came to the field edge thirty or forty feet to my left, quiet and watchful.

The next dove, possibly the highest of the morning, fell right in front of them. I was closer than my bird boy Antonio was, so I walked over to get it. Susan said something I couldn't understand, and when I loosened one of my earplugs to hear her better, I could also overhear the family talking among themselves.

My Spanish is less than rudimentary, but I know a few phrases. The tone I heard was admiring, full of wonder, and two words sounded familiar—*barba blanca*—repeated two or three times.

I picked up the dove and looked at them. One tiny, incredibly beautiful little girl of three or four stared solemnly back. I handed her the bird. "*Mi saludos.*" My compliments. Silently, sober faced, she took the dove. Her mother smiled.

After that, I went on a shooting binge hotter than I'm normally capable of, even dropping one bird neatly onto the little pile of doves Antonio had collected. And for as long as the family stayed, I had an earplug out almost before the birds I hit reached the ground. Each time, more hushed, rapid-fire Spanish; each time, *barba blanca*.

At lunch in the hotel garden, I made a point of asking Susan how *barba blanca* translates to English. "It means 'white beard,' " she said. "Mexicans are very fond of nicknames." I told Chuck and J. W. about the Mexican family. J. W. grinned. Chuck groaned.

"Mr. Editor," I said, "would you consider changing my title on the *Sporting Classics* masthead? To, say, 'Legend-at-Large,' or something like that?"

"How about 'Insufferable Pain in the Butt,' or something like that?" Mr. Editor said.

"Hey, how many magazines have a staff legend?"

"None, if I hear any more about Barbara Blanca."

"That's 'Barba,' not 'Barbara.' "

"Accidents happen. But don't worry; Jones is still here."

We spent the last two afternoons shooting mourning doves at a place I assume is one of the special jewels in Gabino's trove. I assume this because it's hard to imagine a place where you might see more birds. As with afternoon dove shoots everywhere, we were on the ground at three o'clock, grassy rangeland in front of us, mesquite scrub behind, and a cornfield farther back. The first doves showed up promptly at quarter-past, swarming in over the grass, and they kept coming for two solid hours, wave after wave, flock after flock, high, low, everywhere.

With the shooting virtually nonstop, the bird boys scurrying after downed birds and fresh cartridges, and the sheer excitement of seeing so many doves in the air at once, it's as exhilarating as anything you can do standing up. Your gun barrels get hot enough to blister your hand through a leather glove, so you stop for a few minutes, drink a *cerveza*, the bottle cold and sweaty from the ice chest, and watch your friends having just as much fun as you are. Your troubles, whatever they are, seem light-years away.

And then it's over. The flight shuts down as if someone has turned off a great, unseen tap. Apart from the odd lone latecomer rocketing past, the sky is empty but for a few clouds and the soft light of coming sunset. You gather your gear and prepare to toast the day with whatever's left in the ice chest until the van arrives.

At that last moment, waiting for Chuck as he walked down from his stand, I looked up to see two doves coming in behind him, so high they were little more than dots. I pointed to them, he looked, considered, shook his head. They came on, straight to me, and I chose the left-hand bird in one of those snap decisions best summed up by "what the hell."

He was so far up that the front bead covered everything but his wing tips. I swung about two boxcar-lengths ahead and pulled the back trigger. I couldn't say who was the more astonished, I or the dove, but his surprise, if any, was shorter-lived.

I looked at Chuck, still forty or fifty yards away, and pointed to my beard. Even at that distance, earplugs in place, I heard him clearly.

"Aw, jeez," Mr. Wechsler said.

Barba Blanca and the Codorniz

I've TRIED TO MAKE A POLICY of avoiding men who walk up to me in airports and say, "Hi, I'm with you!" while grinning and fumbling with their belts, Even in an airport as unexotic as the one in Harlingen, Texas, such things do not inspire me.

In this case, however, I recognized the voice as belonging to one David Gregory, co-ramrod of Rod & Gun Resources and our host for the next three days. To that point, we'd never met in person. The Dark-Haired Lady looked at him, then at me.

"Are you taking your pants off or putting them on?" I asked. "Either way, a handshake will do."

"Oh, that," David said, grin widening. "Damn buckle sets off the metal detectors."

I could believe this, since the item in question was one of those silver Texas jobs the size of a hubcap. "Well, if we're set upon by *bandidos*, at least we'll have something to hide behind."

The grin now reached well past his ears. "What *bandidos* would dare mess with Barba Blanca?"

"Sorry I brought it up."

About this time, David's wife, Theresa, came up, holding the next generation of Gregorys—Will, age five months, soon to be known as Señor Will. The Dark-Haired Lady, whose need for baby-fixes grows ever stronger now that she's reached grandmotherhood, lit up like a movie marquee. Señor Will, his grin inherited from you-know-who, lit up in return.

Curious how great adventures and special friendships sometimes begin.

Actually, the whole affair was a tapestry of friendship and adventure more complex than most. The bobwhite quail is an old friend indeed—the first game bird I ever knew, the bird my father loved best in those long-gone days when he followed his hard-driving pointers over the southern-Iowa landscape. His love for quail became the map upon which much of my life was subsequently charted, and it has taken me many places where the bobwhite presides and from rough-and-tumble walk-up shooting to the genteel traditions of democrat wagons and hunters on horses.

Had you asked me not so long ago to name the best quail shooting on Earth, I would have waffled between the Deep South—Mississippi, perhaps—and the Texas scrub land, and added by way of footnote that the hunting in Mexico bears looking into. Ask me now, and I could only say that if there's any place in the world with more wild bobwhites than the Mexican state of Tamaulipas, I haven't heard of it.

I didn't know this, of course, when David and Theresa and Will and Susan and I rolled across the border at Brownsville, headed south, but considering the lovely things I've found and felt in the company of bobwhite, a few days in the heart of Mexican quail country were an exciting prospect—all the more so for the chance it offered of sharing something of what my father gave to me, of passing on a part of that precious gift.

David and I had long since concluded that having wives who enjoy shooting with us amounts to considerably more good fortune than we really deserve (a sentiment the ladies would have agreed with instantly if we had let them know it), but for the Dark-Haired Lady, this was to be a milestone. In her progress as a hunter, Susan had yet to close the circle with quail. She had hunted with me at home, where the birds are unfortunately not as plentiful as they once were, had walked up to a dog on point, had felt the thrill of a flushing covey, but the red gods remained perverse, offering her no shots or shots too difficult for one just beginning to translate to live birds what she'd learned from shooting targets. She had, in short, known the frustrations and the vagaries of chance that make up one side of hunting, and now was the time to know how it feels when the balance tips the other way.

The lodge called El Tejón is less than two hours' drive from the border, down Highway 101. In Spanish, the name means both "the badger" and "the bar of gold," only one of which truly fits. You'd be hard-pressed to find a less-badgersome place—or, on the other hand, better quail shooting. Even a bad day's hunting—and I assume there must be one now and then—would work out to about 24-carat, and the good ones are gold, pure and solid.

Each guide has his own personal inventory of special places, their locations jealously guarded secrets of the trade, and he knows exactly what time of day each one will be most productive. Which in turn means that hunting *codorniz* can be an early-morning exercise.

These birds are entirely wild, and habitat therefore is the key to both how many there are and how best to hunt them. In Tamaulipas, the countryside is a patchwork of grassland and grainfields, laced with thickly grown fencerows and interspersed among tracts of classic Mexican bush that range from tiny to vast. Where there's bush, the birds use it as daytime cover, roosting in short grass or stubble nearby and stirring at sunrise to feed their way into the thick stuff. Once there, their safety is absolute, because "thick" hardly describes it. It is a villainous mélange of scrub so densely packed with catclaw, Spanish dagger, jumping cactus, and other blood-letting vegetation that just the sight of it is enough to make a rattlesnake whimper. Neither a hunter nor a dog would stand a chance.

In those places, the trick is to be out at dawn, to catch the birds between their roosts and the thorny fortress. The first morning, we got there too late. After a couple of short and birdless sweeps through a stubble field, David and our guide, Juan Olivera, held a confab in Spanish.

"He says this is a special place he had reserved just for us," David said. "And if the great Barba Blanca is too crotchety to get up in time, he'll have to change the whole plan."

"Tell him to show more respect for his elders."

Whatever David actually told the guide had a decidedly disrespectful tone, and Juan flashed a mischievous smile.

"He says it's not easy working with a legend, but he knows where there are some very slow quail that like to sleep late, too."

A funny man, Brother Gregory is.

As it turned out, he did know where the birds were, and lots of them. David and Theresa had brought along their setter Maggie, a youngster with a sweet nature and a choke-bore nose, but for the most part we hunted in the style known locally as "pushin' bush," in which the guns and the bird boys simply line up a few yards apart and walk the cover, boys switching the grass with their sticks and calling out "*oosh-a! oosh-a! oosh! oosh! oosh-a!*"—syllables that mean nothing in any language except that of quail hunting in Tamaulipas. (A couple of our boys also were expert at imitating the sound of a flushing quail's wings. It works, because covey-living birds take signals from one another, but it made us so jumpy that we had to ask them to quit.)

Surprisingly, you can find more quail pushing bush than you can with dogs. With dogs, especially those whose range is appropriate to big country, you have to go where they go, birds or none. Pushing bush, you work in short sweeps, and if you don't move any birds within a couple of hundred yards, the guide brings up the truck and you simply relocate. Oftentimes, the truck itself will bump up a covey.

Despite Mr. Gregory's promise, we found no slow birds. Mexican bobwhites, like those in Texas and, indeed, all across the South, are smaller than the northern birds I knew as a kid, and they fly like blazes. Their behavior, though, is just as I remember how quail used to be, behavior I had begun to despair of ever seeing again.

At home, quail have responded to years of hunting pressure and shrinking habitat by evolving into hair-trigger maniacs that take off at the first hint of danger and fly clear out of the country on the first flush—which is fine for them, but where populations are slim to begin with, it puts a definite strain on the sport. In Tamaulipas, there are so many birds, so much habitat, and so relatively few hunters that quail just behave like quail. They flush together, fly a hundred yards or so, pitch down as a group, and for the most part stay put until you flush them again.

With birds in such profusion, the shooting is largely covey-rise work. Get among a bevy that's scattered to feed, or find a fencerow where the birds string out in response to the cover itself, and it's a lively dance with singles, pairs, triples, and knots of four or five. Otherwise, you're more likely to put up a whole new covey before you can reflush the last one.

Group living and simultaneous flushes are the bobwhite's great defense against predators, and it works just as well on hunters as on a fox or a hawk. For a while, all those little bodies blasting up at once had the Dark-Haired Lady stymied—that and being unfamiliar at having to keep an eye on so many other people, too. I told her what Dad told me long, long ago: Find your window in advance, where you know a shot will be safe, and don't even look at any birds outside it. When they get inside the window, pick one and ignore the rest. As Dad put it, "You can flush quail in a bunch, but you have to shoot them one at a time."

But finally the circle closed. We had some birds marked down in a little clump of scrub. Susan was focused and ready, and when the four came buzzing out, she swung her old Superposed in a short, smooth arc, and the left-hand bird folded and fell.

She looked around, quizzical. "Me?"

"Mmm-humh. I didn't shoot."

I signaled the bird boy to bring it to me. It was a little cockbird, his white eyebrows and throat bright and clean. Susan stood where she'd been, gun open, eyes wide. I handed her the bird, and she looked it over, smoothing down the feathers.

"How do you feel?"

"As if I've done something not to be taken lightly," she said.

David and Theresa came up, offering congratulations, and the circle, that ineffably sweet, magical circle that is given only to hunters, closed round us all.

Barba Blanca repaid the infidels by being first to breakfast next morning, and we were on the ground at Juan's secret place before the eastern hills showed more than a faint outline of pink. An ungodly wall of bush loomed at our backs. Presently, we lined out and set off through the stubbly grass, moving straight east toward a horizon flaring in flamboyant shades of red and orange. The birds, coming up as singles and pairs, were perfect jet-black silhouettes against that psychedelic sky, climbing fast and looping back for the bush behind us. Looking down the line, I could see little stabs of flame lick out of the others' gun barrels, until finally the rim of the sun cracked the far-off skyline and brought the whole outrageous light show to a close.

"How about that," David said, back at the truck. It was ten minutes past eight o'clock.

"For a while there, it was like being at a Jefferson Airplane concert," I said.

"Jefferson Airplane?" Theresa asked.

"Barba Blanca's been around so long, he can remember when they were Jefferson Biplane," David said. "Don't forget: He probably has socks older than we are."

When Theresa smiles, even her hair seems to get involved. "Well, let's go find him some more slow quail. This is too beautiful a day to be standin' around."

She was right about that. Everywhere we turned that day, we turned toward quail, and it could have been a bloodbath if that's what we'd wanted. It was more fun instead to watch the birds fly and the ladies shoot and to take a few that offered either some particular challenge or the sort of classic shot you can file away in memory like a fine painting whose pigments never fade.

And Barba Blanca got in some licks of his own. We sprang a covey at the bottom of a low, rocky hill, followed them over the top and down the other side. Halfway down, four or five popped up in front of me, tightly bunched. I swung on the right-hand bird and brought down two.

"Barba Blanca strikes!" David shouted.

Twenty steps farther on, I put up a pair. These two were well apart and curling left by the time I got the barrels ahead of the lead bird, and I guess the follower simply flew into the pattern. In any event, it made for four quail with two successive shots, and the others offered gracious applause. Not having a hat to tip, Barba Blanca bowed in return.

I fell into step beside Susan. "Have you ever done that before?" she asked. "Two with one shot?"

"Nope, not once in forty years."

"Nothing like timing," the Dark-Haired Lady said.

That evening, we left Tejón and drove another hour south, to the sister lodge of El Sargento. I don't know what sergeant it's meant to commemorate, but the sergeant in charge is one Eduardo Maraboto, known as Lalo, another renegade veterinarian who chooses to practice the arts of running a hunting lodge and shooting quail rather than the science of animal medicine.

Lalo had laid on a shoot with dogs for the next day. He, David and I, and the crew rolled out before dawn, leaving the women to sleep in and meet us for the afternoon. It was a goodly drive, first on the highways and then along a rocky track that twists steeply among and over and around the hills, but just the sight of Lalo's hunting ground was worth the trip. From the last ridge, the road leads down to a broad valley where the remnants of last year's corn and sorghum lie interspersed with patches of waist-high brush—which, as it turned out, is where the birds were. The dogs, two pointers, covered the grainfields in big, looping sweeps, showing interest here and there but not making game until they hit the edges of the brush.

The first rise brought up as many quail as I've ever seen in one covey. I've heard of thousand-bird bevies of valley quail in certain parts of the Baja Peninsula, but until I see such a thing, those fifty or sixty or seventy bobwhites in Lalo's valley will have to do. Three guns taking six birds on that rise felt like throwing pebbles at a swarm of bees. It was hard to tell exactly how many other coveys we booted out of about five acres of brush—six, at least—but we finished the morning putzing around on a nearby hillside just to watch the singles fly back in.

After lunch in the field, we met the ladies and Will back at the main highway. Among Theresa and Susan and the nanny from El Sargento, Señor Gregory the Younger appeared in grave danger of being snuggled and hugged half to death. His grin was about to subsume his little face altogether.

Had the red gods offered me a chance to write the script for that last afternoon, I would have asked for an abundance of quail for young Maggie and the other dogs to point, good shooting for the ladies, wild country to walk, and good friends to walk it with.

Which is just how it happened. Theresa and Susan did their best shooting of the trip, exhilarated by the birds they hit and content to see the ones they missed go off to fly another day. Toward the end, we stirred up two or three coveys that all pitched into a patch of low bush. Despite being armored to the knees with gaiters that looked at least bulletproof, David and Lalo took one look and chickened out. Susan changed her mind after I harpooned my knee on a clump of Spanish dagger not ten feet inside.

Which left the whole place to Theresa and me and one bird boy, and we covered it twice, once in each direction, stumbling over the rocks, twisting and weaving constantly to stay clear of the needles and hooks—all amid a continuous flurry of quail hammering out in every direction. It was utter chaos, and we laughed and shouted and whooped and hollered until even the bird boy joined in to make the circus bilingual and complete. You could count all the quail we shot on little more than one hand, but not even a mainframe could have totaled up the sum of sheer good fun.

By the time we straggled out, the birds were scattered far and wide, and we all stood by the truck in the buttery late-day sun, listening to them find their ways back together again.

The bobwhite's soft, questioning covey call is one of the sweetest in a world of sweet sounds. I would not be unhappy if it were the last sound I ever heard. There, hearing with my heart, thinking of Dad and Susan and our friends, of cycles turned and cycles still in spin, their voices came like echoes out of time, assuring me that while much is past, much yet remains.

Birds and Bees
and the Spirits of
Agua Lumbre

CAÑON AGUA LUMBRE is a foreboding place, narrow and steep-sided, seamed by a meandering dry wash strewn with stones the size of gourds and pumpkins and sleeping dogs, rounded smooth by ages of rushing water, bleached pale by a blazing sun. Thin patches of mesquite straggle here and there, lending touches of black and faded green. On either side, the Sierra Montserrat, the Serrated Mountains, thrust up a jagged skyline of low, snaggly peaks.

The local people call it Cañon Agua Lumbre, Firewater Canyon, because there they distill an especially fiery form of mescal from the *agaves* that grow in its dry, sandy soil. But in a certain place, Agua Lumbre becomes Cañon Espiritus, the Canyon of Spirits.

The road in begins at the south end, at a tiny village. It qualifies as a road only because it's free of brush and wide enough to admit a vehicle. For an hour we bumped and lurched along, slowly winding among the mesquite, crossing the wash again and again, until Steve Walker stopped the van and pointed.

There, the canyon wall rises sixty feet or more, sheer and gently curving, forming a natural amphitheater. And along it in a forty-yard stretch, the lower few feet are adorned with ancient paintings, dozens of them—streaks and slashes, dots and circles, stripes in undulating ranks and waves, geometric shapes of every sort, painted in pastel shades of orange and brown and rusty red, touched here and there with pink and blue.

They may be a thousand years old, five thousand, or even ten. No one knows how old, nor what most of them meant to the Coahuiltecan people who put them there. Only a few are obvious pictographs: A two-foot oblong with a row of diamonds in the center must surely be a rattlesnake; another looks something like a lizard, yet another, a spider. Two are human figures, no doubt images of the shamans who mediated between the people and the spirit world.

Pointing out a few places where chunks of rock are missing from the wall, Steve told us that this part of the canyon had been sold a few years earlier, and in a fit of greed, the new owners started chiseling out the paintings to sell them.

But then the guardians moved in.

They were watching us even then from an overhang a dozen feet above the center of the paintings, a football-sized cluster of them at the bottom of a waxy mass jutting fang-like from a crevice in the rock. African bees. Killer bees, in popular jargon, aggressive and short-tempered insects that don't cotton to being disturbed or even closely approached.

At full noon in early September, the sun pounds the canyon mercilessly, stealing color from the landscape, fading everything to the shade of old bones. The only sounds were our own footsteps crunching the gravelly floor. Nothing moved except a collared lizard, slithering up the bare rock in search of a shady crevice and solace from the searing sun.

Maybe I have a hyperactive fancy where such things are concerned, but the longer I peered at those remnants of a human past that reaches almost beyond imagination, the eerier the atmosphere became. Out of the silence and the heat and the menacing stillness of the bees, I could almost conjure a vision of ancient people gathering in this holy place, paying homage to gods of wild and terrifying power. The paintings seemed to draw me deeper and deeper toward some connection transcending time.

It broke at the moment I heard two things—an angry-sounding buzz zip past my ear and Steve Walker saying, "Watch it. The scouts are out." Lost in reverie, I had wandered right to the invisible edge of the guardians' comfort zone. The whole hive seemed to grow marginally louder over the *whirr* and *chunk* of David Gregory's camera shutter, and then softer as I backed briskly away.

I tell you this story because there's a connection among bees, birds, and the ancients, or at least there is here, in this desolate Mexican valley. As we bumped back down the road, Steve, a Texan who manages La Loma Lodge and who has spent much of his life roaming the wilderness of Tamaulipas, told us that a couple of years back a game biologist found in a side canyon of Agua Lumbre a whitewing and mourning dove nest site that only the local people knew existed. To the biologists, a nesting area is considered "significant" only if it holds at least 500,000 breeding pair of birds; to anyone's best estimate, the Agua Lumbre site contains upwards of a million and a half pair, all busily going about the task of hatching eggs and rearing young.

But an estimate is probably all they'll ever have, nor is the habitat likely to be much disturbed—because like the holy place of the Coahuiltec, that side canyon is alive with African bees.

Taken together, it's enough to make you believe that nature knows a few things about protecting her own, strategies that we haven't even guessed.

Having done it a few times before, I've come to expect that something out of the ordinary will happen when I head off to Mexico with Brother Gregory or his partner J. W. Smith; something always has. I have to confess, though, I never dreamed it would turn out to be a semi-mystical experience leavened with the possibility of getting whanged by a hiveful of bad-news bees. The whole thing lent a certain spin to the trip, a tone resonating with a bit of Zen.

Actually, a good dove shoot is a form of Zen all on its own, especially in Mexico, where you'll find more birds than anywhere in North America, and especially when it's a mixed bag of mourning doves and whitewings. Add in the opportunity of shooting in a part of the country I hadn't seen before and staying at a spanking-new lodge, and it didn't take much arm-twisting on Gregory's part to convince me I needed to visit La Loma.

It was the newest jewel among some other lodges in Tamaulipas owned by the same people, combining extremely comfortable quarters and splendid food with some of the best—and best-organized—dove, quail, and goose hunting you'll find anywhere. When I went there, La Loma was literally undergoing the finishing touches of construction, and I got a taste of what shows every promise of being some of the best dove shooting this side of South America.

To find both whitewings and mourners together, at least in much of northern Mexico, means a trip in late summer or early autumn. Curiously, the larger, more robust-looking whitewing is the first to skedaddle south at the merest hint of cool weather—but as cool weather is only an unproven theory in Mexico during August and September, you won't notice any shortage of birds, certainly not with such habitat as the nesting area in Cañón Agua Lumbre nearby.

What you will notice is a distinct difference in the way the two birds behave. Apart from hummingbirds and bats, mourning doves probably are the most maneuverable creatures on wings, given to performing aerobatic feats that can leave you breathless. Though no slouches themselves at cutting a dido or two in the air, whitewings rely more on flat-out, hell-for-leather speed. Miss a mourner that's taking evasive measures, and there's no telling where your shot charge actually went; miss a whitewing, and the odds are at least six to one you shot behind.

At La Loma, the whitewings predominate, at least in late summer, but you'll find enough mourners in residence to keep you on your toes. Not knowing much ahead of time whether your next shot will have to follow a bird that's spinning like a gnat or ripping along just at the threshold of Mach 1 lends a dimension you don't find every time.

Sometimes, when the red gods conspire in your favor, the shooting takes on a rhythm and a life all its own—when a dozen or more guns are spread out across the flyway in the delicious almost-cool of sunrise or the brooding heat of late afternoon, and the birds just keep coming in heedless waves. Then, you can lose yourself in the steady throb of gunfire up and down the line as you pick a bird, swing and shoot and then again. Just reaching into your vest pocket for cartridges becomes a hypnotic motion, interrupted every so often while your *palomero*, your bird boy, dumps in a fresh boxful or hands you an *agua mineral* or *cerveza* from the ice chest. You don't realize how scratchy-dry your throat has become until the first swig slides down like a column of liquid ice—but if you can finish the whole thing instead of dropping the bottle halfway through because some dove comes sliding in to give you the mother of all opportunities for an unmissable shot, then you have steadier nerves than I do.

But the red gods can conspire the other way just as easily. I'm not superstitious, but I do tend to take the first few shots of any hunting trip as an omen—even though I know from a lifetime of experience that whatever those shots amount to will be immediately contradicted. So, I should have known what was coming when the first two shots at La Loma—for me, the first two shots of the season of '93—brought down a pair of whitewings as a right and left double. Talk about auspicious beginnings. Then I ran six more without a miss.

By the end of the day, of course, I was wound so tightly, concentrating on centering every bird, that I would have been hard-pressed to hit the proverbial bull in the butt.

By then, I could barely manage to scratch down a bird in every five shots, which naturally only made things worse.

I was looser next morning, though not much, and if Steve Walker and I had not discovered a mutual fascination for archaeology over cocktails the evening before, and if he hadn't volunteered to take David and me into Firewater Canyon at lunchtime, I could be standing down there still, mad-eyed as Rasputin, neck-deep in empty hulls, clench-jawed in a determination not to sleep, eat, or breathe deeply until I shot my way out of the slump.

Which is how I usually deal with a slump until something comes along to thump some good sense into my head, to make me stop thinking about shooting and let my eyes and instinct take over from the churnings of an overheated brain. But the spirits of Agua Lumbre did the trick. The eerie feeling that came over me there in the canyon hung around for days, in fact—so distracting that every puff of wind and every swirl of dust seemed to tell some supernatural tale. If you ever need a way to get your mind off things, try a good dose of someone's commerce with the gods from a thousand years ago and toss in a few hundred nasty-tempered bugs for good measure. It's a sovereign cure for what ails you.

So it got me back on my gun, as the English say, but it also made me something of a vacant presence. David suggested that we go off by ourselves for the last afternoon—possibly because he thought I might start speaking in tongues or chanting to the moon and wanted to spare his other clients the bother of shooting with a lunatic. In any case, the driver dropped us and a couple of *palomeros* off at a pond nestled right at the base of some brush-covered hills.

A water hole has always been one of my favorite places to shoot doves. If the margins offer enough bare ground for the birds to walk about and get their drinks, it'll draw them as irresistibly as a fresh-cut wheat field, and the presence of water is a pleasant, soothing element for me as well. Finding a pond in arid Mexico is a rare treat. Judging from the dozer-scars still visible, this one hadn't been there more than a couple of years.

Long enough for the birds to know about it, though, and we needed only a glance to see that the bare gravel shore was just what they'd like. David set up at the base of the dam, while I climbed high up the slope.

The view was superb—desert flats reaching toward the mountains, looming hazy with distance; the hills rising behind me, dotted with ceiling-high mesquite and manzanilla; the water hole below, long and narrow, gleaming like a strip of fallen sky, its far end out of sight around the shoulder of the hill. Even without doves, it would be a lovely place to watch the afternoon turn to evening.

The *palomeros* told us the birds would come from the front, sweeping over the flats, or from the left, riding high to clear the hills. And presently they began to do just that, mourners and whitewings alike, as singles and pairs.

For all the thrill of gunning under a sky aswarm with wings, something special begins to happen when the pace slows, when each bird becomes a singular event and there's time enough to savor it fully before the next one comes along. As it was, I could call out some incomers heading David's way before they came into his view, could watch from a grandstand seat a little gray shape crumple just an instant before the flat crack of his 20-gauge reached my ears, see the momentum carry it over the top of the dam and skip like a stone across the water. I dropped a few into the drink myself, which proved only a couple of feet deep at that end. Eventually, as the sun poured out its last heat of the day, I stopped apologizing to the bird boys and considered retrieving a few myself. A swim, even from the knees down, grew more appealing by the moment.

When there's not a dove in sight every moment, you scan constantly, usually looking the wrong way when you hear the bird boy say, "*¡Paloma!*" You spin around to find one boring straight overhead and spook it into a whiplash turn. Then you start the gun barrels after it, off-balance on the uneven ground, mount and slap the trigger all in a single motion.

Some you hit; more you miss. But if you're in the right frame of mind, every one of them forges a certain link with an older, wilder world that waits just beyond the bounds of everyday life, a world of birds and bees and an ancient urge to find some means of taking part.

Those are the links that make us hunters, that allow us to find the keen, quiet joys in such simple things as a few doves, a good friend, and a place where time is no more hurried than a shadow creeping across honest earth.

The first stars were just coming visible when we packed up and headed out to the edge of the bush to wait for the truck. One by one they winked on like faint candles, wheeling slowly in a vast, darkening dome of sky—reminders of mysteries that lie close to the surface, of old tales ever waiting to be read.

Black Water, Peacocks, and the Amazon Queen

T HE BRAZILIANS CALL IT *O Rio Mar*, the river sea. We call it the Amazon, a river system more than four thousand miles long, draining an area nearly the size of the United States and carrying one-fifth of all the fresh water on Earth. Its tributaries tumble from the Andes, from the southern scarp of the Guiana Highlands, from the Mato Grosso, and from the Brazilian Highlands, gathering in the great Amazon Basin. It is the lifeblood of a rain-forest wilderness that stretches 1,500 miles across the northern third of South America.

Cartographers seem to disagree over exactly where the Amazon itself begins. Some maps identify it on the far western side of Brazil; others say it begins about nine hundred miles from the Atlantic, at a point where two great rivers meet. I'm inclined to side with the latter view, for although I haven't seen much of the broad, brown Solimões, I have spent some time on the Rio Negro, from its confluence with the Solimões nearly to the Equator, and if it's not the mother of the Amazon, then *O Rio Mar* is an orphan child.

I know of at least half a dozen streams called Black River, but the Rio Negro is the only one that truly fits its name. Cupped in your palm, the water is crystal clear, and it's some of the purest on Earth. In the shallows, bare inches deep, it's the warm ocher of good sherry. Otherwise, with any depth beyond a foot or so, it's as glossy black as a crow feather, a flake of obsidian, or a weasel's eye, stained dark by humic acid leached from the endless cycle of decay on the rain-forest floor.

The Negro is born 650 miles northwest of where it marries with the Solimões, born where the Guaina, which rises in Colombia, meets the Casiquiare from Venezuela. In size and volume, it is second only to the Amazon, and like the Amazon, it flows heavy and strong, without meanders, braiding skeins of channels around islands by the thousand, two miles across at times, a dozen miles at others. In some places it's three hundred feet deep and in others so shallow that even a tiny boat has to throttle back for fear of running aground on the sandy shoals.

Because of the islands, you seldom get any real sense of just how wide the river really is, but you're willing to forego the long view because all those islands are the key to what may be the most productive freshwater fishery in the world. Their shallows and margins and backwaters provide countless miles of edge habitat that supports an incredibly rich variety of aquatic life. Things lurk in the Negro's inky depths—freshwater porpoises, stingrays, catfish as big as four hundred pounds, caiman crocodiles, exquisitely tiny tropical exotics. Things with teeth—*piraña* and dogfish and the barracuda-like *payara*. Things that savage a casting plug or popper or fly—*arowana, sardinata, picua,* and best of all, *tucunare.*

In the Spanish-speaking parts of South America they're called *pavon*; to everyone else they're peacock bass, and they represent a new frontier in fishing, especially fly-fishing.

Some ichthyology: Peacocks are cichlids, not true bass, and there are four different species that qualify as game fish, all marked one way or another with the peacock-feather spots that prompt their common name. At a maximum five or six pounds, the *tucunare-amarelinho*, the butterfly, is the smallest and most numerous. The royal peacock grows slightly larger, and the spotted peacock, *tucunare-paca*, larger still. *Tucunare-acu* are the real bruisers; the all-tackle world record, caught in December 1994, was a yard long and weighed just over twenty-seven pounds. Nobody knows how big they really get.

The royal peacock is the joker in this little deck, because it likes to hang out in swift water. The others prefer backwaters and island edges, places with some underwater structure that's attractive to baitfish, which they often herd into the shallows and attack with a fury that's about what you'd expect from fish with eyes the color of blood. They do the same thing to some appropriate imitation made of wood, plastic, foam, feathers, or hair.

Although their currency as sport fish was minted quite a few years ago, it was for a long time the province of baitcasting rigs and topwater plugs as long as nightsticks. Going against peacocks with fly tackle is a much newer game, one in which the cutting edge is still on the stone. Garrett Vene Klasen pioneered it in Venezuela in the late 1980s and later fished extensively in the Amazon Basin of Brazil. His experience tickled J. W. Smith's fancy, and J. W., being an outfitter always on the lookout for something new, different, and exceptionally good, decided to check it out for himself. In the process, he met Philip Marsteller and the *Amazon Queen*.

A North American who has spent most of his forty years in South America, Marsteller owns Amazon Tours and books sightseeing trips aboard his *Amazon Queen*—an eighty-two foot, triple-deck floating hotel. The upshot is that the *Queen* now is home to fishermen for seven months of the year. As it offers a daily shower, a comfortable bed in a cool cabin, and four-star cuisine, the *Queen* beats hell out of the alternative—which is a land-based camp replete with dirt, bugs, humidity, stifling heat, and a damp tent.

Besides making a comfortable base of operations, the *Queen* offers the distinct advantage of mobility, of covering greater distances and working more fishing grounds than would ever be possible from a land camp. This is especially important when weather patterns send water levels shifting up and down, so that being able to move forty or fifty miles overnight can make the difference between good fishing and no fishing at all.

Exactly where you go depends upon exactly when. Because peacocks are predators, they follow the baitfish, and the baitfish go where they will according to water levels. The rainy season means high water, as much as forty feet beyond the limits of the dry season. In high water, the prey work their way deep into the flooded jungle; the peacocks can follow, but fishermen cannot, so fishing for them is relatively low-water work. However, as the high-water peaks come at different times in different parts of the Amazon system, the fishing season is relatively long. From September through November, the *Queen* plies the Rio Madiernha to the south; from January through March it's the Rio Negro. (Besides making the river incredibly beautiful, the Negro's acidic water also means there are no mosquitoes during the dry season, and that's a blessing because mosquitoes in the tropics can grow to nearly the size of woodcock.)

Regardless of which destination you're facing, your trip begins in Manaus, a three-hundred-year-old city at the confluence of the Negro and the Solimões. Manaus once was the center of the world's rubber trade; now it's home to a million-odd souls, a world-famous opera house, grand hotels, and an international airport five hours distant from Miami. As your plane banks into final approach, you can look down and see the black and tan demarcation where the glossy-black Negro meets the brown Solimões, laden with silt from the distant Andes, and you know you're somewhere out of the ordinary.

The *Queen* is something out of the ordinary, too, especially the canopied upper-deck bar where you can sit in the shade with a drink and think about things while you watch the jungle slide by. And it's a good idea to bring along several things to think about, because the first good fishing grounds are about two hundred miles upriver. Commercial fishermen from Manaus have pretty well cleaned out the lower Negro of anything that might qualify as good sport, so you spend the first day having a good breakfast, a shower, perhaps a nap to recover from your overnight flight, and then you make for the upper deck to tie leaders or sort flies or just wonder at what you see.

A hundred miles or so upriver you begin to see sand beaches on some of the islands, beaches sparkling snowy white in the blazing tropical sun. Here and there, villages line the banks, little gatherings of stilted huts with thatched roofs and only partial walls. Abandoned farms show up as well—grassy corridors cleared from the jungle, to which the trees seem steadfastly unwilling or unable to return. For all its unutterable wildness, the rain forest is at heart a truly fragile ecosystem.

For the actual fishing you and a partner will board one of the little fleet of seventeen-foot bass boats the *Queen* tows behind like a string of ducklings. Each one, driven by a guide who knows the river well, is fitted with an outboard engine and an electric trolling motor. With the swivel-seats removed, both the fore- and afterdecks make perfectly serviceable casting platforms for a fly fisherman.

My first trip up the Negro, in February 1994, was an exercise in experimentation. J. W. had fished the river with a fly rod the year before, with results inconclusive at best. As it turned out, ours were, too, as far as flies are concerned. An airline cock-up sent all my Butoric sailfish flies, 2/0 deceivers, Clouser minnows, big poppers, a couple of reels, spare lines, and various other tackle on some odyssey from which it didn't return till the day I left for home. J. W. had made up a bagful of poppers, and that's what we used.

The butterflies and spotted peacocks loved them, especially some big poppers with dished-in faces that sounded like a flushing toilet when you gave them a good sharp strip. We learned that peacocks are not impressed by finesse. You may own the casting skill to present a fly the size of a starling as delicately as a puff of milkweed floss, but it won't do you any good on the Negro. Peacocks are not into delicacy. The harder you can slap something onto the water, the harder they go for it—especially the butterflies, which hang out in packs and behave like street gangs. Hook one and six more will mob it, hoping to snatch away whatever the fish has found to eat; all your partner has to do is toss something nearby and you'll have a double hookup more often than not. The baitcasters using multi-hook plugs told us of catching two butterflies on one cast time and again.

To my mind, butterflies are the lustiest fighters of the bunch, the Amazonian equivalent of bluegill, muscular and gritty far out of proportion to their size. They'd be a real trip on, say, a 5-weight rig, at least so long as a rod that light remained in one piece. But the thirty-odd butterflies we boated the first day were plenty fun on our 9-weights. Their strike is utterly ferocious, and if your popper lands in a pod of them it's apt to get bounced around from fish to fish until somebody gets hooked. They love to jump, leaping up in a shower of spray and shaking like a dog shedding water. Learning to love butterflies only took a day and one meal. They're superb table fare.

We also learned that our style of fishing stirred great curiosity among the locals. As we worked our way around a lagoon one afternoon, people from a nearby village followed us in dugouts, keeping a respectful distance, exchanging wondering conversation among themselves and with our guide. He finally told us that they'd never seen anyone fish by whipping strange, long rods through the air, and they wondered how it worked.

We had occasion to wonder as much ourselves, because we

also learned that poppers are not the same as topwater plugs where the big guys are concerned. Maybe it's the speed of the retrieve or the vibration or something else, but on that trip the baitcasters hooked all the big *tucunare* but one.

The world fly-rod record was open in the 20-pound tippet class (and may still be, for all I know), so J. W. and I used 20-pound tippets with 30-pound shock tippets to handle the abrasion from the fishes' raspy mouths. We were working down a channel between two islands one afternoon when our guide Natán suddenly took his foot off the trolling-motor switch and pointed to a space between two trees. "*Grande peixe*," he said. Big fish. All I saw was a slight swell at the surface, but Natán knows his stuff, so I made one false cast and slapped my popper right where he pointed. It was gone the next instant in a great boil of water and a slash from the side, which is how peacocks seem to prefer striking. I managed to get it onto the reel at the end of a short run, but then it turned and bored for a brush pile.

Natán said something in Portuguese, which I later figured out amounted to, "Let it run, dummy, and I'll go dig it out of the brush if I have to." At the time, though, all I could think to do was clamp down on the reel and haul back on the rod to force the fish into a turn. My Orvis PM-10 was up to the task, but the class tippet wasn't. The 20-pound mono parted like spider silk, and for all I know the fish hasn't stopped yet. I have no idea how big it was; the head I saw looked about as long as the rod grip, and I didn't see a dorsal fin. Nor did I see the shoulder-hump characteristic of breeding males, so I guess it was a lady, though she was not very ladylike.

A couple of days later one of the baitcasters, a Texan who performs orthopedic surgery to support a major bass habit, came in with a similar story that had a better end. He was fishing the edge of some flooded timber when a sixteen-pound peacock bashed his Woodchopper and headed for the boonies. Armed with a stiff casting rod and 50-pound line, Don reared back as hard as he could and changed the fish's course just enough that it slammed headlong into a tree, knocking itself senseless and burying one of the treble hooks so deeply into the trunk that only pliers could dislodge it. "Aggressive" hardly describes them.

And "exotic" hardly describes the world along the river, where you can look up from fishing to see brightly plumed macaws and parrots winging overhead or watch a four-foot alligator scull silently by. You can listen to the twitter and song of a thousand little birds or hear the faroff siren blare of a troop of howler monkeys. I kept hoping to catch a glimpse of a jaguar lounging on a tree limb, watching us with chilly, sulfur-yellow eyes, but I never did.

The signs of human presence are exotic as well, both those of the native people and those that speak of connections with the outside world. One afternoon, at some place only a few miles below the equator, we moored the *Queen* just off a sandy beach and went ashore for a stroll and stretch. Following a trail that led up from the river, J. W. and I found a little cemetery, presumably used by a nearby village. Some graves were marked with stones, others with wooden markers. A few were covered by sheets of corrugated roofing. Dozens of small, gray-green lizards scurried across the bare, sandy ground. A hundred yards or so beyond, we found the ruins of an eighteenth-century mansion, no doubt once occupied by a wealthy rubber baron; now, only some crumbling walls remain, slowly being subsumed by the jungle. I took away a shard of roofing tile, ornate and obviously handmade, as a souvenir. It still reminds me of the faintly spooky atmosphere surrounding those once-grand remains.

In the end I headed home with a yen for seeing the big river again, fired up for a second go at the peacocks, and sorting ideas on how to entice the big ones with a fly.

Going below the surface with some sort of baitfish imitation clearly seemed the thing to do. That summer, Garrett Vene Klasen sent J. W. a couple of flies meant to imitate Brycon minnows, which he said were important forage for peacocks. He also said they feed heavily on angelfish, and that gave me an idea. After a couple of months' experimenting I came up with a pattern based on Vene Klasen's concept. I called it the Blackwater Angel, and I set off again for Brazil in February '95, anxious to try it out.

Except for a couple of pair of cock feathers for a tail, it's mostly extra-long bucktail tied in an angelfish profile and weighted with heavy lead barbell eyes. It's an ungainly bitch in the air, but it's castable with a big, stiff rod, and it swims beautifully, so the only question left was what the fish thought about it.

Three days into the trip I had half the answer. Little fish shied away, while butterflies and spotted peacocks and the occasional big *picua* seemed to think it was the piscatorial equivalent of canned beer.

It would probably make a more dramatic story if I could say the big *tucunare* took it with slashing strikes and aerobatics, but when we finally found them, they just took it.

In fact, the first one was virtually an accident. We'd nosed the boat into a narrow cul-de-sac, fished a few yards, and were backing out. As we reached the mouth, I flipped about ten feet of leader and line to one side, mostly to get it out of the way of the boat. The fly was virtually at my feet when a bulky shape as long as my leg slid out of the murk, inhaled the thing, and headed toward the far bank.

Having already learned the wisdom of heavy leaders and strong knots, I was using 50-pound mono with a 40-pound tippet and a Pitzen knot for the fly. Nonetheless, I shortly began to wonder if any of it was going to hold up. Some big peacocks run hard and fast and sometimes jump; this one simply twitched its head when I set the hook and cruised off, steadily taking line against the drag. I've never been fastened to anything that felt so incredibly strong—including the Holstein I once snagged with a backcast while fishing for bluegill in a farm pond.

"Bigge fisshe," the guide said. "Put presser."

Having exhausted about seven-eighths of his English, he clicked the trolling motor up a notch or two and swung the boat parallel to the fish.

"Presser, hell," I said back. "There's no way to horse this mother."

"Put presser," he said again.

Right—but it was either apply some pressure or spend the rest of my life in a stand-off, so I palmed the reel and hauled on the rod as hard as I dared. I don't know if it was that or if the fish just decided to change direction, but it turned toward the boat and gave back about half the line before heading off again.

So it went, over and over, until the resistance began to flag and I was able to get it within reach of the guide's long-handled net. It was a hell of a fish, twenty-nine inches by the tape glued to the boat's gunwale. As he hefted it before releasing it back to the river, the guide reckoned nine kilos, almost twenty pounds. Those guys handle a lot of fish, so he was probably close—but even if he added a politic key or two, it was big enough.

So was the twenty-seven-inch specimen I landed that afternoon, taking it on a slender fly that was nothing more than a couple of long white feathers and some green and white bucktail tied onto a 3/0 hook. My partner caught one of about the same size on a similar pattern. Half an hour later, J. W. and his wife, Dawn, fishing from another boat nearby, had a double hookup on Brycon patterns. J. W.'s measured thirty inches, and Dawn's was thirty-three—which probably would have set a new world fly-rod record had she chosen to kill the big peacock instead of releasing it to fight again.

We caught others over the next few days, though none as large as those five, and it was altogether enough evidence to convince me that the hawg-stick-and-snoose crowd no longer has an exclusive on big peacocks.

Either way, it's hot, thirsty work, and by late afternoon you're happy to head back to the *Queen* for a cool shower, a change of clothes, and a tall, cold gin and tonic on the upper deck (purely medicinal, of course; even though you'll want to do a course of malaria prophylaxis in preparation for the trip, the additional quinine certainly can't hurt).

By then, some tasty concoction from the galley is waiting in the dining room on the middle deck. Afterwards, when the pilot cranks up the diesels for an overnight run to new fishing grounds, you can watch the sunset from one of the chairs on the top deck or, as I grew fond of doing, stretch out on the wheelhouse roof with a nightcap to watch the jungle glide past and the tropical moon come up.

Later, when I was in my bunk and lulled to the edge of sleep by the soft throb of the engines, the moonlight stayed with me, gleaming a silvery path across the water like a trail leading to some new adventure waiting tomorrow.

Land of Silver, Land of Wings

IN THE MIDDLE of the sixteenth century, Spanish explorers cruising the coast of South America discovered the estuary where an enormous river meets the south Atlantic, and by 1580 they had established settlements on both the northern and southern shores. Although they named the southern village Buenos Aires, good air clearly was not the main thing on their minds, because they named the waterway Rio de la Plata, "silver river," and eventually came to call the vast country beyond the coast Argentina, "land of silver."

As it turned out, the only significant deposits of metallic silver are far away on the opposite coast, in the mountains of Chile, but it's an appropriate metaphor nonetheless. Argentina is a landscape of astonishing diversity, a million-odd square miles of great mountain ranges and sweeping grassland, forests and glaciers, and the bleak, wind-scoured coast that looks across the Drake Passage toward the frigid wastes of Antarctica.

After four hundred years of settlement, you might imagine that the country had long since revealed all her secrets. But in a land of such manifold riches, discovery is a process, and it was scarcely a generation ago that the word first began to spread: In addition to all her other charms, Argentina offers what may well be the finest bird shooting in the world.

Though I certainly was not among its pioneers, Argentine wing shooting was still relatively new when I made my first trip there in May 1989.

It was a troubled time for Argentina. The national economy was a mess, with inflation running in triple digits—or worse—on a monthly basis. The austral was the monetary unit at the time, and it was fast approaching worthlessness. It exchanged at 106 to the US dollar the day we landed, and at nearly 200 when we left a week later. Nothing for sale in shops and stores was marked with a price tag; you asked, and a clerk consulted a list to see what that particular item cost that day. Twenty-four hours later, the price would be different.

It was a dreadful situation for the Argentines, a windfall for us. The country is especially well known for the superb quality of its leather goods, woolens, and food—all of which was abundant and, on the buying power of dollars, decidedly inexpensive. We had to buy an extra suitcase to hold all our purchases.

The cost of food was ridiculous. A lunch of *parilla*, which is various cuts of beef cooked on a tiny charcoal grill at your table, was about two dollars, including a bottle of good wine. Once—by dining in the best restaurant in our hotel (the Elevage, a five-star establishment) and ordering drinks, appetizers, the most expensive items on the menu, wine, aperitifs, dessert, more aperitifs, coffee, you name it—we finally managed to spend $20 on dinner for two.

The first morning in the hotel, I ordered a Continental breakfast through room service. Presently, a waiter arrived wheeling a linen-draped table holding two pots of coffee and an assortment of rolls, croissants, and other baked goodies piled a foot high on a platter big enough to hold a Canada goose. The bill was 100 australes. I paid it and gave the waiter another hundred as a tip—a total outlay of about $1.70 US. I ordered the same thing the following morning, and two waiters brought it. It looked as if we'd soon have the entire hotel staff serving us.

Which was okay with me, because I was already utterly in love with the Argentines. They are the kindest people I've found anywhere. An old saying has it that if you ask an Argentine for directions, he'll ride with you to show you the way and then walk back to wherever he was headed in the first place. That may exaggerate a bit, but it's not a joke.

We were out walking one afternoon when I decided to cash a traveler's check and went into a bank. Sorry, the teller said, but we cannot; you must cash it at an American Express office.

And where is the nearest one?

"Down there," she said, pointing through the window to one of the city's many round-abouts, where five or six streets all come together. After walking a few blocks without spotting an AMEX logo anywhere, I wasn't at all sure we were on the right street, and after a few more blocks I was sure we weren't. Exercising her high-school Spanish, Susan asked assistance from a nicely dressed woman who was walking the same direction we were.

She smiled, said, "¡Sí, vámanos!" and led us three more blocks and up to a building. In the entryway was an American Express sign the size of a business card. We thanked her, she smiled again, said "De nada," and walked away—heading back in the direction we'd come.

Thanks to the ineptitude of the American outfitter who organized the trip (and who mercifully is no longer in the business), we spent more time in Buenos Aires than we did shooting, but even though I didn't get the story I'd hoped for, I did get to share an important moment in Argentine history.

The second-ever democratic presidential election was impending, and given the economic situation, it was naturally the main topic of interest throughout the country. Election day was a Sunday. We spent most of it walking the *avenidas* of the central shopping district. The shops were all closed, but every few blocks we passed knots of people gathered on the sidewalk outside the polling places, intense in conversation. There were virtually no women among these groups, though every adult citizen was required by law to vote. We never did figure out when or how the women cast their ballots.

That evening we watched the returns on television, able to follow what was happening with our smatterings of Spanish—and not realizing there was an English-language channel two clicks away broadcasting the same thing. Even so, it was clear enough when the final results were announced, because the city erupted in celebration. First came what sounded like gunfire; for a moment I wondered if we were about to be caught in a *coup d'état*, then realized it was only fireworks. The president-elect, Carlos Menim, was staying at a hotel just a few blocks from ours, and soon, through the open window, we heard great crowds of people filling the streets, singing. It was a touching, haunting moment.

Eventually, we caught a domestic flight headed an hour north to Sante Fe, where we met our host, Juan Cavanaugh. Another three hours by car brought us to Esquina, in the southern end of Corrientes province, and yet another fifty kilometers to the *estancia* called *La Pelada*, owned by our other host, Augusto Rohner.

Virtually new and wonderfully comfortable, the main house overlooks the huge river Paraná, far below. Although remote enough that electricity had to be supplied by a generator and hot water by a wood-fired boiler, it wasn't much different from staying at the hotel in Buenos Aires.

The Paraná is a vast riverine wilderness of marsh grass and backwaters. From Esquina we roared upriver for half an hour in a powerboat, turned into a smaller channel, and then into channels smaller yet, winding through feeder streams and backwater pools until I was as thoroughly lost as I've ever been. Finally, the guide cut the motor and nosed the bow onto the bank of a small island. My bird boy led me to a stand of head-tall grass with the center trampled down, where a few old empty cartridge cases scattered on the ground showed that this at least was a place where someone had been before, though how anyone could find it twice was beyond me. The view was the same in every direction—nothing but grass from horizon to horizon.

The snarl of the boat's engine soon faded from hearing, and presently the lower sky filled with what looked like smoke from a grass fire.

"*Patos*," my bird boy said. Ducks.

I've never seen anything like it, before or since. It was all pass shooting as they came over in flocks and scatters—big ducks, little ducks, *suiriri*, *creston*, *patillo*, and a half-dozen other species, all native to the Southern Hemisphere. After the first wave passed, I heard the boat again as the guide circled our island and rousted a new wave of birds from a different direction.

We left that spot late in the morning and headed for a place on the riverbank to build a fire and roast huge slabs of fresh beef for lunch. Winding through the backwaters, we flushed ducks from every pool, hundreds of them at a time. I was spellbound by their numbers—until I happened to look down at the water and noticed that there were just as many ducks scrambling through the low-growing water weeds as there were in the air. It finally dawned on me that it was the end of the molt and about half the birds there were still flightless. Unbelievable.

Next day, I shot pigeons around a bean field not far from the *estancia* and, in the evening, at the edge of a pasture. The numbers didn't match those of the ducks, but there were enough that the shooting didn't have many doldrums.

Then it was over. I left thoroughly in love with the wild beauty of the countryside, with the generosity and charm of the people. And I was determined to see Argentina again.

Then my friend Bob Hunter, one of those people whose surname fits him perfectly, started filling my ear with stories of the fabulous dove shooting in Córdoba Province. Other travelers

Land of Silver, Land of Wings   **187**

told me similar tales, of doves and the wonderful little grassland birds called *perdiz*, with whom I'd already had a brief and tantalizing meeting. So, even though Bob is a persuasive guy, he was preaching to the choir; I was more than ready to go months before we hooked up in Miami on the Fourth of July 1993 for the long flight south.

The old days of economic woe were over. Although he was forced to take such draconian measures as confiscating personal bank accounts, President Menim managed to stem the inflationary hemorrhage. The monetary unit was now the peso, the exchange rate tied one-to-one against the American dollar, and Argentina had become an expensive place to visit. But it was still Argentina, and I was happy to be there.

Córdoba Province lies almost at the geographic heart of the country, and its capital, Córdoba City, is a little more than an hour's flight northwest from Buenos Aires. The eastern side of the province is part of the great Argentine Pampas, farmland that supports a multitude of small grains and grazing herds, interspersed with hilly regions too dry to grow much more than low scrub and dense brush. The combination is ideal for doves.

According to the natural-history books, Argentina is home to twenty-three species of pigeons and doves. The pigeons, some of them huge compared with North American band-tails and blue rocks, are great sport, but the king of them all is *Zenaida maculosa*, the eared dove. With vast areas for nesting, endless grainfields in which to feed, and a climate temperate enough that they can breed about nine months of the year, the little *torcazas* are as plentiful as locusts, and to the farmers of Córdoba, every bit as welcome. Years ago, the government even paid a bounty on them—one shotgun cartridge for each pair of dove feet delivered to the proper authority.

The same deal also applied to the little green parrots that flitter about like flocks of noisy emeralds, chattering continually (for which the Argentines colloquially call them *mujeres*, women). Besides wreaking havoc on fruit orchards, they strew the countryside with twigs of thornbrush, which they use to build enormous communal nests, making punctured tires an almost daily event in some areas.

Consequently, dove shooters are encouraged to bag parrots as well—and in fact, landowners can get a bit testy if you don't. I shot one (parrot, I mean, not landowner), mostly out of curiosity, and then decided to let them be; they're slow-flying, not much sportier than balloons, and pest or not, I rather like watching them sparkle around the sky like clouds of bright-green butterflies. Even their constant chatter has a certain soothing charm.

But don't expect to collect a bounty, even if you knock off a carload of parrots or doves, for that matter. The Argentine government realized some time ago that Córdoba's plague of doves is a marketable resource. So, too, have a growing number of outfitters—among them California gun dealer William Larkin Moore, who has gone most of the others one better by buying his own lodge.

It's in La Granja, about forty kilometers from the airport at Córdoba City, perched on a hill above the village. The house itself was built just after World War II by some German immigrant—most likely one whose former political affiliations promised to make life in postwar Europe decidedly awkward. That, no doubt, is why he chose tiny La Granja, so small that it doesn't appear on even the most detailed atlas maps. At any rate, Bill Moore bought the place and its five-acre grounds a few years ago, refurbished the house, and turned it into a shooting lodge. Now, it's called Villa Sierra Verde, "The House on the Green Hill."

As July is the middle of winter in the Southern Hemisphere, green is only an accent in a palette of tan and brown and the gold of crop stubble—to a bird hunter, the colors of habitat. Exactly which piece of habitat you visit on a given day depends on where hunting-manager Alejandro Hayes and his sidekick

Rafael Muriel think the action will be best. It might be a ten-minute drive from the villa or an hour's journey; in any case, it'll be worth the trip.

The eared dove gets its name from small patches of iridescent feathers on either side of its head. Otherwise, it's virtually a Xerox of a mourning dove without the long, pointy tail. It is capable of about the same speed and has most of the mourner's maneuverability on the wing. Set up some place where the birds are coming in to feed, and the shooting isn't much different from what you'd find in Carolina or Texas—which is to say, doves darting and wheeling in every direction, high and low, this way and that. Start to swing your gun on a tall one, and likely as not you'll have the extra challenge of distraction as half a dozen zoom past almost in your face.

What's different in Argentina from almost anywhere else in the world are the numbers. Gunning a feeding area, you soon notice that the early-morning flurry of activity typical of mourning doves goes on and on as new flocks keep appearing. There's a noticeable lull at midday but still scarcely any time when the sky will be entirely empty of birds. (What you'll be noticing most at midday, however, is the *asado*—a field lunch of sausages and succulent Argentine beef grilled over an open fire, and enough of it to founder a regiment. Even after a nap, your gun handling won't be as nimble as it was before the meal.)

For all the doves you'll see around the grainfields, pass shooting near a roost is the best way to get a sense of just what their numbers really are. Even at that, a sense is all you'll get, because some roosts are so large that any estimate is only a wild guess. At two such places where I shot—one area in the foothills that Alejandro calls The Window and one near La Granja, called Magic Hill—the flights were continuous from early morning to late afternoon.

And from about ten in the morning till mid-afternoon,

they were passing each other in opposite directions, as the first birds out to feed were on their way back while the late-risers were still leaving the roost. I've been some places where doves are abundant, but I've never seen anything like that.

To my thinking, pass-shooting generally isn't quite as demanding as trying to unravel the aerobatics of doves working over a feeding ground. There are exceptions to everything, though, and those are the ones you don't forget.

Like Magic Hill. Magic Hill actually is several hills pushed together, standing with a broad, brushy valley on one side and rolling grassland on the other. The view is splendid, and so is the shooting—especially, I found, at the brow that overlooks the pampas. Doves heading back to the valley come skimming low over the grass to the base of the hill and then streak up the slope and catch the wind currents at the top.

Screened until the last moment by some scrub trees in front of me, they came ripping up like little gray rockets in an almost vertical climb, which gave me about three seconds to get my gun moving before they got into the wind, peeling off and spinning in every direction.

It went on that way for two hours or more, until my head was spinning with the pandemonium of birds pouring through by the scores and hundreds. To those of us nurtured on more modest supplies of game, comments about the possibility of shooting two or three cases of cartridges in a day seem either arrant fantasy or game hoggery of an unconscionable order. But you really can fire that many shots if you want, and in doing so you will molest no more than a fraction of a tithe of all the birds you'll see. For sheer numbers, Argentina is a world of its own, measurable only by its own standards.

Even under the self-imposed restraints of taking only high shots or long shots or the angles you find most difficult, shooting doves in Argentina with a two-barreled gun will give your arms and shoulders a more grueling workout than any health-club weight machine. Spend two weeks opening and closing your gun that many times, and you'd go home with forearms like Popeye's. I shot for only five days and still managed to wear holes in the thumbs of two pair of leather shooting gloves, just from the top lever and safety button.

And it wasn't even all dove shooting, for we spent two full afternoons following Alejandro's ribby, hard-legged pointers as they coursed the grassland for *perdiz*.

Actually, *perdiz*, "partridge," is a misnomer, though that's the word everyone uses, pronouncing it *pear-DEECE*. These are in fact tinamou, ground-dwelling birds native to Central and South America, and they're more closely related to ostriches than to any of the true partridges. Of the fifteen species native to Argentina, I believe only two or three are considered game birds—but the two I know about firsthand are as sporty as any bird you care to name.

They're similar in appearance—marked much like a hen pheasant on top and the color of a woodcock underneath—and different in size. The smaller one, the spotted tinamou, or *inambu comun*, is the size of a gray partridge or a chukar, while the *martineta* is about as large as a hen pheasant.

They're both grassland- and stubble-dwellers, fine runners occasionally willing to hold for a pointing dog, explosive on the flush, and pure blazes on the wing.

I ran into *perdiz* on my first trip to Argentina, flushing a few by chance at the edge of a bean field. I had no idea what they were, but they flew like serious birds, so I shot a couple and gave them to the cook at the *estancia*—and at dinner that evening I found them on a par with ruffed grouse and bobwhite as table fare.

I'm told parts of neighboring Uruguay have even more *perdiz* then Argentina, but I know for sure that Córdoba Province has more than enough to make happy hunters. Besides, filling the legal bag limit of fifteen is no simple feat, even when Good Luck is riding on one of your shoulders and Good Shooting on the other. In addition to being faster than it looks, the tinamou has one odd physical characteristic that sometimes works very much in its favor: Its rump feathers are so long that it appears to have no tail at all. Until you get accustomed to the sight, you can be so focused on this little bird's enormous-looking butt that you stand a fine chance of shooting yards behind.

Otherwise, they'll remind you of miniature sharptails or prairie chickens, capable of as much off-the-line acceleration as quail, and that makes for sporty hunting. If they hung out in coveys instead of singles and pairs, a lot of hunters would keel right over from the adrenaline rush—or I would, anyway. As it is, in the relatively thin cover that spotted tinamou prefer, a keen-nosed dog may make game ten or fifteen yards from the bird in question and the bird's likely to be moving, so there's plenty of time to get yourself wound up like a banjo string before the flush.

Martinetas aren't as startling, which is curious because they flush with just as much enthusiasm. But they seem to prefer taller grass, and walking in tall grass makes a fair amount of noise to begin with, so perhaps there's not as much contrast between the silence before the flush and the actual hammer of wings. Anyway, the difference is noticeable.

I don't know whether they're less plentiful than *inambu comun* or whether we weren't in the right habitat, but in any case, we'd seen only two or three *martinetas* by the time the last afternoon was winding down—among them one presenting such a no-brain gimme shot that even the dog did a double take when I missed it. I wanted one to file away in the little trophy room I carry next to my heart, so I asked Alejandro if we could finish up someplace where a *martineta* was likely to abide. He took us to an *estancia* (small farm) not far off and cast the dog along the edge where an orchard dwindled off into thigh-high grass.

The first sweep brought a wild flush too distant to shoot,

and then another. I'd read that *martinetas* often hang out in pairs. Presently, another offered Bob a shot, and he folded the bird neatly. The light was fading fast, pooling into blue shadows. We should work toward the nearby fence, Alejandro said, and then turn back toward the van.

Hunting pheasants and quail, I always make a point of practicing a little trick my father taught me years ago: Never stop short of a fence; instead, push right up to it and kick it, especially if the cover is thinner on the other side. I've booted up a lot of fence-skulking birds that way. I didn't have a clue whether it might work with tinamou, but there was nothing to lose in trying.

The fence wire groaned and twanged in protest of a lusty kick. Nothing flew, nor on the second try. Figuring the fence wasn't to blame for not harboring any birds, I opted against a third kick, turned away, and jumped half out of my pants when the first *martineta* came flailing up not six feet off.

I don't even remember raising the gun or feeling the recoil bump against my shoulder. But I remember the sight of that straightaway shape tumbling toward the grass and the burr of the second bird's wings as I watched it fly off, silhouetted against the darkening sky.

And I remember walking back through the crackly grass, gun over my shoulder and a plump weight in the game pocket against my back, looking for the Southern Cross among the stars just winking on, thinking about what familiar territories a bird and a dog and a gun create, even here, in this strange and lovely place half a world away.

Part III
Heading East

▶ *England*

▶ *Russia*

▶ *Spain*

▶ *Hungary*

Shooting Days, Pheasant Dreams

AT FIRST, when the single note from the shoot-master's horn has died away, the only sounds are the silky whisper of water from the brook and the dry, brief rustle of leaves that lift and shuffle on an errant wind. Minutes spin past, resolving into faint clicks as the beaters, out of sight beyond the hilltop covert, move slowly into hearing, tapping their sticks against the trees. A cock pheasant slips out of the undergrowth forty yards away, surveys the expanse of green, close-cropped turf, turns tail, and disappears again.

The beaters' sticks are louder now, a free-form rhythm in counterpoint to soft trills uttered now and then. At the stands farther down the valley, the other guns are on their feet, shooting sticks forgotten, gun barrels up, eyes on the bare treetops.

"Over," someone calls, and the first bird appears through the tracery of branches, soundless with distance. Then others, specks against a pearl-blue sky, growing larger, climbing, wings hammering the air or cupped and gliding, curling left, right, tail feathers fanned and streaming. The guns set up ragged volleys.

"Your bird, sir," from the picker-up a few yards behind, the consonants rounded to a musical "Yawh buhd, seh." I pick one among the three or four or a dozen incoming silhouettes, tuck the gun butt under my right arm, push out with my left hand to start the muzzles swinging up along the line of flight, lift the gun to my shoulder in the same motion, block out the bird, remind myself to keep my cheek on the stock, ignore the advice and shoot too far ahead; push out again with my left hand, faster this time, and slap the back trigger the instant the bird disappears behind the barrels. There's a momentary glimpse of scattering feathers, of wings gone suddenly akimbo. By the time the bird arcs down with a thump at the edge of the woods behind me, I have the gun open, ejectors flicking empties to the grass, and pivot a quarter-turn to the right, still watching the hurtling shapes incoming overhead.

My loader, a dark-eyed woman in a plaid wool hat and waxed-cotton coat, drops a fresh cartridge into each barrel. I chunk the gun shut, repeat the ready-and-swing ritual, take a right-curling bird at medium height and, surprisingly, a tall incomer with the second barrel. The loader is ready with two more.

She smiles at me. "Not bad, McIntosh . . . for a beginner."

There's no fooling someone who's watched you miss an ungodly number of shots, only a few of which really are as easy as they look, even to a beginner who feels as if he's fallen into some lovely wrinkle in space and time.

That same lady and I had come off a plane in London at dawn the morning before, in a welter of luggage, bleary from nineteen hours' travel across six time zones. Despite the majority opinion around my house that I can fall asleep anywhere, any time, four hours' dozing in an airplane seat seldom leaves me at my brightest, but the prospect of two days of driven-pheasant shooting in the best English tradition is as good as a night's sleep and a pot of coffee.

Driven-game shooting is not an English invention, strictly speaking, since the idea probably originated with the battues long popular among the nobility of central Europe. But if the old accounts are accurate, the battues often bore more resemblance to guerrilla warfare than to the formal, elegant, and demanding sport of shooting driven birds as it evolved in England a hundred years ago.

Before the 1860s, game-shooting in England was a matter of walking the woods and moors with dogs and shooting birds as they flushed and flew away. Then, about the middle of Queen Victoria's reign, someone, probably a landowner in East Anglia, struck upon the notion of having estate workers do the walking, driving the game toward the guns. The first birds to be shot this way probably were native gray partridge and pheasants, which had been brought to the British Isles nearly a thousand years before.

The driven shoot might have remained a quaint, provincial pastime but for the Prince of Wales, later King Edward VII. The Prince loved shooting as much as he disliked riding and walking, and by 1885 the cachet he conferred had elevated the driven shoot from mere sport to an elaborate social institution. From then until the '14–'18 war devastated an entire way of life, a weekend shooting party at one of the great English country estates was an extravaganza conducted with vast ceremony, replete with five-course meals and costume balls.

Except on the bell-heather moors of northern England and Scotland, where the magnificent red grouse is king, pheasants have always been the heart of English shooting, for these birds, unlike other species, can be reared and released to assure continuing high populations. As the keepers learned the techniques of game husbandry, shooting evolved from a catch-as-catch-can affair involving local birds in whatever numbers nature provided to a system of intense management. By 1900, twelve thousand birds were reared each year in the pheasantries at Sandringham, the royal estate in Norfolk, and untold thousands more at shooting estates all over the country.

Even though the social class that so shaped the sport is now largely gone from England, the sport remains, and shooting rather than farming has become the economic foundation of a great many old estates. It probably is possible, with a lot of work and at least as much good luck, to put together a shooting trip on your own, but not all of the surprises are likely to be good ones. Given the complexities of international travel and the sheer number of small details that can make the difference between a great experience and a disaster, it's wise to work with someone who knows the ropes. Our shoot was organized—and flawlessly so—by Sporting International, a Texas-based company that specializes in hunting and shooting trips over half the world.

Derek Seymour of Cotswold Connections chauffeur service met us at Heathrow the first morning and presently had us rolling across England, bound for Devon, two hundred miles southwest. Like superhighways everywhere, the British motorways are corridors of isolation, where you're walled off from the landscape by guardrails and the speed of travel. But leaving the M5 at Exeter took us into a countryside of hills and hedges, of narrow roads between fields dressed in surprisingly bright mid-December green, dotted everywhere with grazing flocks of sheep and placid, black-and-white Frisian cattle. Skirting the bleak, wild highlands of Dartmoor took us through old, narrow-streeted towns and villages—Sticklepath, Okehampton, Meldon, Lydford, Mary Tavy, Tavistock, finally to Milton Abbott and down a long, tree-arched lane to Endsleigh House.

A rambling, steep-roofed stone house bristling with dormer windows and chimneys, Endsleigh was built in 1811 for the 6th Duke of Bedford, after plans drawn by architect Jeffry Wyattville. Humphrey Repton, at the time one of England's most famous landscape gardeners, designed the flower-lined promenades, the intricate plantings of shrubbery, and the broad, terraced lawns that slope westward down to the salmon-rich River Tamar, separating Devon from Cornwall. The house and its seventy-five-acre estate, now owned by a fishing club, provide first-rate accommodations for Sporting International clients at the Devon shoot.

By evening, when we met in the library for drinks before dinner, we were a full party: two couples from Switzerland, another from America, a Frenchman, an Englishman from East Africa, shoot host Robin Hurt, Susan and I—eight guns in all.

Even devoid of the Victorian excesses that once accrued to the sport, a modern shooting party has a wonderful charm—graceful, good-humored, amiably comfortable amid crisp linen, good silver, crystal, excellent food, fine wine, and dinner-table conversation shifting back and forth among three languages.

There is pleasant ceremony, too, in the shooting itself, customarily done in necktie and sweater, breeks, shooting hat, and knee-high rubber Wellies that are the perfect footgear in a moist and muddy climate. If the bag is to be a large one, perhaps 600 birds or more, you'll use two guns and be assigned a loader. Smaller shoots like ours, with a bag of 400 birds each day, call for only a single gun. You may still be assigned a loader, or if you're fortunate enough, as I am, to have a lady who enjoys such things, your loader might be your spouse.

The rituals are as old as the sport itself. The shoot-master and head gamekeeper walk the land the day before the shoot, planning each drive and setting up a series of numbered stakes where the guns are to stand. Which stand you have might be determined by drawn lots, or the shoot-master may assign stands at the beginning of each drive. Either way, you'll get some splendid shooting.

Few estates now hatch their own pheasants. Philip Tuckett, our host at Endsleigh and owner of Hardicott Estate, where we shot on the first day, told me that the estates now customarily buy the birds as three- or four-day-old chicks, pen-rear them in the first critical weeks, and release them to the woods at the age of two months. There, they grow on special plantings of kale and maize and a daily ration of wheat put down by the keepers. Shooting on a well-run estate reduces the annual pheasant population only by about half, but because there is little natural repro-duction, new generations of chicks are reared each year. The ma-jority of birds shot are sold to game dealers and eventually wind up gracing the tables in English homes and restaurants.

It's the head keeper's job to present the birds at their most challenging. They may be incubator-hatched and pen-reared, but by fall, when the shooting season begins, these birds are as healthy and fit as any wild pheasant anywhere. Depending upon the land-scape, they may fly fifty or sixty yards overhead and might reach seventy miles per hour in full flight. They are not easy shooting. On most drives, you can safely turn and take some shots going away, and those are more difficult yet.

At Hardicott; at Gnaton, where we shot on the second day; and at many others, the coverts were laid out a hundred years ago with shooting in mind. In steep, hilly Devon, strips of woods, called hanging coverts, are maintained along the hilltops, man-aged for the sort of dense understory that offers protective habitat for the birds. Shooting stands are laid out along the narrow, sheep-grazed valley floors, so that the pheasants are well above the guns even when they flush; they're heading for the covert on the next ridge, behind the shooting stands, and by the time they come into range, they are sporty birds, indeed.

The enormous shoots of Edwardian times employed battal-ions of beaters, perhaps a hundred or more; now, with smaller par-ties and more modest bags the rule, there might be twenty-five or thirty, young and old. A few will act as stops, stationed at the ends of the coverts to discourage the birds from simply running out the side door, as pheasants everywhere are wont to do. The rest, at a signal from the head keeper, move slowly through the covert, often following paths cut for generations of beaters long ago.

The trick of it lies in working the covert with only enough fuss to flush the birds a few at a time. A misstep can turn a drive into a wholesale rout. Several hundred pheasants exploding from a covert all at once is an impressive sight but one that doesn't promise much shooting. Pheasants being pheasants, the birds sometimes take a notion to blow out on their own, especially on an estate that's overshot or when shooting days are scheduled too close together. In the best-managed shoots, with shooting days at least a fortnight apart, the birds are alert but not spooky, and experienced beaters can bring off a drive with the delicate precision of a drill team.

Each gun is assigned a picker-up, whose task it is to mark fallen birds and direct his dog in retrieving them when each drive is over. The dogs—mostly Labradors and merry little English springers, with a few golden retrievers and the occasional German shorthair and flat-coat mixed in—are impeccably behaved, always at heel, sitting calmly during the drives but going about their work with great enthusiasm, directed only by hand signals and soft whistles. In two days of shooting, only one dog earned a sharp word of reprimand—in all, better behavior and more skillful handling than I usually see even at formal retriever trials, and I gun a fair number of them every year. With so many eyes at work and so many dogs on the ground, lost birds are extremely rare.

A drive might last twenty minutes or half an hour, depending upon the size of the covert, the number of birds in it, and how they respond. With someone to shoo them up, someone to load your gun, and someone to mark the falls, the only distractions are being always aware to take only the birds within your field of fire and to take them high enough that the beaters and stops are protected. In the slower moments, it's fun to watch your companions at the neighboring stands. At a good stand, when the birds are flying well, you can lose yourself in sheer exhilaration.

Other species of game sometimes appear—wood pigeons and partridge, ducks, and *la bécasse*, the European woodcock, larger than our North American bird and a great prize to the gun lucky enough to bag one. Such is the woodcock's mystique that

"Cock up!" are the only words you'll hear from a beater during a drive. Being borderline goofy on woodcock shooting anyway, I very much wanted to collect a specimen of *Scolopax rusticola*, thereby completing a grand slam on woodcock, so to speak. And I had my chance, a rather long poke at one that appeared in ghostly silence out of the first covert, just as I was swinging on a pheasant overhead. I did hit the pheasant.

It's the pheasants that bring you here and pheasants that bring you back. Taking a high bird in full flight is shooting to be proud of, though you won't spend much time in self-congratulation while they're still streaming out from the covert, the relevant world compressed into an hourglass of sky, gun barrels growing hot in your hand. You'll think of it only later, when three blasts from the shoot-master's horn calls the end of the drive, when you case your gun and walk down to join the others, leaving a bright scatter of cartridge cases in the grass. And later still, in the ineffable influence of a steaming bath and a glass of whiskey that tastes of peat, you'll see high pheasants in your mind.

High Birds
at Molland

I FIND IT a constant source of comfort to know there are places in the civilized world that cannot be reached in any but a round-about way. This is a comfort because almost invariably they are places well worth visiting. Molland Estate is one of them.

Being "centrally located" seems to be one of the great desir-ables of the latter twentieth century, in theory, at least. In fact, being "centrally located" means that it's about equally inconve-nient to get anywhere; I know this because I have for many years lived more or less in the center of Missouri, which is more or less in the center of the United States.

Molland Estate is not centrally located. It's in the fabu-lously beautiful West Country of England, just south of Exmoor National Park, which lies along the Bristol Channel coasts of Somerset and Devon.

To get there from here began with the usual hour-and-a-half drive from the farm to my nearest airport. This segued into a flight to Memphis, another to Minneapolis, and yet another to Gatwick airport, south of London. A half-hour train ride took me to Victoria Station, in the city, and a short trip by taxi to Padding-ton Station, where I caught a British Rail train for a three-hour jaunt west to Tiverton Parkway in Somerset. From there, it was another forty minutes by hired car to the Crown Inn in the village of Exford, where a sweet-natured desk clerk was pleased to serve one highly zombie-like Yank a very large malt whiskey and direct him to his room, a hot bath, and a four-hour nap laced with dreams of planes, trains, and automobiles.

If I'd had the time to spare, I would've broken it up with a day and night in London before heading west, but it was November, a time of year when my life is haunted by the fact that there are so many birds and so little time. And besides, shooting at Molland is easily worth twice the time and effort required to get there.

Molland Estate covers 2,500 acres just over the border into Devon, and the shooting there is managed by Holland & Holland. It proves two things. One is that Holland & Holland does nothing by half-measures; the other is that you can't beat the West Country for sheer beauty and charm.

There is Exford, where horsemen share the early morning streets with cars and lorries, horsemen often preceded by a brace of terriers who, unfettered by leashes, stop at every intersection on one spoken command and do not cross until they hear another.

There is Exmoor itself, a high, often mist-shrouded wilderness of grass and gorse drained by the River Exe—a rolling, starkly beautiful landscape where wild ponies graze in little bands. Lower down, the roads become narrow country lanes cut by centuries of traffic until the roadbed lies the height of a tall man, or more, below the roots of the hedges that line the way.

There is the farmhouse of Great Champson, headquarters for the Molland shoot, a rambling edifice of main house, crofts, stables, and other assorted outbuildings all constructed of the same sturdy stone. Some of the paneling in the house dates to Elizabethan times. If there's a place on Earth where history lives a more active daily life than England, I don't know of it.

And there is Molland itself, all steep hills and vistas cut with coombes and copses, woods and spinneys, and hanging coverts above the valley floors. Every drive has been named—Badgerbury,

Saddleback, Pullworthy Kale, Desmond's Mustard, to cite a few.

Every drive also has a common appeal—pheasants or partridge, or both, flying very high indeed.

To deal with that, my old friends Roger Mitchell and Jan Roosenburg brought for me a lovely pair of Holland & Holland Royal Ejector guns when they came down from London. Roger is Holland's deputy chairman, Jan looks after the company's North American operations, and the Royal Ejectors are the original pattern upon which virtually every high-quality sidelock made anywhere in the world is based. One could hardly ask for better.

Or better shooting, for that matter. The first drive, at Pullworthy Kale, was mostly pheasants at moderate altitude, which was good because it gave me a chance to limber up and relearn the little drill of exchanging guns with a loader. Naturally, I did it backwards at first, passing him the empty gun with my left hand instead of my right, and creating some minor comedy before Peter, the amiable, stolid countryman who loaded for me, set me right.

I also got a small lesson in the ballistic properties of dead pheasants when my neighboring gun killed a crosser that came barreling down at about sixty miles per hour squarely against my left hip. I never saw it coming, and if Rob Peel, one of the instructors at Holland's shooting grounds, hadn't been standing near enough to partially deflect it with a swipe of his hand, I think it would have taken me right off my feet. Read the accounts of shooting parties in the grand old Edwardian days, and you'll find more than a few instances of shooters being knocked unconscious by falling birds. I used to think such stories a bit fanciful; not any more.

Mercifully, there were no more kamikazes, and this, too, was a good thing because the birds got higher and higher with each drive. I don't know how far a three- or four-pound pheasant has to fall before it reaches terminal velocity, but I have a notion some of the Molland birds could do it, and then some. Forty-yard shots are commonplace, fifty- and even sixty-yard birds are not unusual on certain drives. Connecting with a pheasant so far up that the front bead of your gun covers the better part of its body is about as demanding as shooting gets.

The shooting at Molland is nicely varied as well, with partridge to leaven the sport. These are red-legged partridge, *Alectoris rufa*, and they were introduced to England from the Iberian Peninsula during the seventeenth and eighteenth centuries. They're sometimes called French, Guernsey, or Hungarian partridge—mistakenly so because the bird you'll find in Hungary is the rock partridge, *A. graeca*; it's similar to the redleg, and both of them are similar to the chukar.

Which is neither here nor there. The important thing is that redlegs are splendid game for driven shooting. They're smaller than pheasants, of course, aren't as heavy, and therefore don't fly as fast. But they fly plenty fast enough to leave you muttering to yourself as they come over at altitudes that make them look like a flight of bees. The partridge shooting is prime at Molland in September, October, and November, and on certain drives—Dipper, Desmond's Mustard, Barn, Saddleback, and Folly in particular—their numbers will match or exceed the pheasants. Not knowing which will fly over next adds a nice element to the shooting.

And so, as it happened, did Holland & Holland chairman Alain Drache, who joined us for the second day and exercised the streak of Gallic impishness that seems to run in his nature.

"You have stand No. 6," he said to me, "and don't move off the peg." I can't remember whether it was Saddleback or Folly, though "folly" and Stand 6 go well enough together. The drive comes off a tall ridge, and the guns range along the deep valley below. But Stand No. 6 is lower still—a little bowl-like depression perhaps two feet below the valley floor, right underneath a monstrous tree. Whatever birds come over are at nearly vertical when they first appear, splitting along like blazes so that you're behind the power curve before you even begin.

A partridge first, curling right. Push the gun out far ahead, and it falls. Another, boring straight on, forced me off balance and into a miss. So it's on your toes like a boxer, ready to step in any direction, and the next four crumple in a most satisfactory way. For the most part, these are one-shot birds, over and gone before there's even a chance to think about turning for a going-away shot. There were pheasants, too, but none came over that big tree.

I must have looked like a man dancing on a hot skillet. Some of the gyrations were to get balanced for the birds; others, though, were out of sheer excitement.

"It is a good stand, yes?" Alain said afterwards, his grin reaching toward his ears. "My favorite."

Mine, too, especially as I managed to avoid embarrassing myself for once.

If I ever go back to Molland, I'll ask to have that stand again. If you get there before I do, keep it warm for me. You won't forget it. Nor Molland, for that matter.

Misadventures in Mother Russia

For US WHO WERE BORN in the years bracketed by the last great war, Russia was a constant symbol of darkness and dread. Russia was rumored news of Stalin's bloody purges and governance by terror. Russia was Nikita Khrushchev pounding a table at the United Nations with his shoe and promising to bury us. Russia was the catalyst for a race to leave the atmosphere of Earth, for a frenzied gathering of arsenals capable of unimaginable destruction. Russia was the gunslinger of the world, the Iron Curtain a mirror reflecting nightmares.

Russia was enigma and contradiction. It was the delicate beauty of ballet set against a showdown over Cuba when all the world held its breath. It was thick, brooding novels on convoluted themes, the anguish of poets, the cry of exiled voices mourning the loss of something impossible to understand.

Thinking back to a childhood in the 1950s and a coming of age in the '60s, it seems astonishing now, how pervasively Russia loomed in the American consciousness—from schoolroom drills in the art of duck and cover, to Francis Gary Powers and the U2, from spy novels and movies, to the wall in Berlin. Those years play in memory like a photograph in which the bright values of prosperity blossomed against a contrast of shadows teeming with menace. As a nation and a culture, we knew those shadows by a single name. We called them Russia.

But through it all, through the stereotypes of brutal Communism and the louring threat of nuclear annihilation, my imagination teased and tickled with a wish to see Russia for myself, to know something of the landscape and the people and culture and history that seemed irrepressibly to survive beneath the crushing weight of politics and a socialist experiment obviously gone awry. Call it a thriving curiosity or an itch to see the big world outside. Call it perverseness even, or what you will; the fact is, I spent much of my life hoping I could someday visit Russia, if only for a glimpse of whatever reality I might find in the place that so profoundly shaped the world I knew.

Now I've done just that, and I found it a wonder.

Like so much of the good fortune that has accrued to me, my glimpse of Russia came about because of guns and the career I've made from writing about them. It came on the brink of a watershed in modern history, though no one could have known that at the time. It began as one kind of story and evolved into quite another.

The background started a few years ago with David Dees, a Canadian gun fancier who had traveled extensively in the Soviet Union and who realized that no city in Russia offers a more concentrated view of pre-Bolshevik culture than Leningrad, the old capital city of Peter the Great and all the czars and czarinas who followed, the site of fabulous museums housing collections of guns to boggle the Western imagination. So, says Mr. Dees to himself, why not organize a tour focusing on these collections and offer the opportunity to others seriously interested in guns?

A splendid idea, all in all, and Dees set about developing it with care and good sense. Since Helsinki offered the closest access to Leningrad from outside the Soviet bloc, he teamed up with Finnish travel agent Kai Long, a well-seasoned professional at navigating the labyrinthine process of working with the Russians. The two spent many months and great effort setting up contacts and attending to the myriad details that are part and parcel of such a venture.

By the end of 1990, everything was in place and the maiden voyage of the Gun Collector's Tour was scheduled for the following May, an inauguration for which gun writers and photographers would be invited guests. *Double Gun Journal* publisher and editor Dan Coté had no idea he was touching a lifelong dream when he offered me the story, but he may have gathered a clue when I said yes first and asked the details afterward. Maybe some writer with an interest in history could turn down the chance to visit Russia, see gun collections that few Western eyes have ever seen, and get a good story all at the same time—but I'm not the man to do so.

Actually, I would have been happy enough to go by cattle boat, tramp steamer, or hot-air balloon and live in a tent. As it turned out, we traveled on Finnair and assembled at Helsinki's tidy and comfortable Hotel Klaus Kurki. A small group, we were, and a motley one in the true definition of the word: gun writer David Baker, stock maker and crack photographer David Trevallion, David Dees, Kai Long, and I—in other words, an Englishman from England, another who's lived more than half his life in the United States, a Canadian, a Finn, and a Missourian.

The itinerary called for a day touring Helsinki, a night's sleep, and a seven-hour bus ride to Leningrad. Since it's essentially peripheral to the story, I won't dwell on Helsinki except to say that the capital of Finland is a strikingly beautiful city, clean as a new pin, and populated with people willing to go out of their way in treating visitors with kindness and courtesy. I'd like to go there again someday.

For one who doesn't feel as if he's truly visited a place until he's seen the countryside, the bus ride was a welcome treat. At about sixty degrees north latitude, the southern tip of Finland, like Leningrad itself, lies less than five hundred miles below the Arctic Circle, and some snow still lingers in sheltered spots even in early May. On the land route between them—around the Gulf of Finland and down the narrow isthmus south of Russia's Lake Ladoga—the landscape is a sparer, leaner version of northern Minnesota or the Upper Peninsula of Michigan. There are fewer hardwoods and more pines, but the same rolling country where everything that grows seems geared to prosper in a short, treasured summer.

The highway route served another good purpose, as we discovered when the bus reached the Russian border just at midday and drew up next to a restaurant and the Finnish version of a convenience store. Over lunch, Kai Long handed out the paperwork required by the Soviets. Along with our visas, there were forms for listing all the currency, precious stones, and metals we carried—exact amounts of cash and all jewelry. These forms are examined and approved upon entering Russia, and we would be required to submit them and a second version upon leaving. The message was clear: We had better bring out less foreign currency than we took in, and any jewelry not appearing on the first form was likely to be confiscated, no matter if it's your wedding band or the wristwatch you've worn for years. Take no photos and make no jokes, Kai warned. *Glasnost* had not yet reached the border.

Then he directed us to the shop next door, where we each bought a liter or two of bottled water and a few packets of tissues. I'll tell you why in a moment.

Though I'd thought of it most of my life, going into Russia was a grim and almost frightening experience.

Finnish immigration officials stamped our passports and waved us through a gate in the chain-link fence.

We passed through a second gate a couple of kilometers farther on, another chain-link barrier topped with barbed wire, set in a broad swath cleared out of the timber. Ten-foot ribbons of sand ran along either side of the fence. These, Kai told us, were examined for footprints and freshly raked every day.

The immigration center lay just beyond—a squat, ugly, cinder-block building under an observation tower from which armed soldiers scanned the surroundings, sober as radar. There we disembarked and carried all our luggage inside to have our visas processed, our baggage X-rayed. Meanwhile, more soldiers went over the bus inside and out, looking, I suppose, for contraband. The immigration people, all in military uniform, weren't un-friendly, but they weren't smiley-faced, either, and to my ear, even an endearment in Russian lacks any warmth of inflection.

Despite the strict prohibition against taking photographs, our most intrepid shutterbug managed to get a few snapshots by hiding his pocket camera under his coat, while the rest of us—entertaining visions of interrogation rooms and jail cells—tried our best to pretend we didn't know him. (In the interest of avoiding an international incident even after the fact, I won't reveal the name of the guilty party except to say he was the same one who almost got me brained with a broom three days later, for much the same reason.)

After three-quarters of an hour, we were on the road again, rolling through a landscape identical to Finland in natural features but vastly different in its human terms.

The small villages and tiny enclaves of dwellings where the collective-farm workers live all looked as if they once were tidy and well-kept but had gone ramshackle under a careful regimen of neglect. In Vyborg, where we stopped to swap some real money for rubles, we were scarcely off the bus before we were surrounded by urchins hawking trinkets of this kind or that. With two packs of chewing gum (Big Red, appropriately enough) to parcel out stick by stick, Trevallion became a local hero. In return, one of the lads gave him a box of ten-inch wooden matches. The office of currency exchange, on the second floor of a once-handsome building, smelled like a litter box that's got out of hand.

A few miles farther on, we passed through the Russian version of a tollbooth, in the form of a police car parked beside the road with its blue lights flashing, a uniformed cop perched comfortably on the hood. He and our bus driver exchanged a few words, the driver handed over some money, which he had lying ready on the dashboard, and we went on our way.

I asked Rudi, our interpreter, what that was all about.

"Speeding ticket," Rudi said.

Finally, Leningrad—originally called St. Petersburg, changed to Petrograd during World War I, renamed again in 1924 in honor of the spiritual father of Communism (who hatched the philosophical underpinnings of twentieth-century Russia while hiding in a nearby swamp), and now St. Petersburg once again. Leningrad, the glittering city of Peter the Great, built in 1702 on a chain of islands in the Neva River marsh, styled on the pattern of Western Europe.

Leningrad—besieged, starved, and pounded for nine hundred days by Hitler's army. But neither the wartime damage, some of which remains just as it was fifty years ago, nor the seventy-odd years of Communist neglect can obscure the incredible beauty of the baroque and neoclassical architecture, constructed by the finest craftsmen in the world. Simply put, Leningrad is at heart the most exquisitely lovely city in the world.

Which is considerably more than I can say for the Hotel Moskva, or Moscow Hotel, where we alighted into a world as alien as the far side of the moon. Cooperative business ventures were surprisingly well advanced in Russia in 1991, considering that the Soviet Union still existed then, and we were offered the choice—a hotel run by one of the free-market countries known for its efficiency or go the real Russian quill all the way. We all agreed on the latter, in for a penny, in for a pound.

It was a mixed blessing. After having a look around, I asked Kai when the hotel was built. He reckoned the 1960s. I reckoned the sum total of maintenance in those thirty-odd years to be exactly zero. I've laid me down to sleep in some pretty raggedy places but not many quite as ragged as the Moscow Hotel. Shabby is to put it kindly. Falling apart says it better—carpets rippled and ripped, paint peeling, furniture scuffed, upholstery and bedspread threadbare. But the rooms were clean enough, and we weren't going to spend much time in them, anyway.

Remember the bottled water and tissues? What flowed from the bathroom taps, sink and tub alike, was the color of good breakfast tea. In the Queen City of the Worker's Paradise, freshwater lines and wastewater pipes have been laid in haphazard abandon, one atop the other and all crumbling, so that a cupful of city water poured into a stomach not acclimatized to the local bacteria is the equivalent of a gastronomic hand grenade.

And the tissues? Imagine a whole country in the throes of a paper shortage and tell me what paper product would be the first to get shortchanged. As Kai told us at the border, "There's a good chance there won't be any toilet paper in the hotel." He was right. The soap amounted to two tiny, unwrapped bars that looked for all the world like the lye soap my grandmother used to make. The Hotel Moskva is not for the faint of heart.

Or stomach. As I said, I've had some raunchy accommodations knocking around the world, but short of a charnal house or a sewage plant, I can't think of a single place that smells worse than the dining room in the Moscow Hotel. Imagine a kitchen glazed with about twenty years of rancid grease and you've got it. The room is roughly the size of Rhode Island, fitted out with a bandstand and a balcony and enough glitter to stand in for Times Square on New Year's Eve, but I couldn't walk into it and draw a breath without feeling an urge to retch. The menu for the first night, mercifully the only dinner we had there, was leather chicken rescued only by the plentiful application of domestic champagne, which is one of the few things the Russians concoct as well as any people in the world.

In the course of our stay, we found food as good as I've had anywhere—at the Fontanka Restaurant, the Literature Cafe, the Troika, and elsewhere—but I'm told such places are too expensive for the average Russian to even think about. None of them were in the Hotel Moskva. We did have breakfast there each morning (which you should read as "coffee"), and to give you some idea of what the cuisine was like . . . .

On our last day in the country, Trevallion passed me a platter of gray sausages. Made from what hapless animal, I have no idea; they were just gray, the color of wood-ash, and slick with grease. The platter had gone all round the table undisturbed, and it came to me accompanied by one of DT's patentable puckish grins.

I said I wouldn't touch one of those goddam things even if it had a condom on it. He thought I was making a joke.

For getting from place to place, our leaders had hired a van, which proved quite efficient. Relatively few Russians can afford an automobile, and gasoline is hard to come by anyway, so traffic jams weren't a problem. The public transportation system—electric trolley cars—appears to be fairly good, although the cars themselves, like everything else, are shabby and ill-maintained and always so packed with passengers that there must be scarcely room to breathe. Which may not be a bad thing, considering the average Russian's aversion to frequent bathing. At any rate, I was happy to forego the pleasure of a trolley ride.

The Artillery Museum was our first stop on the tour. This is the official military museum, and everything on display is military hardware, from short swords and chain mail to field communication systems to SCUD missiles (which our guide pointed out without any noticeable sense of pride). The collection is huge, extremely well displayed, and interesting enough, but we were into sporting guns, and with that I began to see the complexities of dealing with the Russians.

The Artillery Museum does have a sizeable collection of sporting arms, but they're all in the storerooms and therefore require special access. Being military in nature, the museum is administered by the Army, and we arrived to find the place under control of a new commandant—not, in other words, the man with whom Dees and Long had made their prior arrangements. So, the two Davids and I went off to see the displays while Dees and Long started all over again, explaining through an interpreter why we were there and what we wanted to see, asking permission to photograph the sporting guns, on and on. The commandant, stony-faced as a statue, questioned them over and over about how the photos would be used and where they'd appear, insisting that they ultimately be returned to the museum afterwards.

You'd have thought we were asking to photograph state secrets, but I have a notion the good colonel was simply exercising what little authority Gorbachev's reforms had left to the military. In any event, a couple of hours' negotiation and a bottle of vodka did the trick, and we were led upstairs to the storerooms, there to meet the storeroom curator Jurij Natsvaladze, a civilian and a genuinely kind and friendly man.

If the first part of the visit was an education in Russian bureaucracy, stepping into the storeroom was our initial glimpse of just how vast and fabulous the Russian gun collections truly are. It's a cavernous, dimly lit room perhaps a hundred meters long and about half as wide. Storage cabinets are arranged in ranks along a central walkway, like the stacks in a library, each cabinet double-tiered and literally packed with guns top and bottom. To examine every one would take days, perhaps weeks.

Even the non-sporting pieces are enough to send a collector into raptures. One row of cabinets, for instance, held Model 1866 Winchesters by the hundred. I asked Mr. Natsvaladze where they came from. His answer was simple: "We took them away from the Turks." According to Winchester records, the governments of both Turkey and France in 1870 ordered huge numbers of Model 66 muskets and carbines for their armies. After the last Russo-Turkish war, in 1877–78, the Russians apparently gathered up all the remaining arms and carted them back to St. Petersburg, and I guess they've been there ever since, quietly gathering dust. The Russian Army did much the same after World War II, and rumor has it that there are enough ultra-rare German Lugers socked away in Moscow to ruin the collector's market forever if they all got into circulation at the same time.

The storeroom corridor ends at a barred iron gate, behind which are stored the real gems of the collection. Mr. Natsvaladze showed us some of them: Catherine the Great's flintlock fowler, inlaid with gold and crusted with precious stones; fabulously decorated Colt revolvers once owned by czars Alexander and Nicholas; a sidelock .410 game gun by LeBeau, made for one of Czar Nicholas II's children and perfectly proportioned at about two-thirds scale; a lovely Holland & Holland Royal Ejector double rifle, which I later learned was built for a Frenchman in 1912; a Purdey pigeon gun of 1881 vintage. How either one got to the storeroom of the Artillery Museum is anybody's guess.

When we found the Purdey, Trevallion gave Mr. Natsvaladze his business card, which indicates his former employment with Purdey's—whereupon, Mr. Natsvaladze broke into a brilliant smile and began poking David in the chest, saying "Purr-di, Purr-di." We asked our interpreter to explain that our colleague was Mr. Trevallion, not Mr. Purdey, but I'm not sure the message got through. Before we left, the assistant curator presented David with a copy of a book he'd written on military arms—printed in Russian, of course, and bound with some sort of organic glue that smelled like a buzzard's armpit.

Although Natsvaladze and his assistants were as cooperative as anyone could wish, we had too little time to see more than a few pieces and too little light for good photographs. Actually, none of the places we visited offered anything better than marginal conditions for picture-making, but not even studio shots could capture the scale of it all, the sheer, overwhelming numbers, nor any sense of how incredibly rare many of these pieces are. As a friend and serious collector remarked to me later, "There are guns in Russia that just don't exist."

The Artillery Museum's holdings of sporting guns are minuscule compared to some other collections in Russia, notably that of the Hermitage, and a half-day in the storerooms there was to be the crowning event of the tour. Dees and Long had gone all-out setting up the visit, communicating constantly with the Curator of Weapons, even enlisting the aid of an assistant chief in the Leningrad police department to make certain the curator understood that his cooperation was of considerable economic importance to the city and, for all I know, to the Kremlin itself, as well.

The night before our visit, they even phoned from the restaurant where we were having dinner with a Leningrad university professor and his daughter. (Dinner gave the chief an opportunity to practice his English, which, as the evening went on, finally boiled down to "Let us dhrink!", as he again and again refilled our tiny glasses while proposing ever more florid toasts. Russian vodka, by the way, is excellent stuff, ice cold and silky and available in an apparently limitless supply. Trevallion says I ended up performing a Cossack dance while the band played Russian folk music. I don't recall any such unseemly behavior, and he has no photos for evidence—but he may be right; next morning, my knees hurt almost as much as my head, for some reason.

The Hermitage Museum is a magnificent building, formerly the Winter Palace of the czars, completed in 1762. Standing in the broad cobblestone courtyard in the front, the place where the Bolshevik Revolution of 1917 began, you can almost feel the surging tides of history.

Shortly after, we were all feeling surges of frustration, because the Curator of Arms simply didn't show up. No message, no explanation. We later learned he'd opted for a long weekend at his summer cottage in the border zone, prompted by a rumor that all property in the zone was due to be confiscated. Under the circumstances, we couldn't really blame the poor chap for blowing us off, but it was maddening nonetheless, particularly since we had only the one day and since the bureaucracy is such that his assistant, who was there that morning, had no authority to let us into the storage areas. If Robbie Burns didn't have the Russians in mind when he composed his famous line about the best-laid plans of mice and men, he should have.

By promising not to take photos—a promise we all broke to one extent or another—we eventually prevailed upon the assistant to give us a peek into at least one storeroom, and it happened to be one holding part of the Hermitage's famous and seldom-seen collection of miniatures—tiny Winchesters and Colts and sporting guns built as trinkets for the czars, all fully operational and as exquisitely crafted as the finest jewelry. Other than that, we had to be content with the lovely but unfortunately few firearms on public display, most of them magnificently decorated flintlocks.

In broader terms, though, the Hermitage is a fascinating place. Its holdings of fine art are as good as those of any museum in the world, and the total number of exhibits is astronomical. Someone told us that if you spent two minutes looking at every item on display and didn't stop to sleep, you could see the entire collection in eleven years. I believe it.

With some unexpected time on our hands, we struck off for Gatchina Palace, forty kilometers south of the city. It's a lovely place. The palace and its surrounding park were begun in 1766, built as a gift from Catherine the Great to her lover, Count Grigory

Orlov. Later occupants, the czars Paul I and Nicholas I, added wings and other refinements. The government naturally took it over after the Communist Revolution of 1917, and Gatchina has been a museum ever since. The damage it sustained during World War II (which the Russians call the Great Patriotic War) is still being repaired.

The arms display comprises only a single room, the items mostly antiques and all in sealed glass cases, which made photography that much more difficult. But it was well worth the trip and helped take the edge off the disappointment we all felt at being so close to the hidden treasures of the Hermitage and yet so far away.

As were most such institutions in the USSR, Gatchina was administered by the military, and Trevallion asked a pistol-carrying lady soldier if he could buy some of the museum guidebooks. We never figured out whether the gift shop was closed or whether she was just having a bad-hair day, but in any case her response was decidedly surly. David asked again, waving a five-dollar bill. She grew even more belligerent, and once again, visions of jail cells danced like sugarplums in my head. Fortunately, our interpreter took over at that point, Kamerad Natasha the Nasty cooled down, and David got his books.

He also got a splendid piece of revenge. The same woman passed us on the pathway outside a while later, apparently going off-duty for the day. As she walked away, David turned to take a photo from behind—and caught a thoroughly exquisite moment as she was either attending to an itch or rearranging her underwear. It was not, let us say, a flattering pose.

It had been a long, dry day, so as we neared a village about halfway back to Leningrad we asked our interpreter about the possibility of finding some beer. She allowed as how that could be done and directed the driver to the nearest beer store, which happened to be right on the main highway through town. She went in while we stayed in the van and amused the time by trying to get rid of a drunk in an ankle-length overcoat who came stumbling across the road to pound on the side windows and shout at us. The Russian language is difficult enough when carefully enunciated, so you can imagine what it sounds like spoken by somebody who's thoroughly hammered. Not even the driver could understand what he wanted.

Finally, he turned away, started back across the road, and staggered right into the path of a military truck grinding its way down the highway. The truck never wavered nor slowed, not even when the fender caught our momentary friend and sent him flying, his coat trailing like Superman's cape, to crash in a heap on the dusty road. We were sure he was dead, but in the next moment he picked himself up, shook his fist at the departing truck, and—still shouting in boozy Russian—lurched off on his way. It all happened so quickly, and we were so stunned by it, that Trevallion didn't even get a photograph.

Then our interpreter was back, distributing bottles of beer. As I've said, Russian vodka is superb and Russian champagne is better than you'd expect. But Russian beer . . .well, don't look for it in your local beer shop. It came in bottles fitted with wire bails and ceramic caps, obviously reusable. I'm not sure, but I'd guess the beer was intended to be reusable, too. I do know it tasted like something that had been recycled through about three Russians before we got it. Trevallion remarked that the bouquet and flavor was highly reminiscent of horse piss—which gave us a topic of conversation to occupy the rest of the drive, just speculating on how he knew.

We were due to head back to Helsinki the following day, and despite having only brushed the surface of what there is to see in Leningrad, I was not unhappy at the prospect of leaving. It's a fascinating place, but it's also depressing. Nearly everything is in short supply, and hardly anything works efficiently. I wrote a short note to my family and mailed it before we left, just for the novelty of a letter with a Russian postmark. It hasn't arrived yet.

Anyone who believes that President Bonzo's posturing was responsible for the collapse of the Soviet Union hasn't been to Russia. To all indications, the Communist system simply collapsed from within, too self-centered and too inefficient to survive. The economy was a shambles. The ruble was worthless even inside the country, which is why every bar was packed with working girls, many of whom speak English and most of whom are part-time prostitutes simply because it's the only means they have of getting currency that actually has some purchasing power. I talked with one who was a teacher, another who worked as an executive secretary, yet another who was a computer programmer— all of them pretty, bright young women desperate for some sort of better life.

If nothing else, they are proof that free enterprise is not entirely lacking in Russia—they and the waiters, all of whom have a handy bottle of vodka or pot of caviar to sell on the side. What few goods are available to the general populace seem to go to those who have a source of hard currency. It's a dismal situation, and if you watch the faces on the streets, you soon realize that Russians seldom smile. They just don't have much to smile about. Now that the central Soviet Union is finally down the drain and Leningrad is St. Petersburg once more, conditions probably are even worse.

So far as I know, plans to offer the gun collectors' tours commercially are on hold, which is wise, since no one really knows what's going to happen with those poor, sad people who've been beaten down for so long. If the tours ever get off the ground, though, they'll be an experience no gun-fancier should miss, uncertainties and all.

Besides, your trip might end in the same bizarre way ours did. As we left the Hotel Moskva to board the bus, a six-piece street band was set up on the sidewalk, playing for tips—two trombones, two trumpets, a baritone horn, and a snare drum. Rather than bother exchanging our remaining rubles at the border, Trevallion and I tossed them into the musicians' kitty and added three or four American dollars as well. The leader stopped whatever piece they were playing, looked at the dollars, and asked, "Americans?" David nodded.

The young man signaled us to wait, rummaged through his sheaf of music, and distributed some among his colleagues.

And there on the streets of the former capital of the country so long the nemesis of the world I knew, we were serenaded with "The Star-Spangled Banner," played with excellent skill and at top volume. I cannot describe how strange it felt, and the same feeling comes back every time I look at the photograph David took.

When the last notes died away, we thanked them, turned toward the parking lot, and nearly fell over two women sweeping the street with brooms made of twigs. The older one, shaped like a potato and dressed in a rusty-looking overcoat and apron, had a face any photographer would love. David snapped a picture of her, whistled to get her attention, and snapped another as she looked up.

Clearly, she was not into modeling, for she began scolding us in Russian and brandishing her broom. For our part, not into having our skulls bashed by somebody's grandmother, we sprinted for the bus, hoping she was as slow afoot as she looked. She was, but she was still shaking the broom at us when the bus pulled away.

Not knowing the language, I'm not sure what her objection was, but I do know this: At the border, after going through the same rigmarole to get out as we did to get in, we all felt so suddenly lighthearted that we sent up a spontaneous cheer when the bus rolled through the final gate, out of Russia.

High Birds in
Spanish Skies

THE RAIN IN SPAIN falls mainly somewhere other than the jagged, stony hills of the central provinces. Even in the relatively rainy season of midwinter, it is a spare landscape of olive groves and wild hilltops furred with brush and low trees, sere and starkly beautiful.

Hunter's hills, these are, for all their seeming barrenness alive with the promise of game.

But not always arid. The connecting flight from Paris reached Madrid on the heels of a January rainstorm that left the countryside washed and cool, and muddied the valley flats and benches. As our driver herded the van up the long climb toward Chinchón, I thought about the rubber Wellies I'd left at home in favor of short-topped leather boots that would be perfect for the dry and sunny land of Spain. I decided life would be dull if I didn't outsmart myself at least once a month.

Chinchón, veined with steep, narrow streets, has huddled on this mountaintop for five hundred years or more. At the summit, the looming walls of its old castle still stand, and from there you can see the buildings of Madrid, pale in the distance, thirty kilometers across the plain. In the village center, restaurants and *tapas* bars circle the sandy-floored plaza that twice each year, stoutly barricaded, becomes a *plaza de toros*.

227

Even without the *toros*, it's enough to steal your heart—mine, anyway, and certainly enough to rid me of all fret about the damned boots I hadn't brought. Besides, the charms of Chinchón are simply lagniappe, for in those surrounding hills there is bird shooting of a quality and a level of excitement that you'd go for barefoot, if that's what it took.

Of all Spanish game none is more famous or more numerous than the red-legged partridge. In size, color, and marking, redlegs resemble chukars and rock partridges, and they're also kin to the European gray partridge and the Barbary partridge of North Africa. But apart from populations in southern England, southern France, and the northwestern corner of Italy, *Alectoris rufa* is strictly a bird of the Iberian Peninsula, ranging from the Pyrenees to Gibraltar, from the Gulf of Valencia to the coast of Portugal. You find them in farmland and heath land, but their favorite haunt is just such rough, arid country as the hills around Chinchón.

Like all their gallinaceous kin, they are wonderfully sporty, and as driven game, they are magnificent. Having shot them in mixed drives with pheasants in England made me all the keener to meet them on their traditional turf.

We were a party of ten guns, organized by Jack Jansma of Wingshooting Adventures, an old friend whose ability to combine top-quality shooting with a fair sampling of local culture is little short of uncanny. Jack's pheasant-shooting excursions in Hungary have become near-legendary in recent years, partly for the sport and partly for the camaraderie among a certain hardcore group of us who've made it an annual event.

Thus when Fearless Leader decided to expand his affairs into Spain, it was a foregone conclusion that the Crew would be present for the maiden voyage—Special Ed Smyth and Schnell Eddie Hayes, Joe Pryor and Wayne Latta, Jim Cornetet, Dick Barch, Andre Buise, Jack, and Uncle Bill Teesdale, who himself became legendary some time back by attempting to close his gun while his loader's thumb was in the action, twice.

It was, by any definition, a tough crowd and one not likely to pass up any opportunity to poach one another's birds nor to allow badly fluffed shots to go unremarked—a group with whom I've had more fun over the years than is probably legal in some parts of the world.

At the shooting grounds, we drew for our loaders and *secretarios*, who already had each gun's sequence of stands worked out by random lot. We *hola*'d and shook hands, toasted our hosts and colleagues and the shooting to come with a sip of *vino tinto*, loaded into the vans, and headed into the hills.

Driven shooting follows essentially the same format everywhere, regardless of the game. The gamekeepers have each drive well planned, know where the birds will fly and where to position the guns for the best, and most difficult, shooting. The head keeper's horn is the signal for the beaters to start moving and for the guns to load up; he'll blow it again at the end of the drive to signal that it's time to unload.

What happens between can range from sporadic to frantic, from interesting to electrifying. The guns at the center of the line usually have more shooting than those at the ends, and that's why everyone rotates from drive to drive—from, say, peg 2 on one to peg 5 the next, then to 7, and so on. By the end of the day, you'll have spent about equal time on the hot stands and those where the action may not be so brisk.

When the birds fly high and fast, numbers don't really matter, and for that I've seen little shooting that tops Spanish redlegs. The countryside is ideal for producing high-flying targets, with the birds on the brushy hilltops and the guns on the slopes and benches far below, and though the lighter-weight redleg can't match the velocity of a big cock pheasant, they fly like blazes nonetheless.

They're covey birds, whose first response is to scurry around in the brush ahead of the beaters, gradually gathering in ever-greater numbers. But on the other hand, they don't seem inclined to run great distances, so most drives show a fairly steady series of flushes, a covey here, a covey there, often building up to one great flurry toward the end, when the bunched-up runners collectively decide it's time to boogie.

Either way, they break over the guns at full speed, streaking along in alternating sprints of pounding wings and long glides. Some come zooming down the slopes, hugging the contour. Those you let pass as too low for safe shooting, and you concentrate on the rest, because most often they line out from one hilltop to the next, keeping to an altitude where they look no bigger than robins.

Then you pick your bird, point your leading foot where it needs to be, reach out with your forward hand to get the gun in motion, swing the muzzles through, look a *long* way ahead, touch the trigger, and keep the barrels moving. When it works, it's enormously satisfying to feel the jolt against your shoulder and count off the momentary beat in time between hearing the sound of the gun and seeing the high, fleeting little shape crumple and fall, fall, fall in a long smooth arc to thump down far behind.

Unless you've been practicing high-tower clays (or better yet, high driven birds), getting the hang of it takes a drive or two. If you're tracking flight lines properly, the solution lies mainly in just getting the gun far enough ahead of the bird. When you miss, double the distance in front on the next shot, and then double it again if you need to.

Once you get over a sense of astonishment at how far ahead you really need to be, you can settle into a Zen-like rhythm, lose yourself in the hypnotic, unhurried motion—a bird down, then another, crack the action and turn slightly so your loader can stuff in fresh rounds, never taking your eyes off the birds hurtling over.

Close the gun, bring it up to ready, and repeat the moves: swing and mount and fire.

You can, on these Spanish hillsides, also lose more than your consciousness of everything but birds and gun. Often as not, you're standing on something like a thirty-degree slope, perhaps on about two square feet of semi-shelf your loader kicked into the slant or perhaps not, and if you rush, overswing, try to pivot quickly for a second shot going away, gravity is always there waiting to bite. On one drive, one of our guys—Wayne, if memory serves—tried to make a fast turn, stepped into airy nothing, upended in a graceful cartwheel and landed head-down in a bush a few feet below. As he was not hurt, we, being his pals, responded with all the compassion and solicitous concern of a school of piranhas.

It's a rare drive, at any game, where even the coolest pegs don't produce a few birds. Even so, it's as much fun at the slower times to watch the others, to applaud their good shots and commiserate on the misses.

(It's also sometimes amusing to poach a bit off the guy at the next stand, but *only* if he's your good chum and not likely to get upset; otherwise, poaching is definitely bad form and will earn you no friends among strangers or even casual acquaintances. Among the proper friends and in the proper spirit, though, it can be great fun.)

Every drive is a lovely little world that is born in a moment and dies all too soon, leaving you in the grips of an adrenaline rush. So you help your loader case your gun and gather up the empty hulls, maybe pick up a bird or two to admire, find out how the others did on the stands you couldn't see, and in general try to relive the whole thing until the next drive begins.

Depending on where you're shooting, you might break for lunch at midday or just take a leisurely stop between a couple of drives for *tapas*—cheese and Spanish sausages, fat black olives, succulent thin slices of Seranno ham, this, that, and big jugs of rich, deep-red Spanish wine, all laid out on a tailgate or a folding table. Food never tastes any better—except perhaps for a full-scale mid-afternoon lunch when the shooting day is over. (And you don't hesitate to lunch heartily, even if it is three in the afternoon, because dinner in Spain rarely happens before ten at night.)

As is customary in European shooting, all the birds are laid out in a tableau at the end of the day, arranged in neat rows and ranks. Toasts are offered—to the game, to the guns, to the beaters and loaders, and to all who had a hand. It is a particularly touching way of paying respect to the birds and the traditions they represent. It is the final formality, though not the final salute, for you'll carry the image of them for a long time to come, flying high and strong against the bright sky of memory.

Ancient Honors

DISCOVERY IS TRAVEL'S SWEET REWARD, finding some new place that, unexpected, lays hold of your heart. I went shooting in Hungary in 1991, not knowing what I'd find, and part of my heart is still there, among the pheasants on the Tisza Plain.

Now that the Iron Curtain no longer obscures the view, Hungary is a new world waiting to be explored. It's a world geographically diverse, from the western and northern highlands to the level farmland of the east, and a world rich in history. As a state, Hungary is more than a thousand years old, dating from the end of the ninth century, when Magyar tribes migrated from the eastern plains to establish settlements in the middle Danube Basin, and even now its culture commingles East and West. It's a land of superb cuisine, of *paprikas* and the finest repertoire of savory soups made anywhere on earth; of the strikingly beautiful cities of Buda and Pest, which face each other across the Danube and together form the city known as the Paris of Eastern Europe.

Hungary offers much to the traveler, even more to the traveling sportsman. Her hunting traditions run deep, and to describe the country as a 36,000-square-mile game preserve is no exaggeration. Once it was the private hunting domain of royalty, later usurped by the Communist dictators and bureaucrats. Now, with Communism little more than a distasteful memory, it's available to anyone who cherishes high-quality sport; big game or small— red deer, fallow deer, roe deer, wild sheep, wild boar, hare, partridge, waterfowl, pheasant, woodcock, and more—Hungary has it in bountiful supply.

Perhaps because they were among the chief game of my youth, I have a soft spot for pheasants—*facan*, the Hungarians say, pronouncing it "faatsaan"—and if there's a more elegant sport anywhere than pheasants driven over the guns in the best European tradition, I don't know what it might be. You can find such shooting in England, of course, in Ireland and Scotland and Denmark, and in a great many other places on the Continent. That it should exist in Hungary came as some surprise to me, but like most Americans, I was nurtured on the view that any place beyond the Iron Curtain was as alien as Mars.

Not that I wasn't told. My friend Jack Jansma, who pioneered Hungarian shooting for Americans by establishing the first joint Hungarian-American outfitting company, filled my ear for almost two years with descriptions of shooting on the Tisza Plain and showed me videotape of skies aswarm with birds.

I haven't shot all over Europe, but I have shot on some estates in the hilly west country of England, and as our little van rolled southeast out of Budapest in gathering twilight, I wondered how anyone could persuade pheasants to fly high over a landscape flat as week-old beer. Not to worry, Brother Jansma said, grinning as if he knew something.

Which, as it turned out, he did. And so did I, after a day near the town of Szarvas, which is less than fifty miles from the Romanian border, and two days near Dabas, scarcely forty miles from the center of Budapest. In the Magyar language, *szarvas* means "stag," and although we didn't see any, we saw enough *facan* and *kacsa*, pheasants and ducks, to make up the want. I don't know what Dabas means; maybe nothing. To me, it means "the place where the pheasants stole my heart."

At Dabas, which is pronounced "da-bosh," the shooting day begins about half-past six in the fine, rambling old house that was some nobleman's country estate seventy years ago and now is a shooting lodge. The dining room, cozy with the warmth of a huge, ceramic-tiled fireplace, is the social center, but you'd head there even if it weren't, because somewhere back in the kitchen presides a cook with the touch of an angel—which puts her on a par with every other Hungarian cook. (I don't mean to belabor this, but I'm inclined to think an eating tour of Hungary could all of itself justify the trip.)

After an hour of strong coffee, breads, fruit, cheeses, eggs, sausages, and other stuporously tasty fare, it's a short drive to one of the shooting grounds nearby. As in many other European countries, hunting and shooting are rather tightly governed, and it's available to Hungarians only through membership in a sporting club. Private ownership of land is a concept just now re-evolving as the country emerges from the Communist quagmire, so the clubs lease rather than own the land and manage it for game, usually in conjunction with agricultural uses.

Those two interests kept in balance create an excellent potential. As in Britain and elsewhere, the pheasants are hatched in captivity, reared during the first few weeks of their lives, and then released on the land to mature on their own. By the time the shooting season comes around in November, they're every bit as doughty and tough as any birds you're likely to kick up in an Iowa cornfield.

Having good birds and good land is only a beginning; turning such potential into high-quality sport requires attention and effort and organization. In order to supplement their treasuries, the Hungarian clubs sell a certain amount of shooting every year, and the members themselves conduct the shoots, working as beaters and loaders and pickers-up, all under direction of the chief gamekeeper, a master hunter whose word is the law of the shooting fields. Consequently, your loader might be the local physician, and the village mayor may be among the beaters. Everyone involved has a special, vested interest in presenting the best sporting experience possible.

It shows. High-quality shooting obviously is nothing new to these people, and they've devised some wonderfully clever ways of solving the problem that occurred to me from the start—how to present high pheasants over flat land. Hanging coverts on hills a hundred feet or more above the guns makes high birds easy to come by in Devon and Somerset and Cornwall and Yorkshire and lots of other places in England, but any similar advantages in topography that might exist in Hungary aren't to be found on the Tisza Plain.

You won't, therefore, see many fifty-yard birds, but thirty- to forty-yard pheasants aren't uncommon, and that's high enough for sporty shooting. You'll even find some twenty-yard birds almighty demanding. The trick, which the Hungarians exploit masterfully, is to use any natural feature that might prompt a pheasant into gaining altitude. Flushed in the open at some distance, pheasants invariably will fly over trees rather than through them, so the gamekeepers manage their low, dense holding cover well out from patches of timber and station the guns right at the edge of the woods, where the shots come as the birds are going full-speed and reaching peak altitude to clear the trees.

This is classic driven shooting. If the holding cover is grass or thin brush, the beaters can bring the birds up a few at a time, hens silent except for the staccato clap of wings, cocks with an angry cackle. On your stand, you're constantly aware of your shooting zone—elevation forty-five degrees or higher to protect the beaters, midway between your stand and the next on either side so you don't poach your neighbor's birds.

You let the low ones pass, concentrate on the high-flyers. They tempt you into all sorts of shenanigans almost guaranteed to produce a miss—mounting the gun too soon and riding them in, which means you'll probably stop swinging at the crucial moment, or waiting too long, bending backward off-balance when they're straight overhead.

On these drives, there's more time than you think, time to hear the ragged cadence of the other guns, time to watch their birds fall or fly on unscathed, time to study your own birds winging in, time to focus, to read their flight lines, and then, when they're in comfortable range, time to track your barrels right up their tail feathers, swinging and lifting the gun in one smooth motion. See the muzzles pass through the bird; feel the stock touch your cheek; flick your eyes ahead, letting your leading hand swing the barrels right where you look; and pull the trigger. When it all comes together, the next thing you'll see is the bird crumple into a descending arc and hear it plummet down through the trees behind you, trailing the crackle of twigs. A well-made shot on a high, incoming pheasant feels like the flush of new love.

Some shots can be as unorthodox as others are classic. A major-league power line crosses a portion of a club where we shot—seventy-foot towers strung with thick cables. On one drive, two or three of us were positioned so it stood between us and the holding cover. Flushed more than a hundred yards in front, the birds refused to fly under the wires and were still on the upswing by the time they came in range. Taking care to keep shot well away from the cables made the shooting window smaller still, and going for steeply climbing birds almost straight overhead is sporty stuff.

The low ones can be sporty, too, especially when you're standing in a woodland alley perhaps ten yards wide, shooting as the birds hurtle across the opening overhead. It doesn't take a pheasant in high gear long to cover thirty feet, and the gun who hesitates or is otherwise not on the stick will reap mostly tail feathers. On these drives, when the birds are reluctant to leave a dense patch of woods, the final flush might involve two hundred pheasants all blasting out together in a roar that seems half-deafening even through your earplugs. Visually, such a frenzied rush of flailing wings and long-tailed bodies streaming past can almost make you dizzy.

Which naturally doesn't do much for cool-headed shooting, but that's part of the game. The keepers oftentimes deliberately seek to put an abundance of birds in the air at once, as a means of conserving game while maintaining a high level of excitement, and it works. The exhilaration is genuine, and besides, birds not shot contribute at least as much to the sport as those that are.

Daily bags on these shoots run two hundred to three hundred birds on the average, which is modest by some standards but certainly enough. Some Hungarian clubs can offer much larger bags once or twice a season, but tradition and form make up so much of the appeal of driven shooting that I cannot imagine a thousand-bird day being five times more enjoyable than two hundred pheasants taken the way we do it. In this kind of shooting, numbers rank low on the scale of pleasures.

Weather ranks up or down depending on how much discomfort it brings. Early December on the Hungarian plains is not unlike early December on the Midwestern prairies—often overcast and decidedly weather for long johns, sweater, and coat. That part of the world sees little snow; in five trips, always during the first week of December, I've seen snow twice. And once in a while, as it was the second day of my first trip, you can have a symphony in white on white, one of those eerie, extraordinarily lovely days when every leaf, blade, and twig is rimed in a thick, soft mantle of frost and set against an atmosphere dense with pearlescent fog. The first time, the frost stayed with us all day long. The fog thinned a little at midday but redoubled in the late afternoon, just as we set out for some impromptu duck shooting on a lake near the lodge.

I learned later that it's a sizeable body of water, but that evening, as we ferried offshore in a little motorboat, I couldn't have said whether it was a farm pond or Lake Superior. Thirty yards out, everything simply disappeared in a fabulous haze. A few minutes later, a little island grown with low trees slowly materialized ahead. The whole thing wasn't much larger than a tennis court, but judging from its location and the permanent blinds built around the perimeter, it must be a splendid place for duck on a day when the visibility is good. As it was, the shooting was largely futile. I heard wings aplenty but caught only the merest glimpses of a few birds sliding through the fog, momentary as fireflies. One or two of my companions actually managed to bag a couple; I fired once, as I recall, which troubled me not in the least. Having never been fogbound on a tiny island before, I wouldn't have chosen to be anywhere else in the world at that moment. It was an hour's worth of sight and sound I'll cherish for the rest of my days.

A while later, I felt much the same way about the double-edged warmth of the dining-room fireplace and a glass of *pálinka*, a clear, faintly fruity Hungarian brandy that actually seems to be a form of vodka. Whatever the pedigree, it sometimes tastes like kerosene, but it's sovereign treatment for chilled old bones and a first-class prelude to a dinner that somehow contrives to taste better than the one before.

Such a pleasant assault on my senses and stomach would have been enough, but it turned out that Hungary had yet one more claim to stake on my affection.

I didn't know until our time at Dabas was nearly over that we were the first Americans ever to visit the club where we shot. This has happened a couple of times since, and it always makes me hope we've acquitted ourselves as gentlemen and makes me even more rueful of sharing no common language with our hosts. Hungary's borders have been open for such a short time that few people outside Budapest speak anything but Magyar, and Magyar, like its sister tongues, Finnish and Turkish, is of origins completely different from other modern European languages. Consequently, neither my half-forgotten college French and German nor my poor smattering of Spanish were any help. That is frustrating, because I want to talk directly with these men and women who treat us with such genuine kindness and warmth. I've made a point of learning a few necessities—*puska* and *golyo*, gun and cartridges; *jo*, good; *igen*, yes; *koszonom*, thank you; and the one I was not looking forward to using, *viszontlatasra*, good-bye—but it always feels like much too little.

Hunters, though, can communicate on other levels, purely through love of the sport. After the last drive, the beaters and loaders set to work laying out the birds in neat rows, hens and cocks alternating, feathers smoothed down, each set gently in place, perfectly spaced from the others. Then they surround the tableau with a rectangle of fresh-cut pine boughs and build small pyramidal fires at each of the upper corners. When these grow to a merry blaze, all the beaters and loaders line up on one side, facing the guns lined up on the other.

The gamekeeper offers a toast, thanking us for sharing their sport; we reply, through our interpreter, thanking them. Then, that first time, while we all stood bareheaded in the evening chill, a young man played traditional Hungarian hunting songs on a mellow-voiced horn, wound lovely melodies into the open air in honor of the game, in honor of those who love the hunt, in honor of hunting past and hunting yet to come.

Call that discovery. Call it sweet reward.

Part IV

Heading West

Mixed Bag on the Uncompaghre

"I've got good news and bad news," Jon said, hooking my gun case off the conveyor in the airport at Montrose.

"This isn't a dry county, is it?"

Jon gave me one of his puckish grins and shook his head.

"Then it can't be too bad—unless you plan to make me ride a horse."

"That can be arranged," Jon said, "and if you really want to shoot bandtails, we might have to. That's the bad news. They shifted feeding grounds a couple of days ago, and they're staying up in the hills, probably feeding on mast. The good news is that the doves are really stacking up."

"But no bandtails?"

"We'll see a few stragglers, but we'll have to do some work to find the main flocks."

"The hell with 'em. I've had enough work lately. I'll be happy with doves. What about the blue grouse?"

"Waiting right where they're supposed to be," Jon said.

"I'll bet you say that to all the girls."

Outside, we stowed my gear in the back of Jonny's 'burban while Lefty the Labrador clobbered the side of his crate with a baseball-bat-sized tail, by way of saying hello. Last time I'd seen Lefty, he was rooting ruffed grouse and woodcock out of Jon's old home coverts in Ontario. I opened the crate, rubbed his ears. The tail-bashing pitched to a crescendo. When I stopped, he lay down, sighed, and was asleep before I got the crate door fastened. Not one to get overly excited for no good reason, is Lefty.

A soft-eyed brown face peered at me from the other crate— Katie, Jon's new shorthair, whom I hadn't met before. She accepted her ration of ear-rubbing demurely, and presently we were rolling toward town through the cool Colorado evening, feeling good.

"For a youngster, Kate's coming on like a champ," Jon said. "She's ready to go."

"That," I said, looking south to where the San Juans reared their snaggled, splintery profile against a darkening sky, "makes two of us."

To a hunter, September is flush with promise, a moment on the cusp, the first card in a brand-new game. What follows will be a few months of feeling more intensely alive than the rest of the year can seldom manage to give. The highs will be higher, the lows lower, all of them moments of exquisite worth. At times I've wished I could roam the world hunting year-round, but I don't know if the reality would fit the fantasy. I'm not sure I'd really want to hunt as much all year as I do in the fall. I'd miss the sweet anticipation of September.

The only thing that can make the first real hunting trip of the year any better is when it's a trip into good country with an old friend, and both the Uncompaghre Plateau and Jon Hollinger qualify right to the hilt. Jon's an outfitter by trade, owner of Aspen Outfitting Company and organizer of some of the finest-quality bird hunting available in this country—wild birds in top-notch habitat, mostly on private land for which he holds exclusive lease on the hunting. I know this because I've hunted with Jon before, in the course of some working trips for magazine stories. This was not, however, a working trip, or at least not for me. Jon was working, seeing, as usual, that his clients and guides were properly lined out with one another, this party into the dove fields, another up to the high country for blue grouse. Otherwise, we were footloose, free to follow our whims for any bird that happened to be in season.

I didn't know at the start just how well the Uncompaghre Plateau qualifies as good country—but that was the other reason why I was there. Like many another Midwestern flatlander, I have a hard time thinking of the West in terms of upland birds—despite having enjoyed some excellent hunting within sight of one mountain range or another over the past few years. The more I know of it, the more I'm inclined to think the West will prove to be the last stronghold of truly first-class bird hunting in the United States. There are no woodcock, of course, and no place on Earth will ever match the Upper Midwest for ruffed grouse, but for virtually everything else, the West lies like a land of dreams.

Living as I do in a place that's lost the greater part of its upland trove, the sheer diversity of Western hunting is a continual wonder. Everywhere we turned in the Uncompaghre were places Jon has sought out and established as hunting grounds, places of prime habitat that will offer a whole litany of species through the full range of gunning seasons—this ranch for doves, that one for blue grouse, another for bandtails, others for pheasant; willow-choked backwaters of the Gunnison River for ducks; vast grain-fields for geese; eastward along the Gunnison Valley for sage grouse; on and on. Considering that it's all available within a seventy-odd-mile radius of Montrose and that it's only one of several such places where Jon and his clients hunt, the whole thing can feel a bit overwhelming.

Which is a feeling I hope I never lose, because it's the fuel that makes September burn so brightly. A diverse abundance of game, with its potential for quality sport, is not something to take for granted. Complacency has helped wreck hunting elsewhere in the country, leaving the West as our one last chance to keep the sense of wonder alive on a grand scale.

The promise of country I've never roamed and birds I've never hunted does good things for my own sense of wonder, and in early September, Colorado offers two such birds as legal game—blue grouse and bandtail pigeons.

Bandtails are the largest members of the Family Columbidae native to North America, and they inhabit two separate ranges, one along the Pacific Coast from British Columbia to the Baja Peninsula, and the other in the inland mountain chains from Utah and Colorado south into Mexico and beyond. I'm told they're as strong-flying and sporty as pigeons and doves everywhere; what I know for sure is that they are additional proof of the old wildlife photographer's axiom: Under the most carefully planned circumstances, a wild animal will do whatever the hell it feels like doing.

Unlike others of their kin, bandtails are big enough to make a meal on acorns, and since they aren't tied to a small-grain diet, they don't have to make daily visits to the valley floors in years when the hill-country mast crop is good. According to Jon's own scouting and reports from his guides, the local flocks had been showing up in the lowlands on a clockwork rotation—until about two days before I got there, which on the one hand is the story of my life and, on the other, the reason why it's called "hunting."

As Jon predicted, we did see some stragglers, a few band-tails practicing their aerobatics far out of gun range, as if to remind me of the sort of shooting I was missing out on. We could, of course, have gone after them, searched the hills to learn what habits they were keeping at the moment, but with only a few days to spend and a wealth of other, more predictable birds to enjoy, we opted to let *Columba fasciata* do their thing without us. Besides, they'll be there for a long time, and I'll be back.

For several reasons—one of which is the dove shooting. I knew there were mourning doves in Colorado and once even got into an impromptu dove shoot in the sand hills east of Castle Rock, but that was twenty-five years ago, and I confess I hadn't given much thought to Colorado doves since. It was therefore a pleasant surprise to find the countryside remarkably well supplied with the swift, gray little chaps that somehow always make me shoot both better and worse than I really can.

We had our first crack at them in a classic dove-shooting environment—classic at least for someone who lived for years in northern Missouri, where the wily dove is a close adjunct to animal husbandry. Which is to say, we gunned a feedlot. A big feedlot, just a few minutes outside Montrose, acres of corrals and labyrinthine cattle lanes, miles of concrete feed bunks to sit on, the occasional nose-twitching scent as essence of cowflop eddied in the breeze—and doves by the zillion. With only a few cattle still in residence, all we had to do was watch for a while to see where the birds were flying, take up stands that offered the widest field for shooting away from the buildings, and try not to think about the number of shots fired for the number of birds brought to bag.

As I said, doves have a way of bringing out the best and the worst in my shooting, often at the same time. By the end of the first day, I was not inclined to view a box score of fifteen doves for forty-five cartridges as having covered myself with glory, but mere numbers don't really tell the tale. They reflect neither the sublime misery of missing easy chances nor the splendid thrill of pulling down two sets of right-and-left doubles, each of which offered truly difficult second shots.

Nor again, a day later, gunning a mesa bean field, could numbers even come close to rendering the experience. It was one of those afternoons when nearly every bird that came by was half-suicidal, allowing me to fill a limit with less than a box of shells. That, however, cannot describe a landscape washed in buttery sunlight under a blue-eyed sky, the hazy tops of the Sangre de Christos sawing the eastern horizon, the San Juans in the south, and the massive scarp of Grand Mesa looming to the west.

Hunting is being in places where you wouldn't otherwise

go. It's tramping weary miles through the Gunnison Valley with Jim Houston, retired game manager turned bookseller, who took us out looking for the big grouse that live in the sagebrush wilderness; it's searching for birds in the sage hills higher up, watching a distant rainstorm moving in, getting half-soaked before the squall blows past, and feeling in the midst of it all that there's nowhere else you'd rather be.

Hunting also is a form of surrender to the vagaries of opportunity—or at least bird hunting is, and that's one reason I'm a bird hunter. Big game demands a certain single-mindedness, which I admire but which is not for me. Give me the chance to switch off to some completely different game on the spur of the moment and I'm happy, just as I was when Dale Parker, a horse trainer who's one of Jon's freelance guides, told us he'd seen snipe in the Shavano Valley, right below our dove mesa. After deliberation and discussion lasting all of three seconds—"You wanna?" "Damn right."—next morning found us Jonny (and Mikey) on the spot, combing the moist and grassy banks of Spring Creek.

The Wilson's snipe has more than once been described as the most underappreciated game bird in North America. I can certainly agree with that; trying to paste a charge of No. 9s on a tiny bird flying at high speed in three directions at once is about as sporty as shooting is likely to get—but only someone who's hunted snipe can truly know it, and so far as I can tell, the Serious Snipe Shooters of the World could hold their annual convention in a phone booth and not be much pressed for space.

Snipe are not underappreciated because of their potential for sport; they're underappreciated because getting a good taste of the sport requires attendance in some almighty soggy and difficult places. First, we tried the grassy benches with their pools of standing water two or three inches deep, in part because you'll often find snipe in such spots and in part because we hoped they'd be there, since neither of us was wearing deep-water boots.

It was worth a try, but after a couple of snipeless miles, we had to face some facts: The birds were not in the meadows. If they were there at all, they were in the thicker, wetter stuff along the creek. I surveyed my trusty, battered Bean boots, wishing I'd thought to bring a pair of Wellies. Jon, I suspect, was thinking much the same thing. We looked at each other, shrugged, and headed for the creek.

As it turned out, the only thing Wellies could have done is hold more water. For reasons known only to themselves, the birds were into highly specific habitat that day, which is to say they weren't lurking just anywhere next to the water. Every snipe we flushed came out of a cattail patch, and if you've never been in one, I can tell you that a Colorado cattail patch is no more fun to slog through than one you'd find anywhere else. It's a devilish combination of mud, water, and tangled roots, with stems and blades reaching higher than your head. Wonderful stuff.

But the birds were there. We could hear them twittering off, making their little *scaipe* calls. Once in a while we even got to see one, usually when we were too mired down and off-balance to even think of shooting, or else Lefty, crashing around like a water buffalo, would boot them out in plain sight so we could scatter some aimless shot along the far bank.

Katie, meanwhile, continued to course the wet meadow margins, obviously enjoying the chance to run merrily through the short grass. At one point, Jon looked up as she drifted past in her graceful lope: "What's she doing?"

"Showing that she's a hell of a lot smarter than we are."

Eventually, Katie showed her stuff by retrieving a snipe I flushed and shot on a tiny tributary as we toiled back up to the mesa top. Actually, she fetched it from the rivulet itself, since I managed to drop it in the only water within 200 yards. Jon fished out his pocket camera and took a photo of me, sweat-streaked and muddy to the knees, holding a bedraggled, water-soaked snipe, my face in a happy, utterly witless grin. It hangs in the hall-way outside my office, with other hunting pictures, and people who look at it usually go off shaking their heads.

In the same group is another of Jon's photos of Katie and me, taken on a mountainside a couple of days later and a few miles away. In this one, I'm holding a considerably larger (and drier) bird—the first blue grouse I ever shot.

I love grouse. I love the way they behave, the way they look, and the way they taste. I have an ambition to hunt every species native to North America, and the chance to add a new one seemed lagniappe to an already bountiful feast. By the time we actually set out in search of birds, I'd posed endless questions about blue grouse and their behavior. All of my favorite hunting companions are as intensely interested in natural history—game and nongame alike—as I am, and the more Jon talked, the more intriguing the picture became.

Several things particularly piqued my interest. One is that unlike other mountain grouse, blues migrate to higher elevation as winter draws on, moving from a summer and fall habitat of deciduous forest into high-country evergreens. Another, less surprising but certainly useful, is that a blue grouse flushed on a hill-side almost invariably dives downslope in its escape. And then there's the culinary factor—the purest, silvery-white flesh among all the grouse, Jon said, unutterably sweet and succulent in the fall, predictably turpentiney in winter, from a cold-weather diet of evergreens. Having a notion that nothing dressed in feathers could possibly taste better than a ruffed grouse, I filed this, too, in the memory bank, under "We'll See."

Even though said bank is growing increasingly insolvent with age, I won't forget the first blue, which I shot while standing on a tiny trail that wound around the mountain's contour. First it was a wild flush, far ahead, and I saw the bird pitch into a stand of aspens on the high side of the trail. Jon and Lefty veered upslope.

A few minutes later I could hear them coming down into the trees, and the two dogs must have caught the scent at the same time. Kate, cruising the lower edge, snapped to high-nosed attention just an instant before the bird flushed again.

For a moment or two, there was only a mad hammer of wings, and then a grouse-like shape came climbing through the treetops, bearing straight overhead. A bird hunter judges distance unconsciously, according to the size of the game he's most familiar with, and as the gun barrels caught up and swung ahead, I had one clear impression—either this bird is a lot bigger than a ruffed grouse or else it's a lot closer than it seems. At the shot, the big shape folded, arced, crashed into the underbrush behind me, gave one last drumroll of wings, and went silent. Kate dived in, stubby tail twiddling like a runaway metronome, and presently fetched me a bird, her sweet eyes all ashine.

In hand, a blue grouse cock is more monochrome than a ruff, gray on top and slaty blue underneath, its tail feathers black with a blue-gray terminal band. Like all its kin, it sports bright eyebrow patches, in this species orangy yellow. I've learned since that the race common to the northern Rockies doesn't have the tail band.

It's an impressive bird, nonetheless, for what a blue grouse lacks in intricate dress it makes up in sheer size. From the ones I've seen, I'd guess a mature blue is nearly a third larger than a full-grown ruff, maybe even a bit more.

None of the grouse clan is particularly quick on the takeoff, but blues are no patsies. That first one was the only bird we found in the timber; all the rest were in edge habitat, where aspen stands gave way to serviceberry scrub, much of it shoulder high or taller. Even the ones you see don't give you long to get off a shot, and their habit of diving downhill makes shooting over them all too easy.

A day among the blues seemed fitting enough as an end to the beginning of another season, but as sometimes happens, nature got up some theatrics just to make sure we didn't miss the point. We both had some business in Vail for the next few days and drove up by way of Aspen so Jon could stop off at home to swap gear. We left Aspen in late afternoon on the heels of a rain shower, rolling northwest down the Roaring Fork Valley in a world freshly washed and sparkling. At the edge of town, I happened to glance out the window to the right.

"My God, look at that."

We were at the foot of a rainbow, arching back up the valley, towering tall and brilliant toward the mountaintops in a curving, iridescent shimmer. It looked near enough to touch and seemed to run along beside us. For a mile or more, it kept pace while we watched in silence, as if there was nothing further left to say.

An Arch of Sky,
a Sweep of Space

YEARS AGO, I spent an afternoon cruising Flathead Lake and discussing country with the governor of Montana. It was my first visit to the state, and having spent the previous day in Glacier National Park, I was a bit overwhelmed by the stunning beauty of it all. After listening to my effusions to that effect, the governor solemnly suggested I have a look at eastern Montana as well.

"It's just like this," he said, encompassing the lake and a half-dozen mountain ranges in one gesture, "if you take away the water and the mountains and all the greenery."

I don't recall what I said, but it wasn't very enthusiastic. The governor laughed.

"It is different," he said, "but beautiful in its own way. The bird hunting's pretty good, too."

Because he was a nice man whom I did not wish to offend, I kept my skepticism to myself—for quite a long time, as it turned out, because it took better than ten years before I learned first-hand that the governor was absolutely right.

There is a duality about Montana—spectacularly rugged mountain wilderness and dry, rolling, lonely-looking plains; dense, high-country forests of aspen and conifer; sagebrush hills where cottonwoods huddle in coulees like refugees; mountain goats, bighorn sheep, elk, and grizzly bear; antelope and mule deer. And birds—mountain grouse, sage grouse, sharptails, gray partridge, pheasant, turkey, wildfowl, you name it. If it's a game bird and not a woodcock or a quail, it lives somewhere in Montana.

The longer I hunt, the more convinced I am that my particular fondness for certain birds has much to do with a special fondness for their habitats. In that, hunting birds in Montana for the first time felt like coming home to a place I'd never been.

An early, mid-September snow had swept the high plains the day before, and the melting remnants patched the landscape from Billings north to Lewistown, where we met: Steve Shimek, guru of Travel Montana, Bud Journey, John Holt, and I. Three writers and a State Guy who promised sharptails, sage grouse, partridges, and a bit of trout fishing to boot.

To one born and grown on what once was the great Midwestern tallgrass prairie, Montana's enormous arch of sky is comfortable, familiar. But these aren't the farmlands of home, and here, too, lies a sense of duality. The hills have a fine pitch and angle to them, steep sided and flattened on top, scaling abruptly down into coulees that can feel as pinched as canyons. From the high ground, where the country rolls away in a vast, distant sweep, you feel as if you could fix a course on the horizon and walk forever.

Which is close enough to the truth to give a hunter pause. Shooting birds is one thing, finding them quite another. Freelancing certainly is possible—if you have the time to sort out private land from public, obtain permission where necessary, and scour ranches the size of some eastern states to get an idea where the birds are. A good guide, on the other hand, can save you several hundred leg-weary miles.

We spent the first two days with Larry Surber of D.C. Outfitting, hunting partridge and sage grouse, two birds that are themselves an exercise in duality.

The gray partridge is a European immigrant that became well established in the prairie provinces of Canada and in the western and upper-central United States around the turn of the century. It's a lovely little bird, roughly twice the size of a bobwhite, dressed in gray and buff, with a reddish-brown tail and a similarly colored mark in the shape of a horseshoe on its breast.

Like quail, grays hang out in coveys and flush with a whir of wings. I have a notion they're not quite as quick on the takeoff as bobwhites, although they're certainly speedy enough once underway. They may hold for a dog, or they may simply walk off, leaving the stauncher pointers in a classic though fruitless pose. From what I've seen of them, grays probably are best handled by a wily old pheasant dog.

Their habitat typically has some agricultural component—fields of grain or stubble or even hay—though I'm told they're as likely to be found in sagebrush or grassland. We tried hay fields first, an extraordinarily beautiful spot a few miles out of Lewistown under the Judith Mountains, the Moccasins looming in the west and the Snowy ranges lining the southern horizon. With the hilltops grown ankle-deep in ripening weeds and partially cut hay fields greening the coulees, it's the sort of place where any open-country hunter would be pleased to walk, birds or none. None proved to be the number for partridge that morning, so Larry moved us east to the sagebrush flats.

The sagehen is the largest grouse in North America. Although reports of eight-pound cocks probably are apocryphal, six-pounders don't seem at all uncommon. Hens are only about half as large, but any sage grouse is a bird fit for big country.

Apart from sheer size, the most intriguing thing about sage hens is where they live. They're leaf-eaters, for the most part, indisseverably tied to sagebrush, and if you've never seen it close-up, sagebrush country is a thing to behold. It's a forest in miniature, a knee-high wilderness of stiff, gnarled, woody stems bearded in silvery leaves that stay green year-round. It grows relatively sparsely on otherwise bare, stony ground, and this is a good thing, because you don't get far trying to plow through sagebrush. It's as resilient and springy as a juniper hedge.

In the first few sweeps, we found sign aplenty—big, splay-footed tracks and droppings, both the intestinal variety, which can survive months of weathering, and the black, tarry-looking caecal droppings that signal more recent presence. One of Larry's young pointers finally struck scent in the edge cover where sagebrush gave way to grass, performed a little gavotte to fasten down the strongest thread of smell, and stretched into an eye-rolling point that said, "Birds right there!"

Indeed they were, a dozen or more, and flushing sagehens are a spectacle. Typically, they come up as singles or in twos and threes, lumbering out of the cover like buzzards, big wings chopping. Such ponderous going makes them easy shooting on the rise, but it's a different story once they gain some momentum. Slow flushers, yes; slow fliers, definitely not. Even without a tailing wind, sage grouse can do a mile a minute or better, and those you don't grass on the rise will presently be distant specks, alternately flapping and sailing as prairie birds are wont to do. Those we did hit made hefty mouthfuls as Rojo, Larry's big Labrador, brought them in. Standing on the Montana prairie holding a couple of sage grouse will give you an idea of how Gulliver must have felt, coming ashore at Brobdingnag.

I have yet to know a hunting trip of two days or longer that didn't have a dry patch in it somewhere. This one, as it turned out, had come right at the start, and one birdless morning was a small price to pay for the shooting we got thereafter. Which is not to say that we banged our way across the plains in a continuous cloud of birds; the country is simply too big for that. We trudged our share of dusty miles but always from one oasis of birds to the next—partridges along the edges of wheatfields half-harvested, sharptails in coulees thick with brush, and pheasants not yet in season. The same brushy arroyos sometimes produced mule deer, and hilltop views often showed a sparkle of antelope, flashing their white rump patches in the distance.

After a couple of days, we moved headquarters from Lewis-town to Hardin, 160-odd miles southeast. There, St. Hubert for-give me, I was forced to commit fishing.

That I did not fish for about twenty years became some-thing of a standing joke among those who know me well, but no matter what they might tell you, I've never been averse to a bit of angling now and then, particularly with a fly rod. I prefer shoot-ing, though, and howled at the thought of missing a whole day of it. This cut little ice with my colleagues, rabid fly fishermen and heartless wretches besides. No matter how piteously you whine and plead, when Holt, Journey, and Shimek take a mind to go fishing, you can sooner expect mercy from a hungry coyote. And so off we went down the famous upper-thirteen-mile stretch of the Bighorn River in a couple of dories guided by Dean Barnes of Barnes Bros. Outfitters.

I suppose there's water somewhere on Earth that holds more trout than the upper Bighorn, but unless we're talking about a hatchery, I find it hard to conceive. The only drawback is that you share the river with scores of other fishermen and drift boats, even on slow days. I'm told that stretches farther downriver—from Bighorn to Mallard and Mallard to Two Leggins—offer smaller crowds and bigger trout; serious anglers might prefer one or the other. For my own part, however, the Upper 13 provided good fun and sweet revenge.

While almost literally stuffing me into his spare waders and handing me his extra rod, Holt observed that if angler's luck ran true to form, the non-fisherman of the party should catch both the largest and the most. Modesty forbids me putting too fine a point on it, but Holt was right. Dry-fly purists may scoff, but be-tween a San Juan worm and a little yellow scud imitation, the non-fisherman had himself one hell of a fine time landing a rainbow and three browns, ranging from fifteen inches to better than twenty. Nor was he altogether displeased to hear his colleagues do some howling of their own.

Although the Big Horn country offers the same roster of birds you'll find around Lewistown, we spent the last two days concentrating on what, to my mind, are the king of prairie grouse. Sharptails are tough-spirited, a lot quicker on the flush than sage-hens, more adaptable to agriculture and therefore more abundant than prairie chickens, and almost as unpredictable as their ruff-necked cousins of the woods.

As I've said, big, open-country habitat appeals to me, but it has its frustrations when you're dealing with birds that might be anywhere this side of the horizon. For partridge and sage grouse and prairie chickens, you simply walk the grainfields or the sage-brush or the grasslands, where one spot is as likely to be produc-tive as another. More than the others, sharptails offer the oppor-tunity to hunt rather than prospect.

They're apt to show up in odd places in the morning and evening, when they go out to feed; we found one late-afternoon flock in a grazed-over pasture, pottering and pecking amid a herd of cattle like barnyard hens. Nonetheless, sharptails prefer to spend most of the day holed up in cover—brush, willow brakes, aspen groves, cottonwood scrub, or the like—and since such stuff is not overabundant on the high plains, you can work from one patch to the next with some sense of purpose and a good likeli-hood of moving game.

Sharptails also live in flocks and, if they haven't been hunted hard, seem disinclined to fly great distances from where they flush. Our success may have owed something to the early season, but on the other hand, I saw little evidence of much shooting pressure anywhere David Schaff of Two Leggins Out-fitters chose to take us.

In fact, we spent most of an afternoon chasing one big flock that seemed determined not to leave the long, narrow coulee where we found them, trading instead back and forth between big stands of brush at either end, scolding us with their half-laughing *cuk-cuk-cuk* at every flush. They eventually tired of the trip, or perhaps the scenery, and scattered far over the hills but not before we claimed a half-dozen as table fare. Since the average sharptail weighs about two pounds, a limit of four makes a satis-fying burden at the end of the day.

There are few moments more peaceful than that sweet, sad hour between sunshine and coyote songs, when stillness drifts across the prairie like a gathering shadow—especially to a bird hunter heading carwards. We stayed out late the last afternoon, watching a buttery, coin-faced moon climb slowly up behind the distant buttes, savoring the feeling of connectedness that accrues to a day in honest, wild country.

It's a moment for long thoughts—especially so in this im-mense landscape rich in game and richer still in the sheer sweep of space. In the Midwest and farther east, hunting has largely be-come an exercise of limits and ends—the line fence at the end of a cornfield or the confines of some lonely weed patch not yet dozed, grazed, plowed, planted, paved, or posted. Every year, it seems, we spend more time driving from one scrap of cover to another than actually hunting.

Not so in Montana, where the only effective limits are in the number of times a hunter cares to put one foot in front of the other. Here is country to stretch your legs and your spirit, country big enough to make a man feel tired and free.

Grouse Where the
Buffalo Roamed

I WISH there were one good, crisp word to denote the phenomenon of traveling far before traveling near. It certainly would come in handy for describing, if not explaining, my somehow managing to make some long journeys in search of birds before making some shorter ones closer to home. I spent the first twenty-four years of my life living in Iowa, and yet I was thirty-five before I discovered the wonders of hunting in its neighboring state to the north. The same holds true of its neighbor to the northwest.

Perhaps that omission is easier to understand. When I was a kid, and then a somewhat older kid, South Dakota was the pheasant capital of North America. But in those days, leaving Iowa to find pheasants was like sailing from the Atlantic to the Pacific to find an ocean. With all the pheasant hunting I could possibly want less than an hour's drive from home, South Dakota was simply a redundancy on the roster of places I wanted to go.

For a long time, nobody told me there was anything more there than endless wheat fields teeming with ringnecks, but as I've said before, I believe that certain discoveries come along only when we're best prepared to appreciate them. Thus it was with South Dakota and the grassland birds I have come to love so much.

It started in 1979, when Chuck Post invited me to hunt sharptail grouse. Chuck was information officer for the South

Dakota game and fish department, and I was working for the Missouri conservation department at the time, so it was a sort of busman's holiday among professional colleagues.

As I rolled west toward Pierre through a soft October twilight, the vast open space resonated a familiar chord, touched an emotion rooted in my childhood. To one born near the center of what was the greatest extent of tallgrass prairie on the continent, the midgrass Dakota plains felt a lot like home.

The feeling deepened next day as we trudged across the Fort Pierre National Grasslands south of the Missouri River, and in successive days as we explored the Plum Creek country to the west. Out there, in what the natives refer to as west-river South Dakota (meaning anywhere west of the Missouri), the prairie takes on a wonderful duality—great open reaches of grass and scattered sagebrush cut with broad valleys where cottonwoods line the creek bottoms, and brushy draws offer focus to a hunter looking for birds. Moving down from the windy plains into the coulees is like entering a world where most of the plant and animal life has gone underground.

That trip was the start of my romantic affair with prairie grouse. If there's anything not to love about sharptails, I don't know what it might be. They're hefty, handsome, spirited, hard-flying, and altogether worthy game birds. During the fall and winter, they prefer to spend most of their time near some sort of brush, which is a great help when you're trying to find them.

As the years passed, I hunted sharptails whenever I could, wherever I could find them—in far-northern Minnesota, Montana, and especially Colorado. There, on the high plains and foothills of the northwestern corner, you can find the lovely Columbian sharptail, a sub-race that exists only in about four areas of North America. It's a bit smaller than the standard prairie bird, noticeably darker of plumage, and to my thinking, somewhat speedier on the takeoff. Although abundant in some localized areas, the overall population of Columbians has recently suffered from habitat degradation, and the Colorado wildlife department has reduced the bag limit to only one bird. If the trend continues, complete closure is inevitable. But with luck and some attention from those who manage the land, the birds may rebound to huntable levels once again. I certainly hope so, because they're a delight.

Fond as I am of sharptails, prairie chickens occupy an even deeper niche in my heart, and that, too, is a love affair that began in South Dakota. Well, actually, it didn't; it began when I was a kid, reading of prairie homesteaders shooting chickens by the dozen to feed their families. I read, too, of hunters in the 1870s and '80s filling wagons with them for the wild-game markets in Kansas City and St. Louis, Minneapolis, and Chicago. I shot a prairie chicken myself that first time in South Dakota—just one, but it was enough to bring all the romance of history to life.

Prairie chickens once lived across much of North America, wherever there was native tall- or midgrass prairie. The subspecies known as the heath hen prospered on the scrub-oak plains of the eastern seaboard—or at least it did till European colonists showed up and began hunting the birds for subsistence and destroying their habitat. After 1835, heath hens were known to exist only on the island of Martha's Vineyard, off the coast of Massachusetts. Surprisingly, they hung on there for nearly a hundred years, their numbers continually dwindling as the habitat was ravaged by wildfires, as they were shot by pot hunters, and as they were beset by avian diseases. The last known individual was seen in March 1932.

On the western side of the great hardwood forest, prairie chickens were abundant from southern Ontario to southern Indiana and west all the way to Alberta, Colorado, Oklahoma, and Texas. The densest populations occurred in what is now Illinois, Iowa, southern Minnesota, northern Missouri, Kansas, Nebraska, and the Dakotas. This is precisely the region of the great North

American farm belt—and precisely the reason why the birds have all but disappeared except in the West.

At first, prairie-chicken habitat actually expanded as timber cutting created new open country in the Upper Midwest, and native grasses represented the first stages of regeneration. It took the early settlers some time to realize that native tallgrass prairie, which they first described as the "Great American Desert," is in fact some the richest farmland on Earth. But once they saw the light—and once agricultural technology advanced to the point where they could do something about it—this incredibly diverse biome began to slide into history along the steel moldboard of the breaking plow. With it went the prairie chicken.

To survive in numbers, chickens need native grassland. They need undisturbed open areas to serve as booming grounds, where they perform their eerily beautiful courtship displays; they need clump-growing native grasses as nesting habitat; they need the rich bounty of insects as a summer diet; and they need the equally lush diversity of plant life as food for the rest of the year. Although they can feed well on cultivated grain, agriculture unfortunately cannot accommodate their other requirements for reproduction or winter survival.

Curiously, the region that once supported the greatest population of prairie chickens now supports the greatest population of pheasants. Pheasants are not wilderness birds anywhere in their native or adoptive range and are therefore able to coexist with farming operations in ways that chickens cannot. It's an ironic example of how changes in land use can destroy the habitat of one species and at the same time create habitat for another.

Much as I like hunting pheasants, I'd opt for chickens if I had the choice, both for the nature of the birds and for the aesthetic values of where they live. I took some time in coming to that conclusion, though. Seventeen years, to be exact. I hunted sharptails quite a lot in the meantime and made a couple of brief trips to Kansas looking for chickens. But it wasn't till September 1995, when I got back to South Dakota once again, that it all came together.

Even so, I didn't go specifically for prairie grouse. That fall, *Shooting Sportsman* magazine held its first "Readers & Writers" wingshooting events, two back-to-back pheasant hunts at the Paul Nelson Farm, south of Gettysburg. (If you'd like to do some pheasant hunting that combines first-class accommodations with a mixture of released and wild birds, Nelson's cannot be beat, by the way.)

The writers and editors in attendance had a free day between the departure of the first group of guests and the arrival of the second, and being bent the way we are, we went bird hunting on our day off from hunting birds. Three of us did, anyway—editor Ralph Stuart, writer Robert F. Jones, and I. Ralph had run across a chap in Pierre who guides prairie-grouse hunts and booked him for a one-day gig.

Bob Tinker breeds and trains top-quality English setters and guides bird hunters for sharptails, chickens, and pheasants on about forty-zillion acres of land that ranges from public to private to access-by-permit-only. Bob's a tallish young fella with a go-to-hell sense of humor and a pair of legs any sprinter or hurdler would be proud to own (hurdling, in his high school and college days, is how they got that way, as a matter of fact). Ralph, who's a fit young fella himself, had no trouble keeping up with Tinker and his sweeping dogs. Bob Jones and I, both burdened with considerably more years and a fondness for nicotine, tramped along as best we could. Even so, it turned out okay in the end.

At one of Tinker's secret spots east of Pierre, we found a covey of sharptails that outflanked us with a wild flush far beyond gun range and then hunted up a few singles in a brushy draw. One of these birds crossed in front of me at right angles for as pretty a gimme shot as you could hope for. Being—even by that point—

knee-weary and half-winded, I fringed it with the first barrel and, astonished that it didn't fall, forgot to fire the second.

But prairie grouse are not especially tenacious of life, and as they often do, this one set its wings and sailed the better part of a mile before crash-gliding into the top of a distant rise. Tinker looked at me. "Hope you're up for a walk."

I may not be a candidate for the Boston Marathon, but I'm damned if I'll let someone else fetch a bird I should have stoned at thirty yards, so we struck off while Ralph and Bob Jones cooled their heels. And finally, at the top of the longest slope in the Western Hemisphere, if not the world, lay a beautiful, crisply gray grouse, splay-winged and dead in the grass. I hefted him and smoothed his feathers, turned, and looked back down to where the others waited, then up to an eastern horizon that was all light and space. The ache in my knees faded.

"Are there prairie chickens in this piece of country?" I asked, tucking the bird into my vest.

"How many do you want?"

"Two more birds'll fill my limit, and those guys are entitled to three apiece. You can ask what they want to do, but I want to shoot some chickens."

"I think we can do that," Bob Tinker said.

And we did, and each of us carried away something to remember.

Bob Jones went first, taking a neat double out of a flock that came hammering up in a little basin rimmed with gentle hills. Prairie chickens are not as explosive as quail on the flush, but they're a challenge—even for shooters like Bob, who's no slouch with a gun. Still, once the dogs fetched them in, he stood holding his two birds with a reverence that clearly had more to do with history than with a momentary feat of shooting.

"These are the first prairie chickens I've shot in forty-five years," Bob said as we trudged on up the rise. Later, he told me a lovely story of being six years old, watching his father shovel snow at their home in Wisconsin, and spotting a dozen plump birds puttering at the edge of a patch of prairie grass across the road. "Prairie chickens," his father answered to the inevitable question.

"I want to hold one," said young Robert Francis Jones.

"They don't make good pets," his father replied. "You'll have to shoot it first."

"Okay with me," Bob said. "Because I want to eat it, too."

And there are people who claim themselves unable to understand why other people become hunters.

For our part, Ralph and I each finished the day with unusual efficiency. We'd just crossed a fence and started down a slope toward the vortex where two or three little hills tailed off together. Tinker had just said something to the effect that this was a likely place for chickens to be, when about two-thirds of a good flock flushed almost underfoot. Ralph was the only one in a position to shoot. This he did, twice, and dropped a right-and-left (actually an under-and-over) double of his own.

Then he reloaded just in time in time to see the rest of the bunch take off and thus nailed a limit while standing in his tracks.

Ralph being done for the day, Bob was left with only one to go and I with two. We skirted the hill and swung back toward the truck under assurance from Mr. Tinker that we were almost certain to put up another flock on the way. He was right. This time they came up in front of Bob, and he filled his limit. The rest sailed off in the prairie grouse's characteristic flap-and-glide, angling slightly left, toward the side that I'd chosen as my line of march.

They were understandably nervous from this minor chivvying and flushed a few hundred yards farther on, just as one of the dogs—I forget whether it was Aussie or Scorch—went birdy. From my angle, it was a perfect straightaway flight, and I pointed my leading hand right at the butt of one of the rearward birds and sent him tumbling to the grass.

I had a mark on the fall and walked right to it without taking my eyes off the spot, reloading by feel in case a sleeper had decided to hang back. As I picked up the grouse, the dog came trotting back with a bird in its mouth. I looked, wondering who'd shot it; everyone else was filled out, and besides, I hadn't heard another gun go off. I turned and made a quizzical gesture to Bob.

"Jesus!" he said. "A two-for-one shot—a Scotch double!"

"Whaddya expect from somebody named McIntosh?" I asked, thinking that it's not often the red gods smile so broadly on so many in a single day.

I went back a year later, this time knowing in advance that I'd spend some time with the chickens. *Shooting Sportsman* was to hold another "Readers & Writers" event at Nelson's, with Tim Leary and me representing the magazine. Tim wanted to do a photo essay on prairie-grouse hunting, and I wanted to hunt prairie grouse, so we flew out early and hooked up with Bob Tinker.

Put three inveterate jokesters together, and though the outcome is not likely to have much dignity in it, there will be fun. Bob and I did everything we could think of to make Tim's life difficult, ostentatiously picking our noses or making rude gestures every time he turned his camera on us.

At one point, he asked us to wait while he went on far ahead in order to get a location shot of two hunters walking toward the camera amid the spectacular vista of the grasslands. Bob and I waited dutifully and then, when he signaled, started walking off at right angles.

"Not that way, you assholes! This way!" Tim's voice was a faint cry in the distance.

"He wants us to go that way," Bob said.

"I guess so," I said and, struck with exactly the same idea at the same moment, we joined hands and skipped through the grass like two schoolboys (or schoolgirls) on a prairie holiday.

Forgetting until too late that Leary had a camera trained on us all the way.

We were decidedly more respectful of Mr. Leary after that, hoping that one of us could get our hands on the film before he had it processed and found an editor who'd publish something that looked like an outtake from *The Light-Loafered Lavender Lads Go Hunting*. (We failed, so if you see this shot in print somewhere, be advised that not all photographs are what they appear to be. Tim had done something similar to me a year before, catching me clowning with a pump gun and wearing somebody's dopey-looking hat backwards. He intended it as the cover shot for the premiere issue of a new magazine idea some readers came up with—*Redneck Journal, The Magazine of Road Hunting and Pretty Good Guns*. It's not pretty, but one of the more valuable lessons I'm learning as I enter the latter stages of middle age is not to take myself too seriously.)

We actually were hunting, despite all the foolishness, and the hunting was as good as I'd hoped it would be. We found more sharptails than chickens, which certainly is no hardship, but there were enough chickens to satisfy the connection I was looking for. And then there was that ineffably lovely double point.

We were an hour from the truck, deep into the Ft. Pierre Grasslands, just topping a gentle rise. Aussie and Scorch spun around simultaneously as if lassoed by the noses and went down solid on a patch of grass no larger than a desk belonging to middle management, remarkable only because it stood a bit taller than the surroundings. We crossed a rickety old fence and walked over, stopping for a moment to drink in the sight.

"Man, it doesn't get any better than that," Bob said. We agreed. Tim shot a few frames of film, and then Bob deployed his troops, sending Tim to one side and me to the other. When we were in place, he walked in and kicked the grass.

Nothing flew.

He kicked again, harder, and still nothing flew. We exchanged puzzled looks.

With that, Mr. Tinker hauled off as if going for a sixty-yard field goal, and kicked a skunk.

Fortunately, the impact of a size 12 boot at high velocity was enough to disrupt the little guy's aim, so Bob only got nicked. But it was enough that we didn't have to wonder where he was the rest of the day, and enough to earn him a couple of enduring nicknames—either Bob Stinker or Downwind Bob, depending on which occurs to Tim or me at the moment. It was also good for some speculation on what techniques he preferred for skunk-training his dogs. Aussie and Scorch dismissed the whole thing with the canine equivalent of a collective shrug, as if to say, "You want us to point. We point. Being picky about what it is ain't in the contract."

In some ways, the prairie chicken is an anachronism, more a reminder of what's gone than of what remains. As my old friend John Madson put it in his splendid book, *Where the Sky Began*: "In all of modern America, there is no more lost, plaintive, old-time sound than the booming of a native prairie chicken. And when it is gone, it shall be gone forever. All our television cannot bring it back, and none of our spacecraft can take us to where it vanished."

In the Midwest, where remnant flocks manage to survive in remnant scraps of native grassland, they offer a faint glimpse of how glorious the landscape used to be. Only in the West, on land too poor to plow, can we still find pieces of the picture large enough to get a sense of this country's former vastness. There, where the long views are still long, you can recover some notion of proportion, capture some feeling of how we fit the scale of it all.

Owing to the vagaries of time and events, Missouri has a larger population of prairie chickens than other Midwestern states—perhaps ten thousand birds in all. The numbers have remained essentially unchanged for sixty years or more. There aren't enough to support even restricted hunting (and never will be), but there certainly are enough to watch and wonder at. For years I lived within a scant hour's drive of a booming ground, and it was my annual custom to spend a few March mornings or afternoons there, using my backpack tent as a blind, watching and listening while the cocks perform their courtship rituals. It was like escaping through some rent in time, back to an older world.

Now, though the drive is somewhat longer, the urge to revisit the place is growing once again, just as the prospect of spending more time on the big prairie draws me back to South Dakota. Being in the woods or among the mountains is being on the land; to be out where land and sky share equal space is to feel a balance that's hard to capture anywhere else. Knowing there are sharptails and chickens somewhere between the horizons makes the equation complete.

Epilogue

Rain Songs

THE OLDEST SOUNDS to fall on human ears surely must be wind, thunder, breaking waves, and rain—sounds whose memories flow deep within the nature of our nature and, like Pavlov's bell, set vibrating some inner harp that waits beyond awareness, sounds that touch the level of amniotic dreams.

Though I confess a fondness for all of them, none moves me quite like the sound of rain. I suppose it represents my particular fastening-point to our collective unconscious. If so, that's okay with me. I'm not inclined to worry the notion with too much thought—because what things the sound of rain evokes at the nearer side of consciousness are fully sweet enough.

Oddly for a feeling so old, I know exactly how it began and where, if not exactly when. I was a wee lad that summer, a puppy at my grandfather's heels, probably a nuisance underfoot though he never said so, following him as he followed his high-wheeled walking mower to sickle down the road ditches and the margins of his corn.

Prairie storms can be sudden as a falling stone. Maybe Grandad knew all along it was coming, but I didn't. The first fat drops found us far down the field, their preliminary sprinkle raising the distinctive smell my mother used to describe, perfectly, as wet dust.

"You better beat it for the house," Grandad said, "if you

don't wanna get soused." He always pronounced it "sowzed," and to him it simply was the word for being wet, not a euphemism for getting drunk. I was disinclined to be anywhere except where he was, so I trudged alongside while the wide Iowa sky spilled down on our heads. It came straight down with not a breath of wind, drenching and cool.

By the time we reached the machine shed, I was as wet as I'd ever been in a bathtub, soused in every sense—lighthearted and drunk with some feeling I couldn't name. We stood in the wide doorway, dripping, listening to water hammer the roof. Grandad grinned at me, his gray-stubbled face streaming.

"Why didn't you run?"

"Why didn't you?"

"I kinda like the rain," my grandfather said.

"Yep," I said, discovery dawning even as the words came out, "I kinda like it, too."

I still do. I like to see it and hear it and smell it. And I especially like to hunt on a rainy day.

This is not to say that I deliberately plan my hunting to coincide with the monsoons, nor that a downpour makes me less uncomfortable than anyone else. It's just that a bit of rain can add a dimension not present on more clement days. The world is different in the rain. Colors change. Sounds grow more subtle. The whole atmosphere feels more intimate. Hunting is my connection with nature's vast scheme of life and death, my best opportunity to be a player rather than a spectator, and rain somehow draws me even deeper in.

It makes certain days stand out in memory from among the rest. The sweetest morning of pheasant hunting I ever spent was in fog and drizzle somewhere north of Cedar Rapids, with the corn stubble gleaming. Vision simply stopped a few yards in any direction, vanishing like an old, grainy photograph. The birds vanished, too, one moment flapping, long-tailed shapes and the next only a steady chop of disappearing sound. We didn't see the spooky ones at all, simply heard them go.

The weather cleared just before midday, which improved the shooting immensely, but the bird I remember is the big rooster that came hammering out of the fog, flushed by someone off to my right, all his circus colors saturated with light. The gunshot's hollow boom seemed to linger for a long time, and I walked out to pick him up through a slow fall of bronzy, dark-tipped feathers floating on the windless air. Forty years it's been, but it still plays across my mind intact as a familiar address.

So do some more recent days when rain and ruffed grouse have been the source of pleasant memory. Because I have to drive several hundred miles for my annual northern-Minnesota grouse fix, I'm not much inclined to forfeit many of those precious hours to mere weather. Besides, hunting grouse in the rain is an altogether different game from the one you play on bluebird days. Usually it's a comedy acted out in dripping pine groves so thick that just to see a flushing bird is a notable event, but it can have its moments.

There's a certain place where I especially like to go on rainy days, a narrow old sand road that meanders like a fairy-tale path through the woods. If you follow it a couple of miles south from the highway, you'll come to a patchwork series of tiny hay fields rimmed by brushy woods and connected by a network of trails grown thick with clover. In years when the birds are few, the road and the trails make for an enjoyable stroll garnished with the virtual certainty of a flush or two; in the best of times it's the stuff of a hunter's dreams.

The year that comes to mind most clearly was somewhere between—plenty of birds but still not one of the fifty-flushes-before-lunch years that country produces. A hard rain kept me in until midday, and even before it started to slack off I knew where I was going to spend the afternoon. My partners are fond of describing a turn through the woods after a rain as the equivalent of walking underwater, and they're exactly right. But not so my dear old sand road. There you can stay relatively dry and still stand a good chance of moving game.

The first bird bailed out of a spruce tree no more than a hundred yards from the highway, the wingbeats muffled in the drizzly air. It was the standard tree flush, which is to say he came diving off his limb at a steep slant, and I made my standard tree-flush shot, which is to say I missed him. I don't know where he went, only that it wasn't to grouse heaven.

The next one came from lower down in a big Norway pine, a young one that hadn't learned to flush into the woods instead of across the road, and that bird earned a couple of dozen No. 7s for its folly.

A textbook day so far, but then I wandered off the road to check out a pine grove nearby. I often do this on a rainy day, not because I'm likely to get a clear shot at any birds that might be in the trees but rather on the chance to see a flight line and have a better opportunity on the reflush. It works often enough. So I started circling the grove, pushing through thigh-high ferns and scanning the trees.

Flushing grouse do not normally startle me as much as quail do, even at close range; that's possibly because a single ruff doesn't make as much racket or as much visual confusion as a covey of bobwhites. But two grouse are a different story, especially when they get up almost underfoot while you're looking somewhere else and don't know they're there.

For my money, a genuine double flush is the loveliest sight in grousedom. It's truly breathtaking. This one certainly was, partly because of the perfect synchrony of it and partly because the birds scared me half out of my wits. What they were doing hunkered down in wet ferns I haven't a clue, but the pair came thrashing up in a shower of droplets that surrounded them like an aura.

Of the double flushes I've seen in all my years of hunting grouse, I have been able to turn only one into the even rarer phenomenon of a double kill. And it wasn't that one. Instead, I did what I usually do—fired the first barrel purely on reflex, poking the gun instead of swinging it, all with the usual results. The second shot was better. Killing two grouse does not feel twice as good as killing one, and one double on ruffs ought to last any man a lifetime. But I confess, I've always felt a tiny pang of regret that mine didn't happen that day in the rain.

Much as I enjoy them, rainy days are always somewhere close to the edge, always hold the potential of crossing the thin line between pleasure and misery, and the ones that do aren't easy to forget, either. I still get shivers thinking about the time we ran afoul of the beavers.

It was another day with grouse, in another old favorite Minnesota covert. The rain had almost stopped when we left the car, and as it was already mid-afternoon, Ted and I decided to split up, each make a sweep through a different part of the woods, and by comparing notes afterwards, choose which area to hunt more thoroughly next morning.

I picked a piece of woods I knew well from past years—a sizeable patch bounded on the west by a long pasture and on the east and south by an old woods road, the interior well supplied with stands of gray dogwood, that wonderful shrub with the scarlet-tipped twigs and the little grayish-green berries grouse relish. If the rain truly was over, I figured the birds would soon be heading out to feed.

The woods were wet—fat, crystalline drops hanging on the brush just waiting for someone to come along and shake them loose—so it wasn't long before Tober and I were well-sprinkled, not uncomfortably so but damp enough. By the time we'd checked out the third dogwood patch without moving a bird, I had a notion the grouse knew something we didn't, and a few minutes later, as if on cue, the rain started falling again, chilly and pelting.

Remember Macbeth's line about being stepp'd in so far that returning were as tedious as go o'er? I told Tobe we might as well push on to the beaver pond, make the usual left turn and have a look at one more piece of dogwood that lay between there and the road. After all, you can only get so wet.

This is true, but sometimes we forget how wet that really is. We reached the beaver pond and swung east, taking a meandering course to avoid the thickest, and wettest, brush. The rain fell steadily. A quarter-mile of this brought us to a familiar landmark—the beaver pond. Clearly, we had meandered ourselves into a circle and ended up back where we started. I had felt no need of carrying my compass in woods with such obvious boundaries, and besides, if you walk straight away from the beaver pond, you're headed due east and therefore toward the road. That's just how it is. I'd done it a hundred times before.

We turned away from the pond, thrashed a reasonably straight line through the brush, getting wetter by the minute, and presently fetched up at the beaver pond once again.

I have never been utterly lost in the woods. I have been highly disoriented, though, and never more than I was right then. The rain had not yet escalated quite to a downpour, but it was getting there. In a thick overcast, the sun can be anywhere in 360 degrees of sky, and in the north woods, every direction is north so far as moss on tree trunks will tell you. Standard boy-scouting just doesn't cut it.

The only explanation was that we were going in circles, although that didn't feel right, either. But keying on the pond and the straightaway turn, we headed east again and once again soon found ourselves looking at the beaver pond.

By this time, Tobe was soaking wet and beginning to give me the fish eye. I didn't blame her. I stood for a few minutes, wondering if we'd somehow slipped through a tear in the continuum of time and space and were now in a parallel universe almost but not quite a duplicate of our own. Tobe sat close, shivering and staring at me as if to say, "Pop, I'll go anywhere you go, but wherever it is, could you please make it any place but here?"

"Okay, babe," I said, "here's what we're gonna do: We're gonna go fifty paces east to get away from this bloody pond, turn south and walk the whole length of these woods. It's close to a mile, but we're going to do it, and we're going to find the road and then walk in the rain all the way back north to the car. If you have a better idea, I'm open to suggestions."

She didn't, so we struck off. Fifty paces from the pond, turn ninety degrees right. We navigated in short pitches; find the tallest tree that's straight ahead, walk to it, find the next and walk to that one, on and on. We plowed through brush so thick we could scarcely move, clambered over fallen trees, slogged through low spots. We walked around nothing. Once, going over a blown-down oak, we spooked the biggest buck deer I ever saw out of his shelter underneath. He trotted off looking peevish, and Tobe plodded next to me, never giving him a second glance.

After a year and a half of this, we came to a place I recognized instantly—a dogwood thicket that forms the south end of the cover—and in another hundred yards we were standing on the road, panting and dripping and miserable.

And along came Ted, his rain hood pulled up, gun slanted under his arm, hands deep in the pockets of his slicker. Old Dixie, the greatest grouse-hunting Labrador who ever lived, walked patiently alongside, her coat almost blue with rain. Ted looked at Tobe and me as though we were museum exhibits.

"Find any birds?" he asked, lips twitching slightly under his mustache.

"No," I said, and related our ordeal.

His lips twitched like a horse dislodging flies. "Oh, jeez," he said. "I forgot to tell you: The beavers really went to work in there this summer—built a new dam and a new pond. It's just about a quarter-mile east of the old one. . . ."

I have hunted birds on rainy days from Alaska to Nova Scotia, Mexico to Minnesota, in Europe and South America, but I cannot think of hunting in the rain without thinking of the quail Tober and I found right near home, on the December day that marked the turning of my forty-first year. It came in the midst of the most turbulent, sorrowful period of my life. The cold, fine rain and louring sky perfectly matched the way I felt. We trudged a long way around the edges of muddy fields without finding so much as a feather, and that, too, seemed to fit.

A couple of hours later, heading back toward the car, I was so thoroughly depressed and preoccupied with gloomy thoughts that I almost stumbled over Tobe before I realized she was on point next to a blackberry tangle. Being at least smart enough by then not to stick my foot into vegetation that can stick back, I lobbed in a rock and took two birds out of the covey with as tidy a right-and-left as I've ever shot.

I spoke not one word as she brought them in, gently as offerings. When I took the second, she remained sitting, looking at me with her eloquent eyes.

I looked at her and at the quail in my hands, a birthday dinner, thinking that any world able to hold all at once the perfect love of a dog, the wild freedom of birds, and the unutterable beauty of rain must surely be a world worth living in.

Appendices

Appendix I

THANKS TO CURRENT SYSTEMS of transportation and a goodly number of professional, well-organized outfitters, the opportunities available to traveling sportsmen are greater today than ever before. Depending upon where you go and how much you're willing to pay, you can find hunting, shooting, and fishing that ranges from satisfying to fabulous. And price alone is not necessarily the final measure of quality; in states that have both a great deal of public land and good game populations, you can find superb hunting for no more than gas money, a motel room, a nonresident permit, and enough time to do some prospecting.

Nor is price necessarily the measure of more formally organized, long-distance travel for sport. Quail in Mexico or doves in Argentina are nowhere near as pricey as, say, driven grouse in Scotland or partridge in Spain, but you couldn't find better bobwhite hunting or dove shooting anywhere, for any price.

Though the hunting and fishing available is naturally as varied as the animals themselves, certain common denominators apply to virtually all sporting travel, regardless of whether your destination lies a few hundred miles away or halfway around the world. What follows are some things I've learned over the years, suggestions that might help make your travel more enjoyable.

OUTFITTERS AND GUIDES

Outfitters are essentially travel agents who specialize in organizing hunting and fishing for their customers. Like travel agents who organize sightseeing tours, they are responsible for the infrastructure of a trip—for ensuring that you reach your final destination; that appropriate transportation, lodging, food, and other basic services are available once you get there; and that there are people on hand to see that you get the hunting and fishing opportunities you came for.

Sometimes the outfitter himself is there. J. W. Smith, for instance, personally operates the fishing camps that Rod & Gun Resources sets up in Alaska every summer. More often, though, the outfitter uses the services of a professional lodge or camp owner at the destination end; to again use Rod & Gun Resources as an example, these would be people like Frank Ruiz in Sonora or Philip Marsteller in Brazil.

In any case, the outfitter is at the top of the organizational chain and bears ultimate responsibility for the quality of the services he provides. Obviously, he can't control the weather or make wild animals do anything they don't want to do, but it's his job to see that everything else, everything that can be controlled, is as it should be.

As in everything else, outfitters range from excellent to inept, from meticulous professional to lazy clodpate. The same is true of lodge managers, and you'll almost invariably find like matched with like. Good outfitters insist upon working only with well-organized, well-run lodges that can deliver the quality of experience the customer wants; to do anything else would be suicidal, businesswise.

So one of the keys to a good trip is to book it with a good outfitter, and you can approach this in one of two ways. If there's a certain place or species of bird or fish that interests you, you can search out the outfitters who book that sort of thing. Or you can let the outfitter himself be the basis of your trip and choose what you like best from the menu of what he offers.

Either way, the testimony of satisfied clients is the best recommendation of all. Advertising is one thing, word of mouth another, and if you start with the one, ask for the other. Appendix II lists all the outfitters who were responsible for the trips I've described in this book, and I recommend them highly, every one.

The Bird Hunting Report, a twelve-page monthly newsletter specifically for hunters who travel, is an excellent source of information on outfitters, lodges, and destinations in general. Subscriptions are $45 per year. Contact *The Bird Hunting Report*, 1616 North Fort Myer Drive, Suite 1000, Arlington, Virginia 22209, phone 800-424-2908 (in Virginia, 703-528-1244).

If you're prospecting for an outfitter through advertising, ask for names and phone numbers of recent clients, call a few at random, and talk to them about the experience they had. Advertising is by nature always positive, but you can count on a fellow hunter or fisherman to tell you exactly how it was.

The key questions are: Did your hunting or fishing experience match up with what the outfitter promised? And would you book another trip with this company? Keep in mind that there are some things nobody has control over, but discounting the vagaries of weather and animal behavior, if the answers to these questions are yes, you're most likely on the right track.

Beyond this, ask the outfitter about things that could make the difference between a dream trip and a nightmare. Who's in charge at the destination where you'll be, and how can you reach him if you get stranded in an airport somewhere on the way in? What sort of medical care is available in case of illness or accident, and where? What sort of weather should you expect? How much cash will you need to cover expenses that aren't included in the package price? What's not covered in the package price? What's the typical hunting or fishing day? Are loaner guns or rods available if yours get sent astray inbound?

The list is endless. Just don't hesitate to ask any questions that occur to you. And by all means, if you have a medical condition that might affect you during the trip, or if you have specific dietary requirements, let the outfitter know right up front. If circumstances are such that you might be at risk, or if he can't supply what you need, a good outfitter will say so at the start, and you can reconsider. But outfitters are not clairvoyant, and you can't blame one for not accommodating something he doesn't know about.

The six words you don't want to hear when you arrive at your destination: "There's been a change of plans." Here again, you have to keep in mind that weather and animals are laws unto themselves, but if you've booked a trip to hunt quail and arrive to be told that you'll be hunting ducks instead, somebody isn't doing his job. A good outfitter will change plans in order to ensure that you get the experience you've paid for, but other than that, surprises generally don't turn out to be pleasant ones.

Guides are employees whose job is to put you in touch with birds or fish on a daily basis. They'll be there with you, on the ground. They know the country and the animals, and they're the arbiters of safety and success.

Not all guides are good at what they do. If you draw one who's lazy or indifferent or makes you feel uncomfortable about not being an expert shot or fisherman, don't be shy about asking for another. On the other hand, your guide is only responsible for giving you opportunities; it's not his fault if you miss your birds or dump your casts.

A good guide is a gem with whom you'll be pleased to spend your days. He'll see that you get the best opportunities possible and go out of his way to make you comfortable. He'll try his best to accommodate what you want, but if you wish to attempt something foolhardy, dangerous, or illegal, he won't hesitate to say no, and he has the last word while you're in the field or on the water.

PAPERWORK

At minimum, this amounts to a hunting or fishing permit issued by the state you're visiting. Nonresident fishing permits are generally very easy to come by, and a lot of states offer short-term versions—one-, three-, and five-day licenses. Nonresident hunting permits sometimes take some effort to find, especially later in the season. A few states offer short-term versions of these, too.

For hunters under a certain age, a number of states require proof of your having completed a hunter-safety course. You should check on this well in advance, in case you need to take a course before you go. And don't assume you won't need one just because you're thirty- or even forty-something. Colorado, for instance, requires safety certification of all hunters born after January 1, 1949.

You don't need a passport to enter Canada or Mexico, but you do need some form of identification to enter Mexico, and a passport is probably best. Certainly, you'll need one to go anywhere else. Passport applications are available at larger post offices and Federal Buildings. The cost is $40, and processing can take as long as two months, so don't wait till the last minute if you're going to need one. Passports come due for renewal every ten years.

Some countries require that all visitors obtain visas, which are issued by their embassies in the United States. If you're going to need one, your outfitter will provide the appropriate application forms—but you're responsible for obtaining your own visas and, as with any government paperwork, it can take a while, so don't put it off.

Almost every country requires some sort of gun permit, issued in advance. The outfitter provides the proper forms and secures the permits for you. Some countries—Mexico and Argentina, for instance—require passport-type photos for these, and sometimes for hunting permits as well. For the most part, the cost of gun permits is nominal and included in the package price for a trip, but in a few instances the fees are rather high and may be priced separately. This is the case in Mexico, where a permit allowing you to bring two guns into the country can run as high as $300 to $400. (Unfortunately, the fee is the same if you take only one gun.)

Two crucial points to remember about foreign gun permits: Make sure you list the serial number of your gun correctly on the application, and be *absolutely certain* that the gun you take is the one shown on your permit. This may seem too elementary to even mention, but believe me, discrepancies between guns and permits can be the source of endless hassles, delays, and having guns refused entry or even confiscated. I've seen it happen. Even if you eventually get the problem resolved in your favor, it's a pain in the butt, and your companions will not be happy about having to wait around for hours because you screwed up and brought the wrong gun. It's not the way to start a trip.

One final paperwork-related item that can save some grief is to register your guns with US Customs. The certificate proves that you owned them before you took them out of the country and that you are therefore not liable for paying duty when you bring them back in. Actually, you can register any item—cameras, fishing rods, reels, whatever—and it's not a bad idea to do so for items that have significant value. If you're driving into Canada or Mexico, you can register your guns on the American side before crossing the border. If you're flying, you can register your gear ahead of time at any US Customs office. The certificate is good for as long as you own the items.

AIRLINES

On many trips, your outfitter will make travel arrangements On others, it's up to you. The larger American airlines can take sportsmen just about anywhere in the world, but in some cases you have little choice but to use a foreign line. For example, Varig, the Brazilian national airline, is about the only game in town if you want to fish peacock bass in Brazil, for instance. If you're going to shoot doves in Argentina, you'll have to fly to Buenos Aires first and catch a domestic flight to Córdoba, and it's usually simpler if you take an Aerolineas Argentina flight out of Miami or Los Angeles to begin with. Aerolineas Argentina is a top-notch carrier.

For the most part, foreign airlines are excellent. KLM and Finnair, in fact, are my two favorites in all the world, punctual and very well organized, highly attentive to their passengers' comfort. British Air also takes good care of you once you're on board, but for some reason seems to have perennial difficulties getting off the ground on time. Air France is a bit lax about keeping track of luggage. I've had good trips on Air UK and Aero Mexico.

If at all possible, try to stay on the same airline all the way from your initial point of departure to your destination, because that means you don't have to claim and recheck your baggage somewhere. This is one reason why traveling on KLM is so convenient; KLM and Northwest are part of the same company, and Northwest can take you from just about anywhere in the United States to one of KLM's gateway airports. If you have to switch carriers, it's usually better to do so in the United States rather than in your destination country.

FLYING WITH GUNS

The Federal Aviation Administration allows firearms to be transported on commercial flights as checked baggage only. You are required to declare your guns at the ticket desk when you check in for your flight and sign a tag that says they aren't loaded. Firearms may be transported only in airline-approved hard cases, and the cases must be locked. You may not transport ammunition in the same case.

This, in a nutshell, is all the FAA requires, but like everything else, there are nuances to consider. Policies vary a bit among airlines, and some refuse to transport firearms at all, so you need to check with every carrier you'll be using, in advance. It's no fun to reach the last leg of your journey and discover that Aldertop Air—or whatever company operates the only flights into East

Bunghole—has a no-gun policy. If your outfitter sets up the itinerary, don't worry about it; if you make your own travel arrangements, be sure to have your travel agent check.

"Airline-approved" gun cases cover a lot of ground, and include some abortions I wouldn't trust to keep my gun safe in the back of my Explorer, much less in the gut of an airport's baggage-handling system. In my opinion, nothing made of any sort of plastic is adequate; plastics can be wonderfully tough, but they often get brittle at low temperature—like in an unheated cargo bay at high altitude—and can crack. You want a top-quality aluminum case that's properly padded and on which every latch is also a lock, either combination or keyed. To my mind, for quality, convenience, and durability, Americase is the best.

As I said, FAA regulations require an approved case, and most airlines now insist that it be locked. Both are good regs. How you transport this locked case is largely up to you. You can check it through as a separate piece of baggage, or you can put it inside another piece, such as a big duffel bag or, best of all, a duffel that has a special compartment specifically meant to hold a gun case.

I don't mean to sound immodest, but the so-called gun duffel was my idea; several years ago I designed the first one ever made, which was sold for a couple of years by Countrysport, Inc. I'm still traveling with the prototype bag. Now, you can get good-quality specimens from Orvis and Boyt and probably some others. Galco International makes one that's based on my original design, which, in concept, is still my favorite.

A gun duffel has several advantages. It allows you to combine your gun case with another piece of luggage, and on international flights that sharply restrict the number of pieces you can check, this is good. Better yet, it allows you to transport your gun out of sight. Every gun case looks like a gun case, but if it's in some other bag the risk goes way down. The airlines appreciate this no end, for despite their disclaimers, they're ultimately responsible for the baggage you check. Baggage theft, especially theft of firearms, is a federal offense that the federal government takes seriously, and airlines want your gun to be safe just as much as you do.

This is not to say you won't run into some boneheaded ticket agent who presumes to be an expert on FAA regulations. Just two weeks ago, as I write this in March 1997, a friend of mine, on his way to a quail-hunting trip in south Georgia, was told by an agent in an East Coast airport that the FAA requires gun cases to be carried separately, refusing to let him put the case inside his gun duffel. FAA regs say nothing of the sort, but he didn't object, and naturally his gun case, with a lovely pair of Holland & Holland guns inside, didn't arrive on his flight. They did show up on the next flight, but it cost him several hours of completely unnecessary anxiety.

If any ticket agent gives you a similar line of blather, ask to speak with a supervisor, and keep going up the chain of command till you find someone who knows what's what. And don't buy any nonsense about "airline regulations." Each company does have some latitude in establishing its policies, but I've flown with guns on all the major domestic lines and a good many foreign ones, and I have yet to find one that has a real policy against putting the obligatory tag *inside* the gun case or placing the case inside some other piece of luggage.

This may change in the future. It would amount to utter madness on the airlines' part, but then sanity never was a prerequisite for doing business. At the moment, though, gun duffels are perfectly acceptable, and they represent the best security you or the airline could hope to have.

Certain trips include a stopover in some country other than your destination, and in those cases your gun may be held in airport or hotel security overnight. This is fine, but your outfitter should tell you about it beforehand, just so you can prepare by not packing anything you'll need in the same bag your gun is in.

Some places in the world are just not good places to go if you're traveling with guns checked as separate items of baggage. London, unfortunately, is one of them. Anti-gun and anti-blood-sport mania has been approaching a peak of absurdity in England for quite some time, and I can't tell you how many people I know who've stopped over in London on their way to hunt in Africa or elsewhere and arrived to find that their guns were sent to Bangladesh or Iceland or somewhere equally out of the way. It's purely a matter of airport baggage dispatchers exercising a personal agenda rather than doing what they're paid to do, but it exists and the only thing you can do about it is insist on traveling by a different route.

Even apart from deliberate sabotage, if you travel enough, you'll find yourself at your destination while part or all of your luggage is on tour elsewhere. It happens even with airlines whose employees are honestly trying to do their jobs. I've landed in Mexico without my gun, in Brazil without my fishing tackle, in Spain without my clothes, and lots of other places missing something that was with me when I left home. Your outfitter or his representative should get on this sort of thing immediately. In most cases, whatever's missing will arrive on the next flight, and if you're out of the United States, someone should be dispatched to make a special trip to pick it up. Though late-baggage delivery here at home is generally excellent, that's not necessarily so in foreign countries, and depending upon what's gone astray, it could make the difference between a great trip and a great disappointment.

Policies on ammunition vary. Mexico allows you two boxes of shells per gun; a number of countries allow none at all. If you're going hunting inside the United States, you can transport ammunition by tucking three or four boxes in among your clothing (though *not* in your carry-on bag), but if it's to be a relatively high-volume shoot—doves, for instance—you really can't conveniently carry enough to make much difference. Unless it's a domestic hunt where you probably won't shoot more than two or three boxes, and on any hunt in a foreign country, the best course is to get your cartridges on the spot. The outfitter or lodge will have plenty available, at an average of $9 or $10 per box.

Regardless of the game, 12-gauge is the world standard, though 20-bore shells are readily available almost everywhere. If you plan to shoot a 16 or 28, or if you'll need $2\frac{1}{2}$-inch cartridges, be sure to let your outfitter know well in advance. He may or may not be able to secure an adequate supply. For simplicity's sake, you're well advised to take a 12- or 20-bore gun with $2\frac{3}{4}$-inch chambers and save yourself the hassle.

Fishing tackle, of course, is under no restriction. You can check it through as baggage or carry it on. Having learned the hard way, I much prefer to carry mine, in a rod bag that has a couple of zippered pockets large enough to hold my reels, spare spools, and some flies. I may end up without my vest and waders, but at least I'll be able to fish.

Three- or four-piece rods are less awkward for traveling than two-piece, but if your favorites are two-piece you can still carry them without too much trouble. They'll fit into any plane that doesn't have dividers between each overhead compartment, and if there are dividers or drop-down compartments, a flight attendant can stow them for you elsewhere. Even if they have to ride in the cargo bay, you'll still get them back as soon as you land. It's good for one's peace of mind.

GETTING ALONG AWAY FROM HOME

Your outfitter is responsible for the basic infrastructure of a trip, but you're responsible for some things, too. Changing money, for instance. On some trips it's not really necessary, because there's no place to spend money where you're going, but for the most part it's wise to obtain some local currency anyway—for taxis, pubs, tips, and such.

Generally speaking, airports are the best places to exchange money. The rates usually are better than those at large hotels. The *cambios* you'll find tucked away in various corners of big cities are okay, too. What you absolutely *don't* want to do is change money with somebody on the street. Try as we might to blend in, Americans just seem to stand out, and American dollars are highly desirable in just about every foreign country, especially in South America and eastern Europe. So there's a good chance you'll be approached with an offer to exchange at far better then the official rate. Don't do it. It's illegal almost everywhere, and you're certain to get diddled somehow, so just don't do it. The small fee you have to pay for an official exchange is more than worth what you could lose, to say nothing of spending time in a foreign pokey.

There are lots of places in the world where nobody speaks English. Personally, I think it disrespectful to visit a foreign country without learning something of the language—knowing how to say "hello," "please," "thank you," and how to count are basic requirements, in my view. Find a dictionary in your local library, buy one, do whatever it takes, but by all means don't visit any county without knowing at least a few words, even if you haven't a clue about the grammar. If you make an honest attempt to communicate with people in their own language, you'll be warmly met—except possibly in France, where old nationalistic arrogance still rears its head at times.

Finding someone who speaks English won't be difficult in any large city. Most hotel desk-staffs and quite a few bank clerks know the language. But if you're out in the boonies and need to find an English speaker, look for a kid. A great many European and South American children are learning English, and they're often eager for a chance to practice.

FOOD AND DRINK

Besides the opportunity to see the countryside itself, one of the very best things about travel is the chance to sample the local cuisine. While it's true—to my everlasting disgust—that you can now find McDonald's and Burger King and a bunch of other American chain restaurants all over Europe (and I assume in South America), you're denying yourself a wonderful treat if you don't explore the indigenous cooking. Traditional Hungarian cuisine—especially the savory soups and various forms of *paprikas*—is among the best in the world. The seafoods along the coasts of Spain are fantastic, particularly in the *tapas* bars, where you can choose piecemeal among a vast array of delicacies. Beef in Argentina, salmon in Scandinavia, *cabrito* in Mexico, traditional French and Italian cuisines—all splendid.

English cooking has long been the butt of various jokes, and indeed, the food can be rather bland by comparison, but to my taste it's hard to beat a well-prepared steak-and-kidney pie, or a traditional English breakfast of eggs and bangers and grilled tomatoes, or a pub lunch of, say, ploughman's pocket.

As you'll gather from reading the chapter on Russia, it's the only place I've been where much of the food was simply inedible, but even there you can dine well if you choose restaurants carefully.

With the exception of Mexico, Russia, and parts of South America and Eastern Europe, it's generally okay to drink the water, but it's my personal practice not to do so. Except in good hotels and restaurants, I avoid ice as well, for the same reason. Bottled water is available everywhere, either carbonated (*con gas*, in Spanish-speaking countries) or still (*sin gas*); I'm a *con gas* freak myself, whenever I have the choice, and I use bottled water even for brushing my teeth. You'd be surprised at how much fun even a mild case of diarrhea can subtract from shooting or fishing.

Drink is as varied, and as delightful, as food. European wines are legendary, and there are some exceptionally good ones made in South America as well. In northern Europe, vodka is king, and it's generally superb. The Russians make some excellent champagnes, and the Finns distill a liqueur from cranberries; it's sold under the name Polar, and it's wonderfully tasty. So is the traditional French apple brandy, Calvados.

Eastern Europe can be problematic. The Hungarians are enthusiastic makers of wine, some of which is quite good and some only passable. The national liquor is *pálinka*, which seems to be a form of vodka, and much of it has a decidedly bitter taste. Unicum, the Hungarian liqueur, is flavored heavily with anise; some members of our annual shooting party refer to it as licorice dissolved in kerosene, others like it. I can handle a bit of *pálinka* now and then, but I usually buy a bottle of brandy or malt Scotch at the duty-free shop on the way in.

Needless to say, anyone fond of Scots whiskey can have a wonderful time in the UK. The smaller Scottish distilleries turn out such limited quantities that virtually none of it is exported, and with a bit of looking you'll turn up all manner of malts you never heard of. A lot of chaps preparing for a first visit to Britain ask me which whiskeys to try, and my answer is always, "Try 'em all."

Among Americans, Germany has a reputation for brewing the best beer, but to my taste, nothing can match English beers. There are literally dozens of them, from dark ales and stout to pilsners, and I haven't yet found one I didn't like. Some of the local beers, brewed and sold only in certain areas of the country, are exceptionally good—like Tanglefoot, which you can find in the pubs in Somerset and a few other counties in the West Country. Drink about three pints; you'll find out why it bears the name.

Elsewhere in Europe, the beers are mostly German and Dutch, with a few from other countries mixed in. With some effort, you can usually find some English beers as well—at places like The John Bull Pub in Budapest. It's a great place to hang out.

LUGGAGE, ETC.

Soft luggage—duffel bags and the like—generally are the best choice if you're traveling to shoot or fish. This is particularly true if any part of your trip involves small aircraft, where cargo space is limited and things may have to be stuffed into nooks and crannies. And better two smaller bags than one big monster that's heavy as hell and awkward to handle. With a gun case inside, a gun duffel is fairly heavy to begin with, and it's my opinion that some are too large, which makes overpacking a temptation.

In any event, overpacking is not a good idea. The more stuff you take, the more you have to keep track of. Depending upon where you go, you'll no doubt want to buy some things as gifts, souvenirs, or just to take advantage of bargain prices, and it's wise to save a bit of luggage room for them.

Your outfitter should advise you on what sort of clothing is appropriate for the climate and season, but the one rule of thumb that I've learned from experience is to *always* take something that'll keep you warm (a fleece pullover and pants are perfect) and something to keep you dry, such as a waxed-cotton jacket with a hood or matching hat. Dealing with unusually warm weather is one thing, but there's nothing quite so miserable as being cold or wet, or both.

Otherwise, don't take more clothing than you'll really need, and the fact is, you really won't need many changes of outerwear. If the trip includes any semi-formal dinners or such, you'll have to take a suit or blazer. Otherwise, two pair of field pants, two or three shirts, a game vest or jacket, boots, gloves, and a few changes of underwear will see you through a solid week of hunting in good order. Some lodges offer laundry service, in which case you can reduce the basic list even further. Believe me, the more you travel, the more attractive traveling light becomes.

If you're on any regular course of medication, you'll naturally want to take an adequate supply—enough, in fact, for a few extra days, just in case you get socked in by weather somewhere. Otherwise, you'd do well to have a simple first-aid kit, some aspirin or other painkiller and perhaps a bottle of Lomotil or something equally effective against a touch of Montezuma's Revenge.

Electrical gadgets like shavers and hair dryers will be useless in Europe and South America unless you have a set of adapters to accommodate several different electrical systems and sockets. Taking such things is usually more trouble than they're worth.

Traveling to South America or Europe, I always try to schedule an overnight flight. Four or five hours' sleep in an airplane seat is hardly the same as snoozing in your own bed, but it's usually enough, and the fact that you land in the morning helps stave off the feeling of having somehow lost a day out of your life. If you have difficulty sleeping on a plane, take a couple of Dramamine; even if you aren't liable to motion sickness, it'll make you nicely drowsy.

Coming back from Europe is an ordeal for me. As it's almost always a daytime flight, and as you gain time heading west, I end up convincing myself that I don't need to sleep—and therefore end up being awake for about twenty-four hours in real time before I get home. It's a good idea to allow yourself at least a day before going back to work after a long trip.

All in all, long-distance travel has never been so quick nor so easy as it is now. That doesn't mean it can't be tiring or frustrating when things go wrong. The best thing you can take on a trip is a good attitude. There's no point in getting bent out of shape over things you can't control; delayed flights, bad weather, misrouted luggage, and other such things happen, and getting upset won't change them. Look at every trip as an adventure, sometimes good, sometimes less so. In any case, as long as you're able to get your feet on the ground or in the water with a gun or rod in your hands, you'll likely look back fondly on the whole thing, no matter what.

Appendix II

As I SAID in Appendix I, satisfied clients are the best sources for finding good outfitters. I certainly haven't worked with every outfitter in the business, but I've been with some whom I can recommend without reservation, and that at least can give you a good place to start in booking some hunting and fishing trips of your own.

Each one has been responsible for organizing one or more of the trips I've written about in this book, and I wouldn't hesitate for a moment to go with them again. Most of them offer other destinations and other species of birds and fish than I was after, so be sure to ask for information on all they have available.

Aspen Outfitting Company
315 East Dean Street
Aspen, Colorado 81611
970-925-3406
Fax 970-920-3706
Contact: Jon Hollinger

Holland & Holland Ltd.
32 Bruton Street
London W1X 8JS, England
011-44-171-499-4411
Fax 011-44-171-499-4544
Contact: John Ormiston

Hunts West
139 Highway 10 West
Stevens Point, Wisconsin 54481
715-344-4868
Fax 715-344-1747
Contact: Michael J. Okray

Rainbow River Lodge
November–May
  4127 Raspberry Road
  Anchorage, Alaska 99502
  907-243-7894
  Fax 907-248-1726
June–October
  P.O. Box 303
  Iliamna, Alaska 99606
  907-571-1210
Contact: Chris Goll

Rod & Gun Resources
206 Ranch House Road
Kerrville, Texas 78028
800-211-4753
Fax 210-792-6807
Contacts: David Gregory, J.W. Smith

Sporting International
15608 South Brentwood
Channelview, Texas 77530
800-231-6352
Fax 713-744-5271
Contact: Tommy Morrison

Tinker Kennels
3031 Sussex Place
Pierre, South Dakota 57501
605-222-1014 or 605-224-5414
Contact: Bob Tinker

Trek International Safaris
6601 Southpoint Drive North, Suite 165
Jacksonville, Florida 19065
800-654-9915
Fax 904-296-6438
Contact: Mike Cloaninger

William Larkin Moore & Company
8227 East Via de Commercio, Suite A
Scottsdale, Arizona 85258
602-951-8913
Fax 602-951-3677
Contact: Dan Moore

Wingshooting Adventures
0-1845 Leonard Road
Grand Rapids, Michigan 49544
616-677-1980
Fax 616-677-1986
Contacts: Jack Jansma, Bill Teesdale

There are a couple of outfitters I feel I know just by reputation and word of mouth. I've never hunted or fished with them,
but I've heard so many good comments from their clients that I
feel comfortable recommending them:

Frontiers International Travel
P.O. Box 959
Wexford, Pennsylvania 15090
800-245-1950
Fax 412-935-5388
Contact: Mike Fitzgerald Jr.

Stafford & Stafford
P.O. Box 11196
Jacksonville, Florida 32239
800-383-0245
Fax 904-725-2588
Contact: Ron Stafford

Finally, here's an outfitting company that offers something unique to a specialized clientele. Classic Sports International offers a variety of trips for medical and legal professionals; these blend high-quality hunting and fishing with medico-legal seminars that qualify as continuing-education credit. They aren't for everyone, obviously, but for physicians, dentists, and attorneys they represent a good sporting experience combined with some useful professional education.

Classic Sports International
Spring Valley West
217 South Shields Road
Columbia, South Carolina 29223
800-375-5692
Fax 803-699-2477